DHARMA AND SOCIETY

DHARMA AND SOCIETY

BY
GUALTHERUS H. MEES
M.A. (CANTAB.), LL.D. (LEYDBN)

GYAN

ISBN : 978-81-212-0055-4

Published, 2018

Published by

Gyan Publishing House
5, Ansari Road
Daryaganj, New Delhi-110002
Phone: 011-47034999, 9811692060
www.gyanbooks.com
E-mail: books@gyanbooks.com

Printed at: G. Print Process, Delhi.

TO MY FATHER AND MOTHER

ABBREVIATIONS USED IN THE NOTES:

MBh.	Mahābhārata (Bombay ed.)
Rām.	Rāmāyaṇa
Vishṇu-P.	Vishṇu-purāṇa
Vishṇu	Vishṇu-saṃhitā
Bhāg.-P.	Bhāgavata-purāṇa
Gītā	Bhagavad-gītā
Āp.	Āpastamba-saṃhitā
Yājñ.	Yājñavalkya-saṃhitā
P.	Purāṇa
Up.	Upanishad
Br.	Brāhmaṇa
S.B.E.	Sacred Books of the East

CONTENTS

Preface

To-day East and West are meeting to such an extent and in such a way that it seems as if the well-known words of Kipling are conclusively disproved.

The upholders of ideals of 'meeting' must of course remember that — in accordance with the organic conception of society — Easterners must not turn into cheap copies of Westerners, nor vice versa. It not being our intention to formulate a law, we may but cautiously say that on the whole both Easterners and Westerners will do well to remain what they are, that is to say, keep, as faithfully as is possible in accordance with their inner life, to the ways and forms of expression as handed down to them from former generations.

But both East and West will benefit much by realizing their common humanity and the fundamental oneness of their realizations of Truth and of their aspirations towards the Divine. Next both have of course much to receive from each other. As Romain Rolland wrote in „The Forerunners": „For a long time to come, the intensest joy which man can know on earth, will be derived from supplementing the ideals of Europe by the ideals of Asia". Lord Russell looked at it from another point of view: „Asia must come to the rescue of the world, by causing Western inventiveness to subserve human ends instead of the base cravings of oppression and cruelty, to which it has been prostituted by the dominant nations of the present day" [1]*. Regarding this the trouble is that the East is also taking over the wrong things! It is of course not necessary to enumerate the different benefits of the various Western sciences which — as far as necessary — should be gratefully accepted by the East.*

Perhaps one aspect of the needed change is illustrated in the best and simplest way in the words of a Chinese professor: „The West needs a

[1]) ***Vedanta Kesari***, Vol. XVI p. 89.

temple-bell to rest and the East a bugle call to action". That more is wanted however than this or than a mere interchange of achievements, both cultural and material, I want to demonstrate in these pages. Realization of fundamental oneness, mutual appreciation and inspiration, organic co-operation and cultural synthesis only are of fundamental and real value.

Hindu thought has generally tended to be systematical and synthetical. As the Right Hon. Ramsay Macdonald expressed it: „If one were to turn to any great philosophy or any great system of thought upon which could be built up a harmony between races, a harmony between conflicting thoughts, where could one go to find it more readily than to the great philosophies of India itself? Those philosophies where brotherhood is inculcated, where peace and harmony and co-operation are enjoined; those philosophies which look at the world not in a mere abstract way but as something essentially composed of differences, and yet essentially calling for a harmony of differences rather than a mere uniformity of thought or of action" [1]). *The present book will continually provide illustrations of this.*

It would not be of much use, and it would not be very interesting either, to study dry historical facts and to critically consider the theories, the ideals and the social structures of the ancients, if we were not sure that these old sociological thoughts and facts are still of so much bearing on actual problems, and if we were not convinced that we could benefit much from them in pointing the way to new developments.

In these pages we intend to inquire into the nature of Dharma — the fundamental motive force in the life of man as a social being — in connection with a comparative study of the theory and the ideal of Varṇa ('natural class') and the phenomena of caste in India and incidentally of class in the West. Professor Kern emphasized that „the great point is to distinguish between the natural classes or orders, and castes, which cannot have arisen naturally, but are artificial" [2]). *This special line of study however has been rather neglected* [3]).

We shall further inquire into the inherent tendencies of the social composition, and consider various social-psychological and sociological questions arising out of the fulfilment of duty and the performance of work, especially in reference to, on the one hand, the social theories and

---

[1]) Speech in opening the debate in the Minorities Committee, second session of the Round Table Conference.

[2]) Address to the Royal Academy of Sciences at Amsterdam, March 13th, 1871.

[3]) A book somewhat in this line, but now entirely antiquated, is: B. A. Irving, *The Theory and Practice of Caste.*

ideals of the Hindus, and on the other hand, the historical and actual constitution of Hindu society.

In the first Part, which will be largely introductory, we propose to analyse in the first Chapter the conception of Dharma, as it is found in the history of Hindu Thought, and to try to find out what it means in its aspects and fundamentally, and to define it as accurately as the conception allows. The purpose will not be to test the Hindu theories philosophically or morally, but to show that the fundamental nature of Dharma (and of related conceptions) is a mystic one.

If in the first Chapter, in considering fundamental motive powers and ends of life, we took the individual as point of departure, in the second Chapter we shall deal with the same from the collective point of view. In the second Chapter we propose to analyse the conception of caste—ideal, theoretical, and actual,—to describe the main points of the social doctrine, to consider the conceptions Ārya and Aryan, and to inquire into the origin of caste, quoting opinions and definitions of eminent authorities on caste. The subject of caste being very extensive and moreover one which has been thoroughly inquired into by many scholars, we shall only touch upon those points which fall within the scope of the comparative study of the social theory and actual conditions of caste and class.

In the various Chapters of the second Part it is our intention to consider and clarify some aspects and attributes of Varṇa and caste and to try to throw some light upon some historical and actual social problems and phenomena, both in India and elsewhere.

We shall not test the morality of the various Hindu views and theories, treating those as psychological facts which have influenced the social life of the people. If we give opinions of value, it will be from the standpoint of the graduated scale of Varṇa and Dharma, that is to say, not on the basis of one ethical standard, judging any act to be good or bad of itself, but by assigning to it its relative place in the scale.

We shall take into account the recent developments of psychology. In complement to the sociological conception of the 'social mind', or 'group mind' in the widest sense (concerning the conscious functioning of mankind) we have framed the expression the 'social unconscious'. It is really the same as the 'collective unconscious' of Jung, but is meant to indicate that field of the collective unconscious which applies to the ordinary social relations.

We agree with Professor Giddings' conclusion that the function of social organization, always to be kept in view by the sociologist, is the evolution of personality through ever higher stages until it attains the ideal that we call humanity. That therefore, at every step, the sociological task is a double one — to know how social relations are evolved, and how they react on the development of personality [1]. *In connection with this we have taken as theme the comparative study of theory and reality, of ideal and application, chiefly in relation to Hindu thought and life.*

All the time four categories of facts have to be recognized, and they cannot be too carefully distinguished. First there are things as they really are. Secondly there are things as they are thought to be. Thirdly there are the things as they ought to be, and fourthly the things as it is conceived how they ought to be. In the present book, since our subject does not belong to the field of an exact science, we are almost entirely concerned with the second and the fourth categories. The second category holds the relatively incomplete and inaccurate knowledge of history, philology, psychology and allied sciences which are of use for our purpose. The fourth category contains the ideals, the theories and the conventional, legal and ethical conceptions of the Hindus and of other cultured nations which we shall consider.

Though it is, strictly speaking, unscientific to form any conclusions for the future from the lessons of the past, we feel in rare cases justified in propounding the probability or relative certainty of inferences as to future developments. If not from the past, from what else shall we learn?

The theory of four Varṇas which we shall consider at length in these pages is a special form of the theory of the hierarchic and organic composition of society. As we shall demonstrate, Varṇa can only be translated as 'cultural' or 'natural class'. We have chosen the latter expression, since it is less liable to misinterpretation than the former.

Our first task is to know. *Why? Not for the sake of knowledge, but for the sake of happiness, or in other words, for the sake of the commonweal. Here the scientist must become artist as well, serving, applying, leading, creating, all in one. This lies outside the pale of a book, in which we can only enquire into phenomena and try to discover truths, tendencies and processes, and accordingly try to point the way. Further we must rely on the reader all the time to apply the given information and his conclusions to actual conditions on this planet to-day, to imagine with their help nobler states of interrelation and more efficient forms of interaction than are existent in present day human society, and to put into action forces towards their realization. Nothing has been achieved*

[1]) F. H. Giddings, *Principles of Sociology*, p. 421.

without imagination, and there can be no progress without its help. The science of psychology has proved that there is a great correlation between imagination and intelligence.

There are many to-day who realize that the threads of the tissue of life have for the time being been sufficiently studied, and that it is essential to look at the fabric as a whole, in order to be able to use it. As regards science, it is very pleasing to find out what makes the difference between the theory of A and the theory of B, but it is far more pleasing and practical to find out what is the underlying factor which both theories have in common, and to realize where they complement one another.

The time has come, that there is once more — as so often before in history — a great need to dig up roots, to cut away old branches which have withered or degenerated, in order that new life may burst forth from healthy shoots and from roots newly embedded in fertile soil. As we shall demonstrate in these pages, India will benefit much by realizing once more the four natural classes or Varṇas, and by letting this realization solve the problems of caste. The West will benefit much by realizing the fundamental composition of human society, by clarifying the conceptions of freedom, equality and responsibility, and by making these various realizations contribute towards an improvement of the constitution of Western society. These various points we shall treat of in the various Chapters of Part II.

In the matter at hand we have tried to express ourselves as briefly as distinctness allows, and to evade as much as possible a tedious and superfluous repetition of conclusions. We have to express our regret at not having been able to consult more than the main sources. The material is so enormous that an entirely satisfactory study would take a lifetime.

The first half of the book (up to Part II Ch. III) will perhaps be mainly of interest to students of Hindu thought and social life, the second half besides also in particular to students of Western life. Yet both parts are in all respects intimately connected.

The system of transliteration followed deviates somewhat from the one laid down by the International Congress of Orientalists. It seemed to us more suitable for the purposes of a book which is not in the first place intended for Sanskritists.

I would here express my gratitude to Professor Dr. J. Ph. Vogel for many useful hints. I am also much indebted to him for his invaluable help in comparing a great many of the quotations with the original Sanskrit texts.

ERRATA

Page	*line*	*for*	*read*
21	25	wbout	about
27	28	Treta-yuga	Tretā-yuga
44	7	it	if
54	22	diifferent	different
57	footnote 2	Uma	Umā
83	22	manking	mankind
92	1	ot	to
137	footnote 3	Āp. I: I: 7: 12	Āp. 1: 2: 7: 12
142	12	social-subconscious	social unconscious
192	footnote 1	Young India,	Young India, Vol. I

57 footnote 2. The quotation from the MBh. Anuśāsana-parvan concerns the attaining of Brahmanhood in a *subsequent* life.

137 footnote 2. In Sūtra 5 the Śūdras are excepted.

139 footnote 4. To represent Satyavatī, the mother of Vyāsa, as a mere fisherman's daughter is one-sided. She was a daughter of a king of the family of the Pauravas (Ādi-parvan 63), and born, like her brother, the ancestor of the race of the Matsyas (lit. 'Fishes'), from a fish. The mother was undoubtedly a fisherwoman.

Note. The Preface is not included in the Index.

PART I

Chapter I

Dharma

A. INTRODUCTION. The Western mind, accustomed to make a sharp distinction between morality and custom, and between moral law and statute law, is sometimes surprised at the almost primitive simplicity which the conception of Dharma seems to possess at first sight. But not only Dharma, we have sometimes occasion to wonder at the vagueness of the conceptions of the main ancient cultures, for instance Indian, Greek, Roman or Jewish, about law, convention, religious duty, moral duty, etc. Western science and philosophy have analysed the indeterminate primitive norm into its different aspects, its component parts, distinguishing them very clearly.

Yet this vagueness and many-sidedness has persisted in our modern word 'law', which may mean many things from a local by-law to a natural sequence of the universe [1]). Yet the experts —lawyers, philosophers, sociologists—know the different meanings. In spite of this we forget that the ancients may have known the different aspects of the primitive norm.

For reasons which will become clear in the course of this Chapter, I prefer to speak about the indeterminateness rather than about the vagueness of the fundamental conceptions of the ancients. For indeterminateness does not preclude inner clarity, whereas vagueness is the opposite of clarity.

Science has achieved a marvellous analysis in clearly distinguishing a great number of norms: norms of law, religion, ethics, convention, fashion etc., absolute and empirical, sanctioned and not sanctioned, autonomous and heteronomous, etc.. Yet we are inclined to believe that science has not yet found the fundamental Norm, the basic law, the underlying principle which has ever been

[1]) Similarly in German: Recht, recht, (right in English), Gesetz.

the aim of her search. The individual scientists who were aware of the nature of this principle or basic law had not found it by the ordinary methods of science, but in some other way, as we shall try to prove by exposing the nature of this first principle as realised and conceived by the ancients.

We propose to demonstrate that there is ample proof of this basic principle and law having been clearly realized in the ancient world. As the ancients were unable to define it exactly on account of its very nature, they named it Ṛita, Dharma, δίκη, Mischpat, or something else. They did not always trouble to distinguish it in its different manifestations in society, naming these after the root-conception. They intuitively grasped the basic motive element or will or law, seeing the "inner world" and the "outer world" as one and the same, looking behind the mystery of the subjective-objective, which only the latest development in modern psychology is again succeeding to do. They realized the principle underlying the motive, the means and the end.

In later times they also often mixed up the different aspects of Dharma.

A modern Indian author writes: "Modern Western thought.... has, for various reasons, historical and evolutionary, become disconnected with dharma, religion-law, which in its perfection and completeness is the one science of all sciences, '*knowledge* pre-eminently directed to the achievement of *desired happiness* here and hereafter by means of appropriate *action*' [1])". He continues: "The mainspring of this Western knowledge is mainly intellectual, knowledge for the sake of knowledge, — at least as that mainspring is described by some of those in whose heads it has made progress, especially in science...." [2]). It is indeed true that science in the West has been very much its own end, and that the 'higher mind' or intuition, the organ for direct realization of truth, has not been fashionable in scientific circles. We have also to admit that neither logic nor epistemology can give us a clear idea of this underlying law or principle, which can satisfy us fully.

Yet there are decided signs that a change is coming, in fact, has come already. The materialism of the 19th as well as the rationalism of the beginning of the 20th century have been overcome. We have

[1]) *Vaiśeshika-sūtra* I:1:2.

[2]) Bhagavan Das, *The Science of Peace*, p. 52.

only to read the books of Sir James Jeans to get an insight into the remarkable revolution in natural philosophy [1]).

Eddington, in his lecture to the Mathematical Association on Jan. 4th 1932, spoke about the downfall of determinism in theoretical physics. He mentioned that ten years before every natural philosopher of importance had been a determinist. He stated that modern physics had opened the door to the non-determinism of spiritual phenomena [2]). In my opinion this means the official peacemaking after the long war between natural science and the spiritual sciences in the West, although this war however still rages in the minds of the general public living by 'popular science' and by 'established religion'.

As to the coming attitude to science, we should like to quote the following significant statement of Jung: "Science is not a perfect, yet it is an invaluable, superior instrument, which brings about evil only when it claims to be its own end. Science must serve, it is on the wrong track when it is usurping a throne." [3])

It is to be hoped that sociological thought will develop parellel to the latest trend in psychological science, as expressed by Adler, Künkel, and especially Jung.

The first norm or principle of law and order, which is a dynamic principle and not a static one like 'Truth' (B r a h m a n), 'the Absolute', 'the Self' (Ā t m a n), etc., we propose to study as it was conceived by the ancient Hindus as Ṛ i t a and D h a r m a. We shall inquire also into it as visioned and conceived by some of the other ancient civilizations. Of course this enquiry will be less thorough than the one into the nature of Dharma.

Professor Somló names the principle the **„primitive first norm"**, in which law, religion, ethics and convention cannot clearly be distinguished [4]). I think this name is somewhat misleading, since it makes it appear as if norms have, so to speak, grown out of the earth, instead of, as I want to show, rained down from on high. The name **'primeval norm'** would be more fitting.

In Section B we shall describe Dharma as a mythological person, in Section C we shall inquire into Dharma as an impersonal principle,

[1]) *The mysterious Universe; The new Background of Science;* etc.

[2]) *Lecture* in *Nature,* 13 Febr. 1932, Nr. 3250.

[3]) Wilhelm und Jung, *Das Geheimnis der goldenen Blüte,* p. 10.

[4]) F. Somló, *Juristische Grundlehre,* p. 88. The German expression is *primitive Urnorm.*

Section D will consider Dharma and the ends of life and present some interesting analogies and in Section E the different scriptures of Dharma will be described. Section F will be devoted to the Buddhist Dhamma and Section G to some ancient conceptions of other ancient cultures which seem to be akin to Dharma. Finally Section H will present the conclusions.

The origin of the word Dharma is an introduction to its meaning. Etymologically, the word Dharma is connected with our word 'form', the common Aryan root being 'dhar', meaning to support, sustain, maintain, hold, keep. Sometimes it is also given to mean to owe, as something due to another, or as trust or deposit.

In this connection it is interesting to note that in the English language the words *religion, law, legal, ob-lig-ation* are derived from Latin roots having allied meanings: *ligare, legare, lex.* Dharma as a dynamic principle to some extent came into the place of the static Ātman or Self.

B. DHARMA AS A PERSON. Sometimes we find Dharma as a mythological personage, not man but Deva, that is a superhuman or divine being, somewhat like an Angel. Yet as such we find Dharma only very rarely in proportion to its immense importance as an impersonal principle.

In the Bhāgavata-purāṇa Dharma is mentioned as the father of the fourth Avatāra or divine incarnation [1]).

In the Mahābhārata he is mentioned several times as a deity. The two following stories are of interest. When the lady Draupadī was unveiled and stripped before the eyes of men, Dharma clad her every time in new clothes, and the purpose of putting her to shame could not be accomplished [2]). In this story stress is laid on the moral aspect of Dharma, he was not visible to those present.

Also we find the hero Yudhishṭhira about ascend to heaven. He has to leave his dog behind, for, as it is said, dogs cannot go to heaven. But he refuses to go at all, for he will not abandon the loved and dependent animal. Then the dog reveals himself as an incarnation of Dharma, who has assumed that form to test him [3]). Here also we notice that the abstract moral aspect of Dharma is much more apparent than the personal.

---

[1]) *Bhāg.-P.* I : 3 : 9.
[2]) *MBh. Sabhā-parvan* 68.
[3]) *MBh. Mahāprasthānika-parvan* 3.

In the Bhāgavata [1]) we find a symbolic story in which Dharma takes the form of a bull, and the Earth that of a cow. The bull is trying to go on one leg, because the earth has entered Kali-yuga, the age of discord. In the first age, Satya-yuga, Dharma, or the Spirit of Righteousness, symbolized as a bull, went on four feet, in the second age on three, in the third age on two, and in the fourth and present age he is tottering on one foot. The duties of man varied in the different ages [2]).

In the same story [3]) Adharma is introduced, the opposite of Dharma, the spirit of unrighteousness and evil. He is personified as a person of the lowest caste, disguised as a king. He is kicking bull and cow, till at last a saintly king comes, who drives him away, allotting him only five spheres to abide in: falsehood, intoxication, passion, slaughter and animosity [4]). Or: dice, wine, women, shambles, and later added: gold [5]).

In this story the low caste person disguised as king symbolizes the spirit of the uneducated mass, trying to rule, and maltreating the righteous section of mankind (the bull, Dharma), and not succeeding in bringing about material wellbeing (the earth, symbolized as cow).

Dharma is the incarnated Lord, Śrī-Kṛishṇa, from his lowest aspect as personal God, to his highest aspect as Absolute Truth. Śrī-Kṛishṇa says in the Mahābhārata: "Know that Dharma is my beloved first-born mental son, whose nature is to have compassion on all creatures. In his character I exist among men, both present and past, passing through many varieties of mundane existence, in different disguises and forms, in the three worlds, for the preservation and establishment of righteousness. I am Vishṇu, Brahmā, Indra, and the source as well as destruction of things, the creator and the annihilator of the whole aggregate of existences. While all men live in unrighteousness, I, the Unshakeable, build up the bulwark (setu) of righteousness, as the ages pass away. While entering into various wombs, from a desire to promote the good of creatures, whenever I assume a divine birth, I act in every respect agreeable to my divine character" [6]).

---

[1]) *Bhāg.-P.* I : *16*.
[2]) *Manu* I : 85; *Parāśara* I : 21. For kali-yuga see Part II Ch. VIII C.
[3]) *Bhāg.-P.* I : *17*.
[4]) *Bhāg.-P.* I : *17* : 39.
[5]) *Bhāg.-P.* I : *17* : 38.
[6]) *Mbh. Āśvamedhika-parvan* 54 : 11—17.

Dharma is also identical with Yama, the God of Death, Yama is sometimes called Dharma-Rāja. He is the judge in the world beyond.

Further Dharma is sometimes met with in the scriptures as the father of a particular hero, which may be another way of stressing the righteous character of the hero. Sometimes he takes the shape of some particular saint to test some person. Occasionally he takes the foremost place among the Devas, as for instance at the funeral ceremony of Hariśchandra [1]).

That Dharma, though in the highest sense an impersonal principle, is yet intrinsically personal, because it can be experienced as well as performed only individually, is expressed in the beautiful lines about the 'voice of the man within', the voice of the conscience or of Dharma, which we shall quote elsewhere [2]).

C. DHARMA AS IMPERSONAL PRINCIPLE. The meaning of Dharma as an impersonal principle is very vast, much more so than 'law', as it was translated by the first translators of Sanskrit texts, or than 'duty' or 'sacred law' or 'religion'. All these (and more) translations are found even in recently published books [3]). The meaning of Dharma changed somewhat during the ages. This we shall consider in Part II Chapter II.

Dharma sometimes was:

1. Something like the old Ṛita;
2. The morally proper, the ethical duty, virtue;
3. Good works;
4. Religious duty, religious virtue;
5. The ideal;
6. Identical with God and Absolute Truth; a universal law or principle;
7. Divine Justice;
8. A compromise between the ideal and actual conditions;
9. Convention, a code of customs and traditions;
10. Common law or Law;
11. International or rather inter-tribal law;

[1]) *Mārkaṇḍeya-P.* and *Mbh. Sabhā-parvan 12.*
[2]) See pp. 22, 35 and 132.
[3]) See Mrs. Rhys Davids, *Buddhism, its birth and dispersal,* p. 228.

12. Rules laid down by Brahman authorities for the glorification and elevation of their caste at the cost of the lower castes.

There are some distinctions of Dharma as to its subject and object:

13. The sociological and psychological distinction between Sva-dharma (the Dharma of the individual), Varṇa-dharma (the Dharma of a Varṇa or 'natural class'), Jāti-dharma (the Dharma of a caste), Hindu-dharma, and also between the Dharma for Āryas and that for Anāryas.
14. The philosophical and psychological distinction between Pravṛitti-dharma and Nivṛitti-dharma.

Further there are some attributes of Dharma which have to be specially noticed:

15. Karman.
16. Bhakti.

After considering these various points one by one and after comparing Dharma and Nīti, we shall try to define Dharma with some concluding remarks.

1. At times Dharma appears to be something like the old **Ṛita.** Ṛita is a word for truth, it stands for an impersonal order or law, and is in the Vedas the sustaining principle of the higher and of the lower worlds, that is to say, of the Devas and of the world. In the Ṛig-veda we sometimes find the conception that the Devas are the performers of Ṛita, which has an ethical character. More often we find the view that the Devas are presided over by Ṛita. Ṛita stands as much for a social as for a moral order, the former standing in a subordinate and instrumental relation to the latter.

As to what Ṛita may have meant originally, the opinions differ. Max Müller said that Ṛita, the "right", originally seems to have meant "straight, direct" [1]). He defines Ṛita as the "straight line which, in spite of many momentary deviations, was discovered to run through the whole realm of nature. We call that Ṛita, that straight, direct or right line, when we apply it in a more general sense, the Law of Nature; and when we apply it to the moral world, we try to express the same idea again by speaking of the Moral Law, the law on which our life is founded, the eternal Law of Right and Reason, or, it may be, "that which makes for righteousness", both within us and without" [2]). And further: ".... a law that

---

1) Max Müller, *India, what can it teach us*, p. 64, 66. Notice the etymology. Connected with Ṛita are the word 'rite', and also the Latin 'ordo'.

2) See *Hibbert Lectures*, new ed., pp. 243—255.

underlies everything, a law in which we may trust, whatever befall, a law which speaks within us with the divine voice of conscience, and tells us "this is rite", "this is right", "this is true", whatever the statutes of our ancestors, or ever the voices of our bright gods, may say to the contrary" [1]). Rudolf Otto expresses the same in a different form, stressing its social aspect. He says the word Ṛita comes from the root Ar, to arrange, to order, regulate (German: ordnen) and that it really means the regulated, the ordered. And not so much the state of order and the process, as the principle behind this state and the power that holds and regulates the process. Ṛita is a binding power, constraining to order. It was to be found also in social life, in the life of the clan, of the tribe and of the family. The binding order of morals, customs, laws and manners in the constitution of the social classes and of the labour-communities, in compacts and oaths, in marriage, in the relations of individuals, of clans and tribes, in public law and in private conduct, was also Ṛita, based upon Ṛita. It appeared in social life as the continuation, the consequence and reflection of the cosmic binding order [2]).

Dharma is very much the same in a new form. We shall see this from the definition to follow and from our analysis of Dharma.

The conception of Ṛita was the product of a natural age, of an age in which not much egoistic initiative was yet given to man, the Gods or the cosmic powers being considered to be leading and ruling, an age in which every social happening was considered the natural outcome of a corresponding spiritual happening [3]).

Man still was in contact with these divine worlds, as the ritualistic part of the Vedas shows. As soon as this contact ceased to be an inner one and became based upon the outer ceremonial form, as soon as men began to function at ceremonies no more as souls, but as personalities, Ṛita ceased to be a cosmic power and became a mere rite. A new conception was needed, a new name had to be found for the living experience. And the old Ṛita was reborn in Dharma, which is free from the trammels of ceremonial form, though it can clothe itself in any form it pleases [4]).

Dr. Bhagavan Das defines Dharma as follows. Of all the defi-

---

[1]) *India, what can it teach us*, p. 243.

[2]) R. Otto, *Gottheit und Gottheiten der Arier*, p. 96.

[3]) This was perfect in the Kṛita-yuga, the 'Golden Age of Man', as the scriptures tell. See pp. 43 and 126.

[4]) When the same happened to Dharma, the conception of Nīti arose, about which below.

nitions I have found (and there is no subject of which there are more divergent definitions!), it is the most enlightening. He writes: "That which holds a thing together, makes it what it is, prevents it from breaking up and changing it into something else, its characteristic function, its peculiar property, its fundamental attribute, its essential nature, is its dharma, the law of its being, primarily. That which makes the World-process what it is, and holds all its parts together as One Whole, in a breakless all-binding chain of causes-and-effects, is the Law (or totality of laws) of Nature or Nature's God, dharma in the largest sense, the world-order (cf. the word dharma-megha in Yoga and Buddhist philosophy). That scheme or code of laws which bind together human beings in the bonds of mutual rights-and-duties, of causes-and-consequences of actions, arising out of their temperamental characters, in relation to each other, and thus maintains society, is human law, Mānava-dharma. Yet again: "The code of life, based on Veda (all-science of the laws of Nature in all her departments), the due observance of which leads to happiness here and hereafter, is dharma"[1]. Briefly dharma is characteristic property, scientifically; duty, morally and legally; religion with all its proper implications, psycho-physically and spiritually; and righteousness and law generally, but Duty above all"[2]. This modern Hindu definition forms a good point of departure for our consideration of the various aspects of Dharma.

2. Sometimes Dharma is **ethical.** Dharma as law or convention may have an ethical basis. But here we mean (ethical) Dharma which has no pretentions of being law or convention. For examples we have to look into the more religious scriptures, the Epics and Purāṇas, e.g.: "Harmlessness, truthfulness, absence of the tendency to steal, to be free from the passions of desire, anger and covetousness, activity in the direction of what is agreeable and good to beings, form the course of Dharma common to all Varṇas"[3]. And even Manu, the foremost authority on law, defines the 'tenfold Dharma'[4] as: "Contentment, forgiveness, self-control, abstention from un-

[1] *Vaiśeshika-sūtra.*
[2] Bhagavan Das, *The Science of Social Organisation*, 2nd ed. Vol. I, pp. 49—50.
[3] *Bhāg.-P.* XI : 17 : 21.
[4] Ten often being a symbol of perfection.

righteously appropriating anything, (obedience to the rules of) purification, coercion of the organs, wisdom, knowledge (of the supreme Soul), truthfulness, and abstention from anger, (form) the tenfold Dharma" [1]).

The definition of Dharma given by Mr. Venkateswara in the first volume of his *Indian Culture through the Ages* seems to cover this. He defines Dharma as the discharge of one's duty as rationally conceived as an aspect of social ethics. [2])

3. Sometimes Dharma is taken in the sense of **good works** or **merit** (P u ṇ y a), as for instance in the verse: "The only friend who follows men even after death is Dharma; for everything else is lost at the same time when the body perishes" [3]).

4. Sometimes, apart from being law, convention or an ideal, Dharma may be a **religious duty.** Śrī-Kṛishṇa says in the Bhāgavata: "Whatever promotes devotion to Me is Dharma...." [4]); And the same Purāṇa mentions :"Indeed, there is no Dharma higher than that by which devotion to Śrī-Kṛishṇa arises, a devotion induced by no motive (desire) and unobstructed in its course, a devotion by which the soul becomes pacified" [5]).

5. Sometimes Dharma (also in the Dharma-śāstras) is the **Ideal,** as rendered by the Sages. For instance the conception of the existence of four classes or castes was in later times merely an ideal.

Another example is furnished by verses of this kind: "On account of his pre-eminence,.... on account of his particular sanctification, the Brāhmaṇa is the Lord of (all) the Varṇas." [6]) Or: "The Supreme Lord who dwells in the heart of all creatures, who as the Absolute Ruler and beloved of Brahmans is highly pleased with the worship of Brahmans; therefore let the race of Brahmans be worshipped with sincere and full heart by those that are properly trained and devoted to righteous duties, pleasing to Him. By the constant association and worship of that race a man soon attains the highest state of happiness (liberation from Illusion)...." etc. [7])

[1]) *Manu* VI : 92.
[2]) For the 'voice' of conscience see pp. 24, 35 and 132.
[3]) *Manu* VIII : 17.
[4]) *Bhāg.-P.* XI : *19* : 27.
[5]) *Bhāg -P.* I : *2* : *6*.
[6]) *Manu* X : 3.
[7]) *Bhāg.-P.* IV : *21* : 39—40.

It is clear that Brahmans in these verses wish to be and are pictured as gods on earth. It is interesting to compare these verses with such as will follow under **12.**

6. Sometimes Dharma is seen as **identical with God, or the Absolute,** that is to say with Śrī-Kṛishṇa from His lowest aspect as personal God to His highest aspect as Absolute Truth. We mentioned this already when we considered Dharma as a personality [1]).

As Mr. Subba Rao writes in his introductory to his translation of the Bhāgavata-Purāṇa: "The subject of the whole work is Śrī-Kṛishṇa, called Dharma, i.e. the support of pure righteousness, not an abstract idea, but a concrete reality, whether presented in a definite and seemingly finite form to the limited vision of J ī v a s (indiv. souls) or understood as the omnipotent, absolute, Supreme Being." [2]) Here we find one aspect of that which was seen to be the essential nature and first principle under heading one. Under the following heading we shall discover another aspect.

The Artha-śāstra states: "Dharma is eternal truth holding its sway over the world." [3])

7. Sometimes Dharma is considered to be **Divine Justice,** the (divine) law of cause and effect which will tend to equilibrium, and which will bring in due time the fruits of the karmans or actions. This we may gather from a sentence in Manu, which had to be addressed by the assessors to a judge who acted against the law: "Dharma, being violated, destroys; Dharma, being preserved, preserves: therefore Dharma must not be violated, lest violated Dharma destroys us (another reading puts 'you' instead of 'us')." [4]) Human justice is based on the intuitive recognition of this Divine Justice, or of the Law of moral cause and effect and the Law of Karman. The mistake is that man often thinks that he can take it in hand. It is beyond human power.

"Dharma.... is the ruler of the ruler, namely, Justice. Hence nothing is superior to justice Therefore the weaker seeks (to over-

[1]) Compare also *Gītā* IV : 7.
[2]) See *Bhāg.-P.* I : *1* : 2.
[3]) *Artha-śāstra* III : *1*.
[4]) *Manu* VIII : 15.

come) the stronger by justice, as by a king. This justice is truth." [1])

8. Often Dharma pictures the conventional or legal **compromise between the ideal and actual conditions** at the time when the particular Dharma-śāstra containing this Dharma came into existence. Examples we find for instance in the numerous efforts in the Dharma-śāstras to explain the origin, and the duties of the different 'mixed' castes (j ā t i s) in spite of the ideal of four Varṇas, an ideal at least in later times. We shall revert to this at length in Ch. II and in Part II Chs. II and VII.

9. Quite often Dharma is **convention.** This applies to those portions in the Śāstras which, according to their nature, are not legally enforced codes of customs and traditions. We need not give examples.

10. Much of what we find in the Dharma-śāstras was **law** which may be compared to English Common Law, and has been accepted as law in the complicated modern system of British-India. Manu is still "the foundation of the queer medley of inconsistent systems of jurisprudence administered in the Privy Council and the High Courts of India, under the name of Hindu Law." [2])

The Śāstras provided for the making of new law: "If it be asked how it should be with respect to (points) of) law which have not been (specially) mentioned, (the answer is), "that which Brahmans who are Ś i s h ṭ a s propound, shall doubtlessly have legal force." [3]) Those Brahmans must be considered as Śishṭas who, in accordance with Dharma [4]), have studied the Veda together with its appendages [5]), and are able to adduce proofs perceptable by the senses from the revealed texts. [6]) Whatever an assembly, consisting either of at least ten, or of at least three persons who follow their prescribed occupations, declares to be law, the legal (force of) that one must not dispute." Next follows a description of

[1]) *Bṛihadāranyaka-Up.* I : 4 : 26; quoted from J. Muir, *Original Sanskrit Texts*, Vol. I p. 20.

[1]) As mentioned before Yama is also called Dharma-Rāja.

[2]) *Oxford History of India*, p. 42.

[3]) *Manu* XII : 108.

[4]) I e. while observing the rules of studentship.

[5]) V e d a means the revealed Dharma, the interpretation of the conception *appendages* is doubtful.

[6]) Variously interpreted by the old commentators, see G. Buhler, *The Laws of Manu*, p. 509.

the assembly. [1]) The Brahmans propounded the law, and the King, or the committee of rulers had to execute. [2])

Dharma is considered to be the fundamental principle of the jurisdiction: "Dharma, evidence, custom (Charitra, to be found in the tradition, Saṅgraha), and edicts of kings are the four legs of law. Of these four in order, the later is superior to the one previously named." [3]) However "whenever there is disagreement between custom and Dharma or between evidence and Dharma, then the matter shall be settled in accordance with Dharma." [3]) But a clever reservation was made against possible imperfections of revealed Dharma: "Whenever Śāstra is in conflict with rational law (Dharmanyāya, king's law), then reason shall be held authoritative; for there the original text (on which the Dharma has been based) is not available." [3])

The letter of the law was recognized as dangerous: "Chhala-dharma is misinterpretation of the text and an attempt thereby to follow the letter of the rule." [4]) And in one of the Dharma-śāstras we read: "If there is a conflict between two legal points, equity should supersede law. The rule is that a Religious Code is superior to a Legal Code."

Law was constantly changing and adapting itself in India, until English law arrested this process. Institutions once found to exist, or perhaps only found by books to have existed, the facts having been long since reformed, became thus stereotyped. Sir Alfred C. Lyall gives a notable exemple of this in the history of the Brahmo Samaj. The Brahmos disapproved of the common Hindu marriage ceremonies, but for a long time it was not safe for them to disregard them; because any omission of the customary rites might invalidate their marriage in an English court of law. [5])

The question of equality of rights we shall discuss in Part II Chapter VI D.

11. We have noticed already the universal aspect of Dharma. Mānava-dharma is the Dharma of the human race. [6])

[1]) *Manu* XII : 108—111.
[2]) *Vasishṭha* I; *Vishṇu* III : 2; *Āp.* II : V : *10* : 13; *Manu* VII : 35, 144—5.
[3]) *Artha-śāstra* III : *1*. See also p. 35.
[4]) *Bhāg.-P.* VII : *15* : 13.
[5]) A. C. Lyall, *Asiatic Studies*, Vol. I pp. 8—9.
[6]) See S. V. Ketkar, *An Essay on Hinduism*, pp. 29, 11—13.

S a n ā t a n a-d h a r m a is Eternal (or universal) Dharma. As a consequence of the conception of the universality of Dharma rules of **international law** came into being. Of course they were as yet **intertribal** and not international in the modern sense. We shall deal with various points regarding this in Part II Chapter I, and only want to mention here as an instance the rules of war. Manu enjoins "When he (the king) fights with his foes in battle, let him not strike with weapons concealed (in wood) nor with such as are barbed, poisoned, or the points of which are blazing with fire. Let him not strike one who (in flight) has climbed on an eminence, nor an eunuch, nor one who joins the palms of his hands (in supplication), nor one who flees with flying hair, nor one who sits down, nor one who says "I am thine." Nor one who sleeps, nor one who has lost his coat of mail, nor one who is naked, nor one who is disarmed, nor one who looks on without taking part in the fight, nor one who is fighting with another foe, nor one whose weapons are broken, nor one afflicted with sorrow, nor one who has been grievously wounded, nor one who is in fear, nor one who has turned to flight, but in all these cases let him remember the duty of honourable warriors." [1]) And Gautama says that of course captives may not be killed, neither messengers or musicians, and the king who kills an antagonist, whose horse or charioteer has been shot dead, commits sin. [2]) These rules of chivalry, which seem to have been no mere idealistic dreams, but have probably been followed to a large extent, compare favourably with modern warfare, which by its very nature has outgrown all possibility of adapting itself to rules of personal combat. And, as we shall see later, war was a matter of the warrior caste almost exclusively, in those ancient days, and it could happen that in one place there was a battle, and that in the distance husbandmen were tilling their fields or gathering their crops quite peacefully, not directly concerned about the outcome of the battle [3]). The above mentioned rules of chivalry were broken in many stories in the Epics. In this they show their relationship to the rules of modern international law.

12. Sometimes rules of Dharma were invented by categories

[1]) *Manu* VII : 90—93; see also *Yājñ.* I : 326; *Baudhāyana* I : 10, 11, 18, *Gautama* X : 18; *MBh. Śānti-parvan* 65 : 10, 95 : 12—13.
[2]) *Gautama* X : 18.
[3]) See p. 146.

of Brahmans for the **glorification and elevation** of their caste at the cost of the lower castes in order to spiritually dominate them more efficiently. Especially the Parāśara-saṃhitā is full of this: "The blessing of a Brāhmaṇa ranks equal with the merit of all pieties combined." [1]) "Whatever a Brāhmaṇa enjoins is Dharma. He who disobeys the dictates of a Brāhmaṇa should be regarded as a Brāhmaṇa-killer." [2]) "A Brāhmaṇa shall not be made to pay taxes." "The three castes shall remain under a Brāhmaṇa's control." [3]) "Brāhmaṇas are the locomotive sanctuaries, solitary and givers of all boon. Verily the sins of the polluted are washed away by the waters of Brahmanic words. The word of a Brāhmaṇa is the word of a God. A Brāhmaṇa is a moving pantheon, his words can never be falsified." [4]) "The Brāhmaṇas are visible deities. The Brāhmaṇas uphold the world. By the favour of the Brāhmaṇas, Devatās (superhuman beings or gods) reside in the celestial region." [5]) This last sentence is the culmination of priestly arrogance.

They invented moreover terrible punishments at times to enforce their position, punishments of hell and evil reincarnations, and bodily and social punishments, not even to mention the lesser penances.

But some scriptures neatly put side by side descriptions of the Brahman as he ought to be and of the Brahman as he sometimes really was. [6]) And Manu, being well aware of actual conditions, for the protection of Dharma says things like this: "Even if thousands of Brahmans, who have not fulfilled their sacred duties, are unacquainted with the Veda (the revelation), and subsist only by the name of their caste, meet, they cannot form an assembly (for settling Dharma)." [7])

13. There are some distinctions of Dharma as to its subject.

A. Sva-dharma is the Dharma of the individual, which is manifesting itself under the limitations of his former life or lives, of his previous actions (k a r m a n), hampering his present unfoldment, and which is the inmost law of his being pointing to his

[1]) *Parāśara* VI : 51.
[2]) *Parāśara* VI : 57.
[3]) *Vasishtha* I.
[4]) *Parāśara* VI : 60—61.
[5]) *Vishnu* XIX : 20—23.
[6]) *Śankha* XIII : 1—8.
[7]) *Manu* XII : 114; also *Vasishtha* III.

particular line of evolution as an individual member of a group. The Sva-dharma determines the Varṇa according to the principle: "according to the social behaviour of a man his Varṇa is manifest". [1]) It originally determined the class in India, but with the degeneration of the caste system, the caste began to fix the Sva-dharma, which became subsidiary. In Part II we shall revert to this at great length, as also to

B. Varṇa-dharma, the Dharma of the Varṇas.

C. Jāti-dharma is the Dharma of a Jāti or caste.

D. The distinction between the **Dharma for Āryas** and the **Dharma for Anāryas** is a sub-variety of either Varṇa-dharma or Jāti-dharma, according to circumstances. [2])

In modern Hinduism some more distinctions have arisen which are worth mentioning.

E. The Dharma of a particular social group manifests under the limitations of the karman of that group, hampering the present full unfoldment. It is the inmost law of the group, pointing to its particular line of evolution by performance of its group-duties as a member of the whole family of groups in society.

F. The Dharma of a nation or **of a state.** For instance the Dharma of a nation at some particular time is the fitting expression of the inner life of that nation in its social forms and in its behaviour towards other nations. If a nation expresses itself in a way inferior to its ability, this means that it is doing badly according to its own standard, and if it persists in its expression it lowers its standard in the scale of standards.

Hinduism recognizes no universal ethical standard. The standard varies according to the degree of development of the individual or of the group. It varies even according to the stages of life of the individual (as systematized in the Āśrama system) [3]) or of the group. In subsequent Chapters we shall revert to this at length.

14. There is also a distinction of Dharma as to its end. There is a philosophical distinction between **Pravṛitti** and **Nivṛitti-dharma.** Pravṛitti-dharma is Dharma which leads man to the pursuit of selfish worldly aims, and consequently to deeper bondage and ignorance. It may be called 'involutionary Dharma'.

[1]) See p. 59. See also "whoever upholds his own duty" on p. 128.
[2]) See Ch. II C.
[3]) See Ch. II F.

Nivṛitti-dharma is unselfishly performed work for the good of the whole. It is performed without the desire for consequences. It may be called 'evolutionary Dharma' [1])

The aim of both is pleasure or joy, but of the former it is egoistic pleasure, of the latter it is pleasure in the harmonious working and interworking of the individuals and groups of society. It is experienced by identification with it after the realization of the underlying unity.

Manu defines them as follows: "The acts prescribed by the Veda are of two kinds, such as procure an increase of happiness and cause a continuation (of mundane existence, pravṛitta), and such as ensure supreme bliss and cause a cessation (of mundane existence, nivṛitta). Acts which secure (the fulfilment of) wishes in this world or in the next [2]) are called pravṛitta (such as cause a continuation of mundane existence); but acts performed without any desire (for a reward), preceded by the acquisition of true knowledge, are declared to be nivṛitta (such as cause [eventually] the cessation of mundane existence)." [3]) The definitions as given above represent conceptions of modern Hinduism.

In connection with this it is logical that it is the Dharma of the performers of Nivṛitti-dharma to know the nature of Dharma; from the others it has to be kept secret, since they will never understand it clearly. Manu says: "The knowledge of the Dharma is prescribed for those who are not given to the acquisition of wealth and to the gratification of their desires; to those who seek the knowledge of Dharma the supreme authority is the revelation (Ṡ r u t i)." [4]) We shall come back to this later.

We have seen that Dharma may mean a great many things, and it will be clear why I do not attempt to translate the word.

Some Hindu scriptures enumerate in one breath a number of the forms of Dharma as described above. For instance in the following verses we can recognise several: "Bhīshma who knew the truth, described (discoursed upon) them (the various courses of Dharma), O sage, as contained in the several Ākhyānas and Itihāsas; described the Dharmas which are laid down according to the nature of men,

---

[1]) S a t, Being, is differentiated into Pravṛitti, Nivṛitti and Mukti (liberation from Illusion).

[2]) That means also works performed with a view to attain heaven are included!

[3]) *Manu* XII : 88—89.

[4]) *Manu* II : 13.

their Varṇa and Āśrama or stage of life; the twofold Dharmas, Pravṛitti and Nivṛitti, laid down with reference to the conditions of renunciation or attachment; the Dharmas or duties of charitable gifts, those inposed upon Kings, those leading to salvation, those laid down for women, and those that delight the Lord, and in general he described Dharma, Artha, Kāma and Moksha, and their accessory means, — he described all these distinctly, without confusion, both briefly and in detail." [1])

15. Another conception, related to Dharma, which has — like Dharma — reached the West in a one-sided way, is **Karman.** Karman means action primarily, secondarily it consists of the fruits of actions inseparably connected with their source of action, viz. the person, and bound to return to that source in due time to re-establish the equilibrium broken by that action. We recognize the same principle of divine justice or Law of Equilibrium mentioned in **7.** In the present treatise we cannot go deeper into this or into the doctrine of reincarnation, which forms really a part of the doctrine of Karman, or rather is its logical outcome. [2])

Dharma is Karman, but much more than that, for it is not only the tendency due to past and present work, but also the divine tendency hidden in the inmost being of man, to unfold in the future. Dharma is the law of his unfoldment, the divine inner potentiality, If Karman implies law and bondage, Dharma holds the element of Divine Grace and the principle of freedom. Karman is a law of cause and effect, Dharma is largely ethical and religious.

16. Sometimes we find that the added element which makes from Karman, Dharma, is **Bhakti,** Love. Some scriptures state that Dharma without love will be mere labour. [3]) So Bhakti is here stated as an attribute of Dharma.

Bhakti is love to God, to the Guru, to the Brahmans, perhaps to the king. But primarily to God. In Hindu philosophy stress is laid on Love without more. Love to God is put before all. Love of humanity is a natural outcome of it, and does not occupy the foremost place in the minds of the people. Only if Bhakti is stated as an attribute of Dharma it implies love of humanity, brotherhood. To allow ourselves a diversion in the spirit of modern Hindu thought,

---

[1]) *Bhāg.-P.* I : 9 : 26—28.
[2]) See also p. 45.
[3]) *Bhāg.-P.* I : 2 : 14.

we might say that love to God, that is love experienced religiously, to Life, that is love experienced mystically, to the neighbour, that is love experienced socially, and the love that returns from God as Divine Grace, from Life as the gift of joy in living and moving, from the neighbour as an act of brotherhood, is of one nature

The doctrine of Bhakti gives as highest stage of Bhakti the merging of the triad of love, lover and beloved into one And Śāndilya defines perfect Bhakti as the unbroken feeling of the Universal Self in one's own self [1])

All 'lower' manifestations of love (love for a form, that is to say, not for the One behind the many and in the whole, but for a part) are only stages on the way to the highest love Fellow-feeling, the consciousness of kind, brotherhood, the horizontal view of humanity, all of which conceptions we shall discuss in Part II, are all aspects of the nature of love In social conduct the essential ethical factor is not the "this is right and that is wrong", but the degree of sociality As we shall see in Part II Ch VI, the vertical composition of society and the horizontal composition of humanity must be clearly distinguished Sociality concerns both, love in each of its aspects, brotherhood, comradeship, good fellowship, etc., is only connected with the latter

Dharma without love will be mere labour [2])— I think in these days many people are 'merely labouring'

Our analysis of Dharma having come to an end, we cannot conclude without a few words wbout Nīti. It is impossible to draw a hard and fast line between Nīti and Dharma They were not thought to be opposed, but were taken as complementary, and also had much in common Dharma was based upon the Revelation, Nīti derived its authority from its innate worth and was less imperative in its tone In later Sanskrit literature and in the various vernacular literatures Dharma has received the meaning of 'religion', and Nīti that of 'morality' [3]) Dr Ketkar writes that the influence of the writers on Nīti must have been a great check on too extravagant claims of Dharma [4])

'Dharma' is very ancient It is found in the Ṛig-veda. [5])

[1]) *Nārada-sūtra* 18
[2]) S Subba Rao, *Srimad Bhagavatam, Vol I p* 7
[3]) S V Ketkar, *The History of Caste* Vol I p 128
[4]) Early Nīti teachings are found in the *MBh Sabhā parvan* 17
[5]) Eg Ṛig veda X 90 15

From the above enquiry it is clear that Dharma, as we stated at the beginning of this Chapter, is the underlying motive principle in the social evolution of humanity towards the manifestation and demonstration of the soul, or in other words, of the basic oneness of mankind.

Dharma is realized spontaneously and in a new light by the individual at each step in his evolution, and it points the way to the next step. At each further step it shows itself more divested from personal factors in the sense of separative (egoistic) endeavour, and yet manifests more intimately and actively through personal factors as individual specialization for the common good. In other words, it tends to manifest the mystico-social unity through the individual in his limitations of time and space (Karman). To this process we shall recur in Part II in full detail.

Dharma is seen by men according to the different stages of their development, or to the colour of their character, which is related to the special field they are working in, and the special psychological angle from which they are wont to look at it. The religious man will see Dharma as the divine law of God, the ethical person will see it as the inner principle that affords standards of good and evil, the lawyer will see it as law, as a plan of protection of right and security, the psychologist will stress tradition, common law and the social mind, the philosopher will see in it the consciousness of kind or the consciousness of unity, by its nature impelling man in the long run to manifest 'kindness' or unity, the idealist will see it as the ideal, the realist as the law behind the existent show of life, the practical mystic will see in it the force impelling to brotherhood, building the community and bringing about harmony in unity.

But in truth it is the principle at the bottom of and contained in all these manifestations, and underlying all these conceptions.

To speak in terms of Indian Philosophy: Man in truth or in essence *is* perfect, but as we see him in form-life by means of the senses and the mind dependent upon the senses, and as he manifests himself 'most imperfectly' in the mirage show of life (M ā y ā) that the senses and the mind dependent upon the senses become aware of and build up, how can one expect clarity and exactness! Only direct realization, the higher 'vision', may reveal truth and bring about inner clarity. In the Māhābharata we find: "The holy men of old.... had an *intuitive* perception of all Dharmas." [1])

[1]) *MBh. Vana-parvan* 183 : 63.

To continue this line of thought: Dharma in truth is 'perfect', but as it manifests in the mirage show of life (the material world, the emotional world and the mental world) of which the senses and the mind of man are aware, it takes shape in imperfect forms, and man may become aware of it only according to his limitations in time and space (of Karman). Individual man becomes aware of Dharma according to the degree of alignment of his true Self to the outer world and to his personality, or in other words according to his stage of development as a social-mystical member of the whole, as a human being in society and as a spark of life in the cosmos.

Like anything else people have tried to misuse the name of this basic principle for egoistic ends. No greater sins have been committed in history than those in the name of virtue, no greater cruelties than those of religious enthusiasm turned to extremes of fanaticism, no greater injustices than those in the name of justice.

In accordance with the nature of Dharma as we have shown it to have been conceived by the ancient seers, it has not only to be grasped mentally, but it has to be realized in its pristine natural singleness. This is the prime requisite. Next its aspects have to be mentally analysed and clearly distinguished. The Hindu doctrine is that all the time man has to open up all his inner faculties in order to be instrumental to Dharma. To the extent he is not able to realize Dharma intuitively, he has to perform the Dharma of his class, his family and profession, as ordained by Karman. If he has not yet any subjective realization, he must follow duty and work in society, as laid down in the scale by people wiser than himself, as a child follows a particular school and not any other, because his parents thus deem the most advisable. If later he gets the subjective realization, it may overrule the decisions and opinions of the others, and change the course of his life.

It is clear that Dharma implies action and can never mean a flight from work. But here we must remember that there are many kinds of action, ranging between physical labour and the emotional, mental and spiritual work of a hermit or sannyāsin. The hermit, though living apart from his fellowmen, may, according to Hindu doctrine, influence the thoughtworld of man and the general spiritual standard of the time. If he does, he performs his Dharma, if he does not, he is a useless unit of society and as lazy as the labourer who lies down to sleep beside his work.

A change of work — according to the theory of Dharma — may

either be a flight from work (non-social and thus against individual development) or — as we mentioned above — due to a flash of direct realization of personal Dharma.

How does man become aware of Dharma? To say it again in another way: Not from books of law and ethics, nor from sacred scriptures, nor by means of scientific theories. Nor does the enlightened person act because public opinion or a special group of people expect it from him. But he becomes aware of an urge within himself, and, because it demands satisfaction, he follows, he obeys. The religious man will call it listening to the voice of God and obeying it. The ethical man will call it doing his duty and obeying his conscience. The practical sociologist will call it following his calling. The philosopher will call it doing the logical next step. The mystic will call it obeying the need of his heart. The types, like all psychological types, will of course overlap. To all types of men 'it' speaks in some way or another and for all of them 'it' takes of course the 'right' form for them. They all are right, as they all know. But as a rule few people are aware that the others are also right. If I may be allowed here to express a personal hope I should like to say that it is to be hoped that the tendency which is so prevalent in Western society of laying down the law for others, judging others according to one's own standard, and of attaching more weight to public opinion than to individual freedom, may gradually be modified and mitigated by greater aptitude of understanding of each other's special work and place in society, as organs with their special functions in the organic whole — as expressed by the theory of Dharma and Varṇa. We shall recur to this at length in Part II. It is most desirable in our days that the students of the different sciences, the religious people of the different sects, the philosophers of the different schools, the psychologists and many more types of workers will once more realize their common basis and will be once more connected by threads of understanding and appreciation. The sociologist — among others — has here an important task as mediator. The sociologist must, in order to efficiently perform his work, be on the one hand a seer of unity and oneness, a mystic (which much-feared word, perhaps on account of the word-associations with 'mystery' and with 'misty', might be translated with caution as 'direct beholder of unity') and on the other hand a practical applier. If he is a *true* mystic, not one of the sloppy type, he cannot but be also a true practical applier. I only make the distinction because the notion of some is that a mystic is a vague and impractical dreamer, and that of others that a practical man cannot be a mystic.

If for anybody, these two requisites count for the sociologist. His Dharma is to form a connecting link between different people and groups of heterogeneous make-up, to be an educator of public belief and of public opinion and to be an invoker of socializing tendencies from the social unconscious.

In a way of course it is the Dharma of all people high up in the scale of social development, and we are watching to-day many of the leaders of science, philosophy, religion and literature doing exactly this work, in the lecture hall, on the platform, in the pulpit and in their writings. Yet their work is coloured by their special branch of work, and it is the task of the sociologist to unify, synthesize and adjust their achievements, criticizing them from a sound scientific standpoint. The modern social-psychologist has taken largely the place of the prophet and mystic of ancient times, because the needs of the present day require it. But I believe that fundamentally his task is exactly the same.

I have stated my personal views, because they seem to me to be part and parcel of a renewed realization of the primeval norm, Dharma or however we may call it, a rebirth which we are at the present time watching in course of development. In various Chapters of Part II I shall come back to this.

D. DHARMA AND THE END(S) OF LIFE. Because social life is largely the visible outcome of thought, religious belief and experience, and realization of truth, it is necessary here to describe the aims of life in the world, and the end of life as a whole (or better: as a co-ordinated unit) as pictured by the ancient Hindu philosophers. What is more important than studying motive powers in society, and so to understand the causes of actions.

The scriptures propound a fourfold end: Artha, Kāma, Dharma and Moksha. They are psychological tendencies which have to be purified and perfected, or in other words: socialized. Artha is the trend to (perfection of) wealth and material wellbeing. it is and has to be manifested as subsidiary and subservient to the second: Kāma which is the trend to (perfection of) feeling and desire, of sensuous and sensual experience [1]), this is and has to be manifested as subsidiary and subservient to Dharma, the trend to mental (incl. moral) perfection. All are subsidiary and subservient to Moksha, spiritual liberation. [2])

Saying it in Christian terms, we might perhaps call Moksha the Kingdom of Heaven, and Dharma, in its highest aspect naturally (ruling Artha and Kāma), the Kingdom of Heaven *on earth*, for which few are chosen, since most see Dharma only in its lower aspects.

Others will hold that also Moksha or Mukti (the state when all ignorance with its bondages is destroyed, and truth shines unveiled) may represent a life on earth. It is then merely a difference of terminology.

In the different periods of Indian history Dharma, and not Moksha, came on the whole foremost as ideal and was considered as supreme. [3])

In this place only the relation of the four ends is of importance. Of course Artha and Kāma are subsidiary. Manu says: "Let him avoid (the acquisition of) wealth and (the gratification of his) desires, if they are opposed to Dharma, and avoid also those acts of Dharma which are opposed to and hurt the feelings of the general public, and lead not to joy, even in the future." [4]) And Dharma is the means of attaining Moksha, only by performing one's work does one attain spiritual insight and liberation, not by running away from it. The Bhagavad-gītā proclaims this again and again and the Bhāgavata states: "He who has his mind and intellect cleansed by the performance of his own Dharma and has fully realized My nature, attains knowledge and wisdom and in a short time reaches Me. This is the righteous course of conduct of those that are in the pale of the Varṇa and Āśrama system: And that course united to devotion to Me becomes the best means of attaining Moksha." [5])

It is interesting that — like there are four Varṇas and four Āśramas — so there are four ends of life. Must we put them side by side with the four stages, pictured in the Varṇa system and in

---

[1]) "The end of Kāma is not the gratification of the senses, but the benefit of Kāma is only to that extent to which it contributes to the support of life." (*Bhāg.-P.* I : *2* : 10). (In re Artha: *Bhāg-P.* I: *2:* 9).

[2]) See also p. 73.

[3]) See Part II Ch. II B and Ch. VI C.

[4]) *Manu* IV : 176.

[5]) *Bhāg.-P.* XI : *18* : 46—47.

the Āśrama system? If we do, it is very interesting to watch the result. I have not found a single instance in literature where this analogy was tried, but probably it was originally implied in the system. When arranging them thus, we get, beginning 'at the bottom':

1. The Śūdra-varṇa, labourers — Artha, wealth — Ist Āśrama, of the Brahmachārins, learners and students.

2. The Vaiśya-varṇa, merchants, etc. — Kāma, desire — 2nd Āśrama, of Gṛihasthas, householders.

3. The Kshatriya-varṇa, the kings, nobles, and military men — Dharma — 3rd Āśrama, of Vānaprasthas, who spend their time with sacrifices.

4. The Brāhmaṇa-varṇa, priests — Moksha, liberation — 4th Āśrama, of Sannyāsins, those who have renounced all. [1]) The analogy should of course not be carried too far.

Only in the last case it is absolutely clear, and do the stages correspond. In 1 and 2 they correspond pretty well. In 3 it is less clear, though even here there is a remarkable correspondence: the military man sacrifices his life in the world, the nobleman sacrifices socially, the Vānaprastha sacrifices spiritually. Of course we do not want to prove that the three lines — of Varṇa, ends of life, and Āśrama — do or ought to correspond exactly. All we want to show is that we find a similar and analogous fourfold division of grades in the life of mankind as a whole, in the life of individual man, and in the end(s) of life. And also in historical sequence, as pictured by the composers of the Purāṇas, where they mention the sequence of four Ages in their chronology: *1.* the Satya-yuga or" Golden Age" in which Dharma goes, symbolically speaking, on four feet; *2.* The Treta-yuga, in which Dharma goes on three feet; *3.* The Dwāpara-yuga (2 feet); *4.* The Kali-yuga or "Age of Discord", in which Dharma goes only on one foot. For our analogy the order has to be reversed. At present we are in the Kali-yuga, the most materialistic of the Ages.

We can extend the analogy a little and compare the four stages and the four ends of life with the fourfold man of Indian philosophy: I. The body (symbol: earth), 2. The body of feelings and emotions (westernized under the name: astral body; symbol: water), and 3. The mind (symbol: fire), all three to be co-ordinated under 4. the soul or true man.

[1]) See pp. 79—82.

The lower three, Artha, Kāma and Dharma are sometimes called the spheres of the three Guṇas [1]), here we have another analogy, which lies too far in the metaphysical field to concern us here, like also the four Yoga paths.

A further very interesting analogy is the old doctrine of the temperaments or psychological types of Galenus: (taking the words in their *original* meanings, and not in the popular) 1. Melancholici, 2. Phlegmatici, 3. Sanguinici and 4. Cholerici, based on the ancient doctrine of the four elements: 1. earth, 2. water, 3. fire and 4. air.

Popularly Artha and Kāma are not seen in their perfected form, but in their imperfect manifestations, and represent respectively greed and lust; like Dharma may be popularly merely a rule of law or convention, perhaps far from 'right'. [2])

What is attained through the pursuit of this fourfold end? It is happiness, which can be expressed again in a scale of four degrees, well-known to all: health and wealth — pleasure — happiness or joy — bliss.

But the sages who compiled the old scriptures saw everything in its due relation and proper light [3]). Systematization and clarity were their ideals. The end of life was not a heaven of delight! "The chief end of life here is not the attainment of heaven popularly known to be the result of pious duties, but it is the desire to enquire into Truth." [4]) To be short, it was a matter of consciousness, here and now.

Since Dharma is for our purpose the most interesting and the main end of life, we shall now consider it with greater attention.

The performing of Dharma is the cause of happiness. [5]) The performing of Dharma means the performing of the individual duties of class and Āśrama, as realised by personal experience in the more developed stages. It brings as fruit happiness in one or more of its forms, (according to the alignment of the other ends to Dharma): health and wealth, pleasure, happiness, and bliss. The

---

1) *Bhāg.-P.* I : *8* : *27*.

2) *See Manu* IV : 176, quoted above.

3) "To act solely from a desire for rewards is not laudable, yet an exemption from that desire is not (to be found) in this world: for on that desire is (even) grounded the study of the Veda and the performance of the actions, prescribed by the Veda." (*Manu* II : 2).

4) *Bhāg.-P.* I : *2* : 10.

5) In popular mythology this is symbolized in that the three sons of Dharma are Śamā, Kāma and Harsha, Tranquillity, Love and Joy (*MBh. Ādi-parvan* 66 : 30).

ancient Hindus never racked their brains about 'the greatest good of the greatest number', or about the question whether the happiness of the state or the happiness of the individual comes foremost. They mentioned simply: happiness. Probably because they saw that in truth the individual can be only perfectly happy (in all its four grades and aspects) in a happy society, and that society as a whole can only be perfectly 'happy' if its individual members are, like man's body can only be in perfect health if all members and organs are well functioning and healthy (which is in truth the same). It is like the question: which came first: the hen or the egg?

Dharma, even if perfectly performed, becomes fruitless and worthless if considered subservient to wordly objects: "He shall not fulfil his sacred duties merely in order to acquire the worldly objects (as fame, gain and honour). For when they ought to bring rewards (duties thus fulfilled) become fruitless." [1])

To the school of the Mimansists Dharma is whatever act is instrumental to the attainment of the highest Bliss. Considering what we wrote above, this is the logical conclusion. Also the 'three lower degrees' of happiness are imperfect manifestations of Bliss, which is perfect. Or, from another angle: the 'three lower aspects' of happiness are reflections of Bliss.

Bliss is not the aim (heaven forbid!), but it is the goal, and the stages of life are the steps to this goal. [2])

The definition of Dharma by Swami Vivekananda, the great monk, looks to me one-sided. He mixes up in this definition happiness as goal and as end. He says: "Dharma is that which makes man seek for happiness in this world or the next. Dharma is established on work; Dharma is impelling man day and night to run after, and work for happiness." [3]) But means and end is Dharma, goal is Mukti.

The religious way of expressing it is that all Dharma ultimately points to God. "All knowledge [4]) finds its end in Vāsudeva; all meditation refers to Vāsudeva; all Dharma ultimately points to Vāsudeva, and all attainment culminates in Vāsudeva." [5]) Vāsudeva

[1]) *Āp.* I : 7 : 20 : 1—2.

[2]) Manu also points to bliss as the goal of him who follows Dharma (*Manu* II : 9).

[3]) *Complete Works*, Vol. V, p. 349.

[4]) The School of Qualified Monism puts: "Knowledge of Matter and Spirit."

[5]) *Bhāg.-P.* I : 2 : 29.

is Śrī-Kṛishṇa, the incarnated Vishṇu (God). [1]) And the mystics know that this incarnation *is* 'life', social life in its highest aspect seen from a cosmic point of view." On the disposition of the limbs of His Person, the worlds stand arranged,. . . ." [2]) The Gnostic Christians had a similar teaching, about the limbs of the body of the Cosmic Christ. We discover in it the organic theory of life, and consequently of society, which we also find in the verses explaining the origin of the classes. [3]) In accordance with the above performing Dharma pays. To conclude with a personal deduction: Dharma brings happiness and profit if all discharge their own duties, regardless of their rights, to the community and their social group, if all nations discharge their duties, regardless of their rights, to the world as a whole. This sounds Utopian, and it *is* Utopian, but even then it is a matter of great encouragement and cheer that at the present day so many persons, and statesmen of various nations are beginning to see, from sheer economic reasons of profit, that peace and co-operation are best. This may save the world from chaos, save the League of Nations from failure and make it go on doing its work on the basis of profit till the time comes that more altruïstic factors can have their say.

Dr. Bhagavan Das wrote: "On the eve of the Mahābhārata war, the Ṛishi Vyāsa cried, and cried in vain: 'I cry with arm uplifted, yet none heedeth. From Righteousness flow forth abundantly both Pleasure and Profit. Why then do ye not follow Righteousness?' But they heeded not the cry, and the result was that which they fought for, the pleasure and the profit of all combatants, were drowned in a sea of blood. A terrible lesson for all the ages that may follow." [4]) And he adds in a footnote in the 2nd edition of this book: "And yet, as Hegel said, the only lesson of history is that men never learn from history. Since the above was written in 1909—10, a far greater war than even the Mahābhārata war has taken place, in 1914—18, ..."

But, since the great war was only yesterday, and for the above mentioned reason we may have confidence in man's nature, if — in this case — only in his mental powers; for after all, man is too

[1]) Christians say: All paths lead to Christ. Christ is the way and the goal.

[2]) *Bhāg.-P.* I : *3* : 3. See also pp. 53—54.

[3]) Quoted Ch. II B.

[4]) *The Science of Social Organization*, p. 50.

intelligent a being to jump headlong into an abyss for the second time in one lifetime, even granted that wars are made by the profiteering few.

E. THE SCRIPTURES. It is very difficult to fix approximate dates to the ancient scriptures of India, for they were written down ages after their birth, since tradition at first admitted only oral transmission from Guru to disciple as we shall see.

It is however even far more difficult to say when the early periods of the ancient Indian and pre-Indian, or of the Aryan and Dravidian civilizations began and ended. All the first Western Orientalists, who lived not so long ago, telescoped millenniums into centuries and centuries into decades in a heroic attempt to put up with the year 4004 B.C. of the Bible for the Creation! [1])

Indian History begins to show approximate dates from the seventh century B.C. Before that the only sources of history are literature and archaeological evidence, for in earlier times there are none of the other sources: inscriptions, coins with their stories, evidence of foreign travellers, or historical annals which may have existed. Of the latter there were few in India, for the interest of the Brahmans was engaged in other pursuits, and the annals of the kings, who were interested to preserve their own doings to posterity, have perished almost completely in consequence of the climate, including insect damage, and of the innumerable political revolutions. [2]) The first foreign evidence are hearsay notes of Herodotus and Ktesias in the 5th century B.C. Later several Greeks and many Chinese wrote reports of their travels and experiences and of Indian customs and laws. Not even the expedition of Alexander the Great is distinctly mentioned by any Hindu author. Truly, the ancient Indians were no historians in the strict sense. For early times our historians have to content themselves with the ancient traditions, laid down in Sanskrit Śāstras (including astronomical observations and other evidence), and with the evidence of ancient remains.

Before describing the Dharma-śāstras, we shall say a few words about the scriptures in general. They are mainly of two types, the Srutis and the Smṛitis. The Srutis (revelation) contain

[1]) C. Johnston, in *Prabuddha Bharata*, Vol. XXXVI p. 195.
[2]) *Oxford History of India*, p. XIX.

the eternal laws of spiritual life, which — like natural laws — cannot be changed. They are contained in the Vedas. The Smṛitis (tradition — recollection) contain rules and regulations relating to man's conduct in society. These are subject to changes demanded by the needs and requirements of the age. The existence of a great number of Smṛitis shows that social usages have changed from time to time. The Śāstras, which are Smṛitis, are textbooks. There are Śāstras of Dharma, of Nīti, of Artha, of Kāma, etc.

It is for some difficult to believe that many of these scriptures, which were only written down at such late dates, since it was not considered proper to commit the sacred knowledge to writing, were really composed ages before Christ. It is however an undoubtable fact that they were transmitted by memory for thousands of years, and even now they are learnt from the mouth of the Gurus, and not from manuscripts or books. Max Müller went so far as to say that if every M.S. of the Ṛig-veda were lost, the whole of it could be recovered from the memory of the Śrotriyas. [1]) He calculated that a student of the Ṛig-veda has to learn in the eight years he is living with his Guru, ten books, containing nearly 30.000 lines, each line reckoned as 32 syllables. [2])

A Chinese Buddhist, I-tsing, who visited India in the 7th century, and spent about twenty years there studying in different monasteries, speaks of the high degree of perfection to which the memory of both Buddhists and orthodox Brahmans attained. He has seen Brahmans, he says, who can recite the 100.000 verses of the four Vedas, handed over from mouth to mouth. [3])

It was in early ages not considered proper that the sacred verses were committed to writing, to preserve the esoteric sense always imperfectly expressed in form. The Celtic Druids just like the Christians in the early centuries after Christ kept secret their creed and did not allow publication. And in the second place, especially in later times, the Brahmans forbade to put them to book, to preserve their privileges as (the only) teachers [4]). The art of writing was only used for more utilitarian purposes. The fact that later law-books threaten with severe punishments persons who copy the Veda, or learn it from a Ms. shows that Mss. existed, and

[1]) *India, what can it teach us*, p. 208.

[2]) Only the 1017 or 1028 hymns of the Ṛig-veda equal in bulk the Ilias and Odyssey together.

[3]) J Takakusu, *I-Tsing, A record of the Buddhist Religion*, p. 182.

[4]) G. S. Ghurye, *Caste and Race in India*, p. 147.

it is indeed known that in the first century Sanskrit Mss. were taken to China and translated there. [1])

The Dharma-śāstras were not law-books in our sense.

Nobody can doubt for a moment, as Bühler writes, that the Dharma-śāstras are manuals compiled by the teachers of the Vedic schools for the guidance of their pupils, that at first they were held to be authoritative in restricted circles, and that they were only later acknowledged as sources of Dharma applicable to all Āryas. This fact is fully acknowledged by the Hindu tradition. [2])

These "Dharma-śāstras proper", of which there are some 24, took their present form sometime between 500 B.C. and 400 A.D. The most important ones are the Manu-saṃhitā, the Yājñavalkya-saṃhitā, the Baudhāyana-saṃhitā, the Nārada-saṃhitā, the Gautama-saṃhitā, which is very old, the Āpastamba-saṃhitā, and the Vishṇu-saṃhitā, which has very ancient parts. The original Sūtra of Manu or Mānava-sūtra was lost and has not been recovered yet. The later metrical code of Manu has been compiled from it, and took its place. What Dr. Robertson wrote about it, though long ago, is still the opinion of modern students of that remarkable code: "With respect to the number and variety of points the Hindu code considers, it will bear a comparison with the celebrated Digest of Justinian, or with the systems of Jurisprudence of nations most highly civilized. The articles of which the Hindu code is composed are arranged in natural and luminous order. They are numerous and comprehensive, and investigated with that minute attention and discernment which are natural to people distinguished for acuteness and subtlety of understanding who have been long accustomed to the accuracy of judicial proceedings and acquainted with all the refinement of legal practice. The decisions concerning every point are founded upon the great and immutable principles of justice, which the human mind acknowledges and respects in every age and in all parts of the earth. Whoever examines the whole work cannot entertain a doubt of its containing the jurisprudence of an enlightened and commercial people. Whoever looks into any particular title will be surprised with a minuteness of detail and nicety of distinction which, in many instances, seem to go beyond the attention of European legislation; and it is remarkable that

[1]) M. Müller, *Op. Cit.* p. 213.
[2]) G. Bühler, *The Laws of Manu,* (S.B.E. XXV) p. XI.

some of the regulations which indicate the greatest degree of refinement were established in periods of the most remote antiquity".[1])

Other Śāstras that are of use for our purpose are the Artha-śāstra, a (rather Macchiavellian) manual of political science, attributed to Kauṭilya, the Minister of Chandragupta. It was written in Sūtra style sometime between 321 and 300 B.C.

Further the Epics and Purāṇas, mythological, and, perhaps to some extent historical scriptures that present the social, the ethical, the religious and the ideal aspects of Dharma. Some of these, like the Bhāgavata-purāṇa at its very beginning, claim to be the scriptures of the highest Dharma, *the* scriptures on Dharma. Professor Rapson says about the Purāṇas: "We cannot escape from the only possible conclusion that the Purāṇas have preserved in however perverted and distorted a form, an independent tradition, which supplements the priestly traditions of the Vedas and Brāhmaṇas, and which goes back to the same period. [2])

We shall also use Buddhist and more recent scriptures and works as authorities on Dharma.

The scriptures form the sources of Dharma. But there is another source: personal realization. Manu says: "The whole Veda is the first source of Dharma, next the tradition and the virtuous conduct of those who know the (Veda further), also the customs of holy men, and finally self-satisfaction." [3]) Or a parallel line: "The Veda, the sacred tradition, the customs of virtuous men, and one's own pleasure, they declare to be visibly the fourfold means of defining Dharma." [4]) In the first three sources we recognize some of the aspects of our analysis. The last source is personal experience, inner approbation, which has always to attach its seal to everything to give it its full worth.

We shall here only give a few examples out of the many cases where reference is made to conscience, the voice of the 'man within'. "Thou thinkest 'I am alone'", says Śakuntala, the deserted wife, to King Dushyanta, when he refuses to listen to her appeal, "and knowest not the ancient seer (Muni) seated in thy heart, who

---

[1]) W. Robertson, *An historical disquisition concerning the knowledge which the Ancients had of India*, p. 217.

[2]) *Cambridge History of India*, Vol. I p. 302. Pargiter gives a similar opinion in *Ancient Indian Historical Tradition*, p. 334. The name 'Purāṇa' implies 'old'.

[3]) *Manu* II : 6.

[4]) *Manu* II : 12.

knoweth the evil deed — in his presence thou committest falsehood. A man having committed sin thinketh: no one knoweth me. But the gods know him and he that is the inner man." [1] Or: "That violator of Dharma ignores the Devas (Divine Beings) and Me, the Ātman present in his own self." [2] And the well known Buddhist lines from the Jātakamālā: "The fool thinks himself alone and commits sin. But I know of no lonely place at all. Of a bad action my 'Self' is a witness far more sharp-sighted than any other person."

Not all Dharma has been revealed of course. Manu speaks about the "secret portion of these Institutes" [3] and treats after that of doubtful points of law and interpretation of law, and of unforeseen cases.

Yet sometimes we also find the view that the Śruti contains everything, and that all truth is contained in the Veda. From very early times the Hindu doctors appear to have been conscious of difficulties in the interpretation or application of their theory, and sometimes their books contradicted one another. One of the earliest expedients was to suppose the loss of passages in the most ancient portion of the scriptures. [4] "If you ask", says Āpastamba, "why the decision of the Āryas presupposes the existence of a Vedic passage, then I answer, all precepts were originally taught in the Brāhmaṇas, but these texts have been lost. Their former existence may, however, be inferred from usage. It is not, however permissable to infer the former existence of a Vedic passage where pleasure is obtained by following custom, he who follows such usage becomes fit for Hell." [5]

F. THE DHARMA OF THE BUDDHISTS.

It is not really necessary in this place to give an exhaustive analysis of the theories of Dharma of the Buddhists and of the Jain Schools, and to mention where these differ from the Dharma of orthodox Hinduism described in the main above. However since Buddhism had such far-reaching social effects, we shall touch upon those characteristics of Dhamma, the Buddhist interpretation of Dharma, which have a practical bearing.

1) *MBh. Ādi-parvan* 74 : 28—29.
2) *Bhāg.-P.* XI : *18* : 41.
3) *Manu* XII : 107.
4) H. S. Maine, *Dissertations on Early Law and Custom*, p. 17.
5) *Āp.* I : 4 : 12 : 10, quoted by Maine.

What we shall say about it, may be taken on the whole to be also representative of the Jain conceptions of Dharma.

Defined in another way we find the main aspects of our analysis of Hindu Dharma back in the Buddhist books. For instance Buddhaghosa, who did not claim originality in the matter, writing in the fifth century A.D., gave the following analysis of Dhamma [1]), in which we shall recognise some of our points in another guise:

(*1*) The Doctrine, as a verbal, or literary composition to be learnt and mastered. (*2*) Condition or cause. This is illustrated by the quotation: "Dharma-analysis is knowledge concerning conditions."[2]) And the Piṭaka phrase: "Investigation of Dhamma is insight into cause." [3]) (*3*) Right, or righteousness. (*4*) Phenomenon. The Pali word here used means non-entity, non-substrate, non-soul-ness. It means that a mental object, a state of mind is a phenomenon.

This meant that insight into Dhamma (not a question of soul, nor of mind, but realization in the "higher mind"), as we read in the Sutta-piṭaka, meant "the discernment of an eternal, orderly, conditioned sequence of things, the which, when thoroughly grasped, swept out of a man's thoughts all speculation on the beginning of life or its ultimate end, or on its present nature as entity or soul." [4])

From this we see that these Buddhists also recognised (the same that we indicated at the beginning of this Chapter), that the immediate knowledge of Dharma must come first and is supreme. And that religion, metaphysics, logic and philosophy of law come only in the second place and are synthesised under it and by it. As to those sciences, it is not our intention of "sweeping them out of our thought". We merely want to bring forward that intuitive realization of truth (if one does not like to call it 'perception') rules and overrules the way of the senses and the lower mind. Yet must this realization, not to fall into error, (concerning those who might delude themselves about their 'intuition') always be tested by

[1]) Taken from Mrs. Rhys Davids, *Buddhism*, (1st. Ed.) p. 49.

[2]) *Vibhanga* (*Abhidhamma-piṭaka*).

[3]) *Buddhism*, (1st Ed.) p. 78.

[4]) *Saṃyutta-nikāya* II : 25—27, 60, quoted from Mrs. Rhys Davids, *Buddhism*, (1st Ed.), p. 50.

[4]) Enlightening information on Dharma is given in the Chapter on Dharma of Mrs Rhys Davids' *Śākhya, or Buddhist origins*, and in *Buddhism, its Birth and Dispersal*. Dharma is considered as theory of no-soul, as the law of causation, as moral law, as ideal, as cosmic order, as doctrine, as standard, etc.

common sense and logic. These Buddhists called the ordinary mind process speculation, which indeed it is, for it is founded upon assumed axioms, which cannot be said of intuitive realization, if this is in truth what its term implies. Dharma is seen directly: "...the wise know Dharma in the very self. Here I have a Fellow-Student, ever knowing, ever seeing." [1])

What, now, are the social implications of Dhamma? Here of course we have to touch upon Kamma, the Pali equivalent of Karman. We read in the Jātakamālā that "Kamma affects all creatures, even down to the grass". Also we read that "My kamma is my possession, my kamma is my inheritance, my kamma is the womb which bears me, my kamma is the race to which I am akin, my kamma is my refuge." [2]) In short, it has to do with every kind of action and phenomenon with which we are concerned and we recognise in this enumeration many different elements. The karmic factors (saṃskāras) are the background of all evolution, and they can be divided in several categories, of which social karman is one, devided again in karman of family, karman of race, etc. Mr. Suzuki writes in his *Outline of Mahāyāna Buddhism*: "Everything done is done once and for all, and its footprints are generative, good or evil. No deed can be done without leaving some impressions either in the individual or supra-individual (that is the collective) consciousness. [3]) No act remains traceless, but lives potentially or actively in the world of minds and deeds". And only by putting into action counter-karman may Karman be neutralized and equilibrium be re-established. Here we have the doctrine of Karman in a few words. We cannot devote more space to this seemingly simple, but in fact very complicated doctrine. Of course what we mentioned is not typically Buddhist, the Hindu doctrine comes close to it.

Evil brings suffering, "the accumulation of evil is painful" (this is specially stressed in Buddhism), and "if a man does what is good, let him do it again; let him delight in it: the accumulation of good is happiness." [4]) Good and evil deeds can of course only be performed in the world, in the psychic world community called Dharmadhātu, the 'region of Dharma' or spiritual universe, not an

[1]) *Gradual Sayings* I : 132f. From *Buddhism* (Rev. Ed.), p. 88.

[2]) *Aṅguttara-nikāya, Pañcaka-nipāta.*

[3]) This covers probably the "collective unconscious" of Jung plus the "social mind".

[4]) *Dhammapada* IX : 117, 118.

imaginary 'moral region', but a state of consciousness, which is the expression of the One Dharmakāya, which is literally the 'body of the Dharma' and means pure consciousness, beyond body or form or attribute.

Contrary to the current belief in the West, Buddha did not teach a flight from the world and a negation of life, as we shall indicate in Part II, Ch. II and VI.

Interesting is the clear distinction which is made between letter and spirit of the Dharma, we find often in the Buddhist scriptures: "The doctrine of Dharma, which is glorious in its spirit and glorious in its letter."

For practical purposes the Dhamma is defined as the 'Noble Eightfold Path': 1. Right comprehension, 2. right resolutions or aspirations, 3. right speech, 4 right acts, 5. right way of earning a livelihood, 6. right efforts, 7. right thoughts, and 8. the right state of a peaceful mind, or right rapture. [1])

Perhaps the attitude to Dharma of the ordinary Buddhist is expressed best in the following verses: "Let a man's pleasure be the Dharma, let him delight in the Dharma, let him stand fast in the Dharma, let him know how to inquire into the Dharma, let him not raise any dispute that pollutes the Dharma, and let him spend his time in pondering on the wellspoken truths of the Dharma." [2]) And in a more sublime setting it shines from the following opening of a Sūtra: "All aspirations of the Bodhisattvas, countless as Ganges sands, are comprehended in the great aspiration — taking refuge in the Dhamma." [3])

In popular belief Dharma took a personified form as Dharma-Rāja, the king of the dead as a king of justice. He is the Yama-Rāja of the Hindus and corresponds very much with Osiris, both have the symbolical weighing ceremony. The same we find in the 10th book of Plato's Republic.

But, as we saw above, in ordinary Buddhism, Dharma is the Path, and for men on the Path more important than the Buddha, as we may gather for instance from the words of the Tibetan saint Milarepa to his desciples: "Personal love and regard make ye think that I must be an Incarnation; but towards the Dharma ye commit

[1]) T. W. Rhys Davids, *Dialogues of the Buddha*, Vol. II p. 226. P. Carus, *The Gospel of Buddha*, p. 33.

[2]) P. Carus, *The Gospel of Buddha*, p. 149.

[3]) *Srimāla devi Siṃhananda*, from K. Saunders, *Lotuses of the Mahāyāna* p. 53.

the great sin of doubt and scepticism.... It is by the great power of the Sacred Dharma alone that I have been able to attain such spiritual advancement as to be very near Buddhahood in the latter portion of my years, although I had been guilty of such heinous sins in my youth and early manhood...." [1] [2]

In Part II Chapter II we shall describe some of the changes wrought in the constitution of Hindu society by the propagation of Dhamma by the Buddhists.

G. SOME ANCIENT CONCEPTIONS AKIN TO DHARMA. That some of the ancient cultures had discovered and realized the Principle which the Hindus called Ṛita and Dharma, we shall try to show in this section. For lack of time and space we shall have to confine ourselves to some of the most important cultures of the ancient world and leave out others like the Chinese, the Egyptians, etc.

Among the ancient Hebrews there were conceptions which were similar to those of the Hindus. In the Tora we find that the attributes of God are identical to Love and Justice. For those two divine attributes there is one word, T s e d a k a, meaning divine justice as well as divine love, meaning love to God as well as love to the neighbour. This divine justice, which is a law of nature, and consequently requires no sanction of worldly power or violence, can for this reason only be essentially the same as the law of Karman, and also essentially the same as Dharma, since Tsedaka is also divine grace, and human charity and benevolence. Its social implication is a complete giving of oneself to God and his work in the world in service and love. [3]

The Jews distinguished clearly between this divine justice and human justice as an outcome of law [4], which can never be natural law; which needs to be enforced and is only a phantom of justice really. The illogical and cruel Talio doctrine which may have been older, may have existed side by side, developed from the more primitive instincts and may have become joined to the other

[1]) Ed. W. Y. Evans-Wentz, *Tibet's Great Yogi Milarepa,* p. 233.

[2]) That on the Path the truth is essential and not the Buddha, may be gathered also from the *Mahāparinibbāna-suttanta* II : 30—35 (S.B.E. Vol. XI).

[3]) *Jüdisches Lexikon* (Berlin) Vol. V p. 1476.

[4]) *Op. Cit.* Vol. II pp. 1024—1025.

doctrine thereby pushing it to the background as soon as the realizations of justice and law became vague, and then it must have come to the foreground. This is however all speculation.

Sin brings about guilt, that is a duty to God to right the moral wrong, to restore the inner balance, according to Jewish doctrine.[1]) In this we find the same which in Hindu Philosophy is often expressed that the only true way to destroy one's sins or bad Karma is by prayer and meditation. The *outer* adjustment, the social reparation or satisfaction must be the natural result of this inner process.

"The greatness of the guilt is not measured by the social results but depends upon the motives and on the amount of energy required for committing the sin." The sinner "hopes for the Grace of God only after he has removed the sinful motives from his soul."[1]) In this we again come to the root of Dharma.

The T o r a (lit. "doctrine") offers law, morality, and religion as a unified whole[2]), requiring acceptance as such, being divine revelation. Because it was not man-made it cannot be repealed by man, except if particular rules have become obsolete because the original conditions have fallen away or have become entirely altered. As a whole they can only be fundamentally altered or repealed by God himself, which will happen according to Jewish belief "in the days of the Messiah", when the Jewish ritual will lose its binding power. In this we recognize, according to the "Jüdisches Lexikon"[3]) the fundamental difference between two kind of rules. Partly is this difference covered by the distinction between M i s c h p a t t i m and C h u k k i m, the former meaning the clear regulations of legal and moral duties coming forth from the "natural light of the human intelligence", the latter being the divine injunctions, the meaning of which is hidden from man, according to Jewish belief. This distinction we find again in the distinction between reasoned law and revealed law, according to Dr. Wiener, the writer of this particular article.[4]) In spite of this distinction both are fundamentally the same: before the distinction

[1]) *Op. cit.* Vol. IV p. 1410.

[2]) Judaism knows no division between civil and religious law. Also ethics is codified law (*Op. cit.* Vol. IV, p. 1262).

[3]) Vol. II p. 1106.

[4]) Another distinction, not of great interest to us, is that between M i s c h p a t and D i n. Mischpat is usually unwritten law and Din written law (*Op. cit.* Vol. IV p. 1262).

was seen the same underlying law or order, and basic principle, which we mentioned in connection with Dharma, was realized, it was similarly not to be mentally understood, yet to be innerly grasped. (Or could it not be realized by man at all, according to Jewish doctrine?) Perhaps it was originally grasped, and later held not to be understandable (which indeed *mentally* it was not), and it became a crystallized dogma, a secret system of a far-removed God. And not to be touched or changed — unless the Messiah came! Now if this is taken to symbolize the Messiah in every human being, it would mean that, at a certain moment in their psychological unfoldment, men could perceive and grasp that hidden Principle, not with the lower, but with the higher mind. And if it is taken to mean a Messiah really, it may be a forecast of a period of revival, of fresh law, revealed in man himself, a period of a new Buddha, to speak in terms of the former section of this chapter, or — on a smaller scale any period of revival. [1])

In this prohibition to repeal or abolish these divine laws we find another and an extreme formulation of the warning which we shall mention later on, that no outer organization or constitution should be changed before its mind picture has become changed. Perhaps this warning has to be enlarged in keeping with the above prohibition, that it is unwise even to change the mind picture before the vision has again dawned.

To conclude we may mention that this Principle was — of course — seen as universal, and we consequently find even traces of the formulation of a kind of international law, like in India. We quote the three following illustrations from the "Jüdisches Lexikon." [2]) "All foreigners are loved by God and everywhere the Tora places them on a par with Israel." (*Mechilta, Ex.* 21 : 8) "Cursed be he who violates the law of the foreigner, of the orphan and of the widow." (*Ex.* 23 : 6; *Lev.* 19 : 15; *Deut.* 16 : 20; 27 : 19) "Who violates the law of a foreigner has equally violated the law of God." (*b. Chag.* 5*a*) [3])

But the tribal spirit of the Jews does not seem to have made them adhere always faithfully to all these norms in later times.

Some of these ideas we should like to have confirmed by deeper studies of Jewish law.

---

1) See Part II Ch. II E.
2) See Vol. II p. 1025.
3) Cf. Part II Ch. I.

Somló, quoting Jhering, points to the conformity between *Dharma, Mischpat*, δίκη and the *Tabu* of several primitive peoples. [1])

The Greek δίκη contained, like Dharma, all the provinces of life: convention, morality and law. Who lived according to it was δίκαιος. who did not was ἄδικος without distinction between the rules of law, of convention, of religion or of ethics, according to Jhering. [2])

"Δίκαιος is the man, as he ought to be; ἄδικος, his contrast, is scorning the law, as the godless, the evil, the impertinent and the shameless man. Of course this does not mean that the Greeks who, like other civilized peoples, were not able to do without law, *had not grasped correctly its conception.* They even distinguished between the divine and the human (θέμις and νόμος). But what is essential is *that they have continually preserved that indeterminate general conception of* δίκη, and that they cannot even miss it to indicate that which is in conformity with law (τὸ δίκαιον) or against it (τὸ ἄδικον)." [3]) Exactly like the Indian conceptions of dharma and adharma.

Jhering calls this lack of differentiation, *"which one should expect least of all of such an eminently gifted philosophical people"* as the Greeks, a characteristic indicating a low stage of development. He is right in so far as that a stage of clear differentiation is of course much higher than one of deficient differentiation, provided the underlying principle — whatever name one likes to give it — is continually clearly realized. But if this basic, in its realization and manifestation unifying and synthetic principle is no more perceived, the loss is of far more weight than the gain of the scientific distinction.

I tend to believe that the existence of the endless variety of theories of law and the state, which are advocated at the present time, many of which are opposed to one another or one-sided, is a clear sign that "the Principle" is no more realized. Another sign is the loss of harmony and balance between the various special sciences, religion and the various schools of philosophy. Yet all the sciences, religion and philosophy are based upon truth and the desire for knowledge of truth. In the One Principle, either in its static aspect (truth) or in its dynamic aspect (Dharma) is their common ground. Again, a stage of far-going specialization is only

---

1) F. Somló, *Juristische Grundlehre*, 2nd ed. p. 123.

2) Jhering, *Der Zweck im Recht*, II 4, pp. 40—41, quoted by Somló.

3) The italics are mine.

a step forward if the balance and the unity are preserved, and if all the special branches realize their organic function and personal importance in the one body. At the present day many of the schools of law, of ethics, of religion, of sociology may be considered to stand side by side. Professor Bolland and many others had good cause to rage against unhealthy specialism.

We may conclude that the Greeks, like the Hindus, the Hebrews, and also the Romans, as will be shown later, in the dawn of their great cultures saw life as a whole, saw the inner and the outer world as one, recognized not only, but realized the underlying law or principle and consequently were in that respect further advanced than the present age. However, in the present age signs of the search for and renewed realization of this principle are to be noticed.

The myth of the 'Golden Age' found all over the world among ancient cultures as wide apart as the Egyptians, the Greeks, the Romans, the Hindus and Iranians, the Jews, the Chaldaeans, the Scandinavians, the Irish Celts, the Chinese, the Mayas, Red Indians, tribes in the Pacific, in Australia and in Africa, etc. etc., seems to embody the remembrance of a state of perfect social balance, harmony and happiness due to the perfect realization of this primeval norm. Since we are in this book mainly concerned with India, let us quote only one typical example from Indian literature: "In the Kṛita-yuga [1]) Dharma proceeds on all four feet as supported by the people of the time, and, O King, the four feet of the powerful and perfect Dharma are truthfulness, mercifulness, tapas [2]) and charitable gifts. Then the people are contented, full of compassion, friendly to all beings, possessed of tranquility and control over their senses and endurance, finding delight in Ātman [3]), regarding everything with an equal eye and mostly engaged in excercising their own faculties to practice self-control." [4])

The gradual loss of the vision of the primeval Norm corresponds to the 'Fall' of man, a gradual development of egoistic feeling, *thinking* and acting against the interests of the cosmic life and of the human community, or, in other words, of God and of the tribe. [5])

[1]) Which we may call the 'Golden Age'.

[2]) Asceticism: self-discipline, contemplation and spiritual striving.

[3]) The Self.

[4]) *Bhāg.-P.* XII : *3* : 18—19.

[5]) See p. 126.

At the later stage of the great known cultures of the ancient past the vision was only vouchsafed to the leaders of the race. Then the priest, the scientist, the doctor, the mathematician, the artist, the philosopher, were more or less all combined in one person. The students of life then approached the great mystery of truth by all the roads available, they studied truth in all its aspects, they naturally had to look for a basic law, it this was not their starting-point which is more likely. The conflict between the different approaches and branches of study was of much later date, when rival groups of people had taken their special branches.

As long as the basic law and first principle and basic Norm (however we like to call it — I decline to give it merely one name) continued to be realized, it satisfied the most urgent desire for knowledge of truth, entailing happiness, and it served in the second place as a synthetic factor, as bridge from one science to another, from science to religion, from science and religion to art, and so on.

Owing to the far-going specialization that began in the classic past and extended itself dangerously in mediaeval and especially in modern times, the desire to know and consequently the vision of this basic law or essence was lost, at least generally and officially.

That the Hindus, not to mention the others, were able to specialize besides realizing the principle of order and fundamental oneness, their systematic philosophy of life, dating from the Ṛig-vedic Age, and their achievements in the different sciences prove indeed. In the field of religion the Devas or superhuman beings, all aspects of the Supreme Essence of Life, or the One God, and grouped under Him, were psychologically far more real and socially far more effective than the abstract Truth of modern philosophy and the abstract God of established religion or theology, mostly found by logic if found at all, or accepted as a dogma.

To give an illustration from the Ṛig-veda (from the later literature hundreds of illustrations could be quoted): "He who has given us life, who is the creator, He who knows all the places in this universe— He is one, and He is the only name-giver of the gods,. . . ." [1])

Professor Barth writes about those Vedic gods, who were masters close at hand and far more serene than the old German, Greek or Roman gods, as we have come to know them, and lacked most of their human shortcomings and defects: "He (man) must be sincere

[1]) *Ṛig-veda* X : 82 : 3, see also *Ṛig-veda* X : 129.

towards them, for they cannot be deceived. Nay he knows that they in turn do not deceive, and that they have a right to require his affection and confidence as a friend, a brother, a father .... How could it be permitted to man to be bad when the gods are good, to be unjust while they are just, to be deceitful when they never deceive! It is certainly a remarkable feature of the hymns that they acknowledge no wicked divinities and no mean and harmful practices.... In striving to be 'without reproach before Aditi and the Ādityas' the Vedic bards felt the weight of other duties besides those of multiplying offerings to the gods." [1])

To return to Greece. The Greeks believed that even the gods were ruled by Anangkè, Necessity. Aeschylus pointed to this in his Prometheus. In a way Anangkè and Karman cover one another. Anangkè is deterministic, Karman is inevitable, it is an inexorable law. But if we consider the two conceptions more distinctly it is evident that they are opposed. For Anangkè is a supreme principle or being, Fate. And Karman, as subsidiary to and part of Dharma, presupposes free-will. Karman may be modified by counter-karman. [2]) Also Determinism and guilt cannot be reconciled. Yet Karman is very much deterministic (in its sense of inevitable) as regards those who have not yet realized their spiritual freedom and still live largely as slaves of their personal desires. They are ruled by their own nature like by Fate, and the exercise of their freewill is negligible. In the following quotation from the Tibetan work "Karma's Proclamation of His Omnipotence" this freewill is attributed only to the enlightened. All beings, even the gods (who need not be enlightened) are ruled by Karman. Here the conceptions of Anangkè and Karman somewhat correspond. "The Buddhas and the Arhants alone have discovered my true nature, in its very essence, and have triumphed over me. All other beings but live under my despotic rule: I put them to death and I make them to live; I am the deity who giveth them prosperity they enjoy, and I bring about the doing of good deeds and of evil deeds among mankind. *Gods*, emperors, kings, rich and poor, strong and weak, noble and ignoble, brute creatures, and the happy and

[1]) A. Barth, *The Religions of India*, p. 32 sqq.

[2]) And so Karman may in the long run be overcome or get exhausted. In the MBh. we find that the heroes after the exhaustion of their Karman are reunited to the Godhead, of which they were incarnations (Avatāras). *Svargārohana-parvan* 5.

the unhappy spirits existing in this world and in the upper and in the lower worlds — all these I elevate or cast down to their respective states. I humble the high and exalt the low, *according to their several works*. Therefore am I, indeed, the God who ruleth this *phenomenal* Universe." [1])

To conclude this chapter a few words about the conceptions of the Romans. In Rome the distinction between law on the one and convention plus morality on the other hand became clearly seen and applied. Boni Mores were both the precepts of convention and the moral rules which were not yet clearly distinguished, or at least did not develop their own terms. Distinction was made between Fas, divine law, and Ius, human law. For our purpose the oldest conceptions which our students of law have been able to trace, are the most interesting. Muirhead defines Fas as follows, after making the remark that it is very difficult to define its nature and limits": by Fas was understood the will of the gods, — the laws given by heaven for men on earth." [2]) From this definition which is very vague, one may conclude many different things, and consequently it is safe not to conclude anything at all. But he continues: "Among a people that believed so profoundly as did those early Romans that in the gods they lived and moved and had their being it could not fail to be regarded with the utmost consideration and to exercise an influence more potent than any merely human rules. So far as can be gathered from the scattered references to it, it occupied a higher place and had a wider range than these last." Next Muirhead gives some examples of actions which Fas allowed but Ius forbade. An exhaustive enumeration of what fell within the Fas is impossible, he writes. We find in the Fas also the universal element: "There were but few of its commands, prohibitions or precepts that were addressed to men as citizens of any particular state: all mankind came within its scope. It forbade that a war should be undertaken without the prescribed fetial ceremonial, otherwise it was not a *purum piumque bellum*, but an act of violence by the invaders, which their gods had not sanctioned, against others, who were equally god-protected." "It required that faith should be kept even with an enemy when a promise had been

---

[1]) W. Y. Evans-Wentz, *Tibet's Great Yogi Milarepa*, p. XIV. The italics are mine.

[2]) J. Muirhead, *Law of Rome*, p. 14.

made to him under sanction of an oath. It enjoined hospitality to foreigners, because the stranger guest was presumed, equally with his entertainer, to be an object of solicitude to a higher power." [1]) In these injunctions of the Fas we recognize norms of universal ethics plus of universal religion, which were tried to be formulated as a kind of international law naturally including the national law, for no fundamental distinction was seen between self and others. As such it was rather an attempt to realize universal law than international law in the modern sense, which makes a great difference. The same applies to the Jews and to the Hindus. **'Universal law'**, and not **inter-national law**; we recognize the fundamental principle again. [2])

The moral and religious norms we recognize also in that Fas punished murder, because it was the taking of a god-given life, in that it punished the sale of a wife by the husband, for she had become his partner not only in things of the world but also in things divine, etc. etc. Very little seems to be known about the manner in which the rules of Fas were enforced, Muirhead writes [3]). "Were the offenders left to the gods or were they excommunicated and declared sacer?" It is not known. [4])

If they were "left to the gods" it would indicate that the Romans recognized the same basic law or order which we have so often mentioned. I should not be surprised if it had been the older practice; in connection with what we saw concerning the other civilizations, it would be logical. This is made probable since the *original* meaning of *Ius* seems to be just 'law', as a binding rule of action. [5]) The

[1]) Cf. pp. 41 and 83.

[2]) See pp. 16, 41, and Part II Ch. I.

[3]) *Op. cit.* p. 16.

[4]) Excommunication, if the sinner was declared sacer, was the devoting of the sinner to the infernal gods (to his *karman*, G.H.M.), and the forfeiting of his estate to the service of the deity primarily offended. The homo sacer was an outcast in every sense of the word, it was pollution to associate with him, he could not take part in any of the institutions of the state, civil or religious, whose life the gods would not accept as a sacrifice, but whom nevertheless anyone might put to death with impunity as no longer god-protected. (Muirhead)

[5]) *Op. cit.* p. 17. Recent philologists derive it from the Sanskrit yu or yuj from which Yoga is also derived), meaning to join, to bind; from which some deduce as the significance of ius "that it binds", the "bond of society" etc. (See references in Clark's *Pract. Jurisprudence* p. 16—20). (M. Bréal identifies it with yos of the Vedas, which he interpretes as "the divine will".

meanings of *Ius* as 'justice', 'right', appear later — probably when the true meaning of Fas was forgotten, or rather when insight into what it stood for was lost.

When the Roman priests began to excommunicate people, they cut themselves off from the elements of Justice and divine Grace in Fas, by taking the karman-element into their own hands. They did not see any more that no priest can morally judge any person absolutely right, like no judge can apply the law in absolute justice. And as soon as they thought they could, they lost the vision of what had been called Fas (or perhaps it was the other way round), which then became a man-made concoction of different kinds of norms, just like Dharma had become. Priest and judge may only take measures to protect the community against anti-social conduct of its individual members.

As Muirhead wrote: "These precepts of the Fas therefore were not mere exhortations to a blameless life, but closely approached to laws, whose violation was visited with punishments none the less effective that they were religious rather than civil." This makes us almost believe that Fas, if it had ever been a word for the essential principle or fundamental law, must have been so at a very early period, and perhaps not been so clearly grasped by the Romans as by the other ancient students of life that we have mentioned in this chapter. But we know very little about these things.

H. CONCLUSION. From the above chapter we come to the conclusion that this principle or basic law which we have found hidden to a greater or lesser extent in Ṛita, in Dharma, in Mischpat, in Δίκη and in Fas is apriori knowledge, and as such it might be a matter of Epistemology. But it is more than that, for it is not knowledge in the ordinary sense, neither is it an axiom which could be posited. Also it is not the "consciousness of causality", it is more than that.

It is apriori knowledge, and by its very nature it cannot be defined. According to the psychological make-up of man, he will give it different names: — God — Law — Order — Life — and he will mention many attributes — Love — Justice — Consciousness — Causality — Equilibrium. We shall not attempt to write anything more about that, which, if mentally pondered upon, appears the greatest secret in the universe, not possibly to test empirically or to find rationally; and which yet may be perfectly manifest and clear to the man who does not identify himself with his mind (neither with his feelings of approval or disapproval owing to sensations of personal sympathy or antipathy), but knows his mind to be an instrument, and who realizes this indefinable Principle to be of one nature with his very deepest and truest being, and ruling it (for it is One, and ruling all) and *as such capable of being grasped and known — and manifested.* And not science or the conclusions of others can give absolute certainty (this is even 'unscientific'), but only personal realization.

To conclude with a fitting quotation from a great Buddhist: "The essence of all things is one and the same, perfectly calm and tranquil, and shows no signs of 'becoming'; ignorance, however, is in its blindness and delusion oblivious of Enlightenment, and, on that account, cannot recognize truthfully all those conditions, differences, and activities which characterize the phenomena of the Universe." [1]

---

[1] Aśvaghosha, *The Awakening of Faith,* Suzuki's transl. Quoted from W. Y. Evans-Wentz, *The Tibetan Book of the Dead,* p. 154.

Chapter II

Varṇa and Caste

A. INTRODUCTION. The first difficulty that presents itself when studying the caste system is to answer the question: what do we mean by the word 'caste'? Which Sanskrit word does it represent? Must we take the word 'caste' to mean the ideal system that was pictured and drawn up by the old social leaders and which we find in the ancient scriptures, or must we understand that 'caste' represents historical and actual social conditions in India. The word has been applied in both senses. Much confusion was caused by mistranslation of words by the first translators of Sanskrit texts. And like they translated 'Dharma' by 'law', which is a onesided translation, as we saw, they translated 'V a r ṇ a' by 'caste', and spoke of the 'four castes' as if only four existed. But in reality thousands of castes exist, developed out of the original 'J ā t i s'. Manu already distinguished 48 Jātis [1]), and at the present day there are thousands. [2])

If in these pages we refer to 'caste' we mean the ultimate development of Jāti, according to the historical and actual conditions. And if we mean the ideal and theoretical class-system as pictured by the ancient sages, which formed the basis of Jāti, of caste, we shall use the word Varṇa.

Some social and religious leaders both in the past and at the present time consider the ideal system as the real and proper caste system and regard the existing system as a degeneration. Some exalt

---

[1]) *Manu* X : 8—42.

[2]) 2300 castes exist among which inter-marriage is prohibited. Most of them are only small, there are about 40 with more than a million members (C Bougle, *Essais sur le régime des castes*, p. 32) A recent author mentions more than 3000 castes (N. K Dutt, *Origin and Growth of Caste in India*, Vol. I, p 3)

'caste' to the skies and mean the theoretical system of Varṇa. Others condemn the system in most abusive terms and do not see the basis of Varṇa. The Indian Government rightly does not use the names of the four Varṇas except Brahman in dealing with actual social conditions. In Europe the current conception is that four castes exist in India, and everything applying to Varṇa and caste seems to be mixed up in Western thought.

It would remove much misunderstanding if modern writers in East and West would once and for all accept the above distinction of Varṇa and caste. The existing confusion of terms would then come to an end.

To distinguish the different conceptions provisionally and inclusively: *Varṇa* (Chāturvarṇya) is the Hindu ideal and theoretical picture of class based on Dharma. *Caste* represents historical and actual social conditions in India and elsewhere. At one time in early history the classes must have corresponded closely to the Varṇas. *Jāti* sometimes means Varṇa and sometimes caste, we have to be careful with the use of the word. [1]) If we use it at all, it will be in the sense of caste as it exists in India. A modern Hindi term which has evidently been derived from it is Jāt, which is used side by side with Jāti. [2]) This Chapter will form the introduction to the different studies that are to follow. In Section B we shall inquire into the birth of the conception of Varṇa, in Section C we shall consider the origin and the history of the conception Ārya. In Section D we shall mention the causes which brought about caste, and quote some opinions and definitions. In Section E we shall quote from the Dharma-śāstras the duties of the various Varṇas, finally saying in an Appendix a few words about the Āśrama system or order of life.

The social constitution, as manifestation of Varṇa and Āśrama, is for the Hindus an aspect of k r i y ā, a term of the Nyāya philosophy, meaning the active aspect of consciousness. Another aspect of kriyā is found in the ceremonies of the exoteric or established religions.

The theory of Varṇāśrama evolved from the thoughtworld which knew Ṛita, the worldorder [3]), and Purusha, the Cosmic Man. [4])

---

[1]) Ghurye, *Caste and Race in India*, p. 51.

[2]) Sometimes Varṇa is used in the scriptures in the sense of caste or offspring, which is confusing: e.g. *Manu* X : 27.

[3]) See pp. 9—10.

[4]) See pp. 53—54.

B. ORIGIN AND BIRTH OF VARṆA. That 'Varṇa' implies more than just a caste or a social class we gather from a line in the Mānava-dharma-śāstra: "The 4 Varṇas, the 3 worlds, the 4 Āśramas (orders of life), the past, the present and the future, are all severally known by means of the Veda." [1]) The Veda is then not mere scripture, but "the eternal eye of the Manes, gods and men; the Veda ordinance is both beyond the sphere of (human) power, and beyond the sphere of (human) comprehension; this is a certain fact." [2])

Swami Vivekananda writes: "The system of division into different Varṇas is the stepping-stone to civilization, making one rise higher and higher in proportion to one's learning and culture." [3])

To avoid confusion let us begin by stating that we have not rendered 'Varṇa' as 'class', because 'Varṇa' presents the theory and ideal of class, and the word 'class' at once suggests historical or actual classes, or 'population classes'. We have translated Varṇa as 'natural class', when we have translated it at all. The word 'order', sometimes also taken for 'Varṇa', we have in these pages only applied to Āśrama.

We have to apologize if our distinction of Varṇa and caste is not always quite in accordance with Hindu traditions or current opinions. Manu and others sometimes use Varṇa in the sense of caste. In our endeavour to throw some light on the social composition and on the social constitution [4]) we feel however not only justified, but also constrained, to bring some order in the chaos of conceptions and applications of the words.

The theory and ideal of Varṇa probably originated in the earliest Indo-Aryan ages. In Ṛig-vedic times there were classes that had not yet grown into castes. There were priests (Brāhmaṇa), nobles and warriors (Rājanya or Kshatriya), commons (Vaiśya or Viś) and servile classes (Śūdra). Professor Kern held that the fourfold division of classes was older than the most ancient Indian documents. [5]) The facts on which the theory of Varṇa was built up existed. Originally there were only two Varṇas, of Āryas and of Anāryas (non-Āryas). This we shall consider more in particular in the next

---

[1]) *Manu* XII : 97.
[2]) *Manu* XII : 94.
[3]) Vivekananda, *Complete Works*, Vol. V, p. 439.
[4]) See Part II Ch. IX E.
[5]) H. Kern, *Indische Theorieën over de Standenverdeeling, in Verspreide Geschriften* XIII : 1.

Section. But a fact is that while the Indo-Aryans were still in the Punjab they were already divided into classes: Brāhmaṇa, Rājanya and Viś.

(In the Ṛig-veda is only one passage in which the four classes are mentioned. It is the famous Purusha-sūkta hymn which has been the subject of much contention. Whether the hymn is a later addition to the Ṛig-veda, as some maintain, or not, is immaterial to our inquiry. By quoting the hymn we shall see that the general view that the hymn has for its subject a cosmogony or theory of creation is undoubtedly correct. The poet represents creation as the result of immolating and cutting up the "embodied spirit", the Divine Man, Purusha, "the soul and original source of the universe, the personal and life-giving principle in all animated beings" [1]). "Into how many portions did they divide this Being whom they immolated? What did his mouth become? What are his arms, his thighs, his feet now called? His mouth became a priest (Brāhmaṇa), his arm was made a nobleman (Rājanya), his thigh was transformed into a farmer (Vaiśya), from his feet sprang the servile man (Śūdra). The moon was produced from his mind, the sun sprang from his eye, air and fire proceeded from his mouth and wind came from his breath. The intermediate region was produced from his navel, the sky from his head, the earth from his feet, and space (lit. the quarters of the sky) from his ear; thus did he frame the worlds." [2])

In later times Brahmans took up this Vedic creation theory and based upon it and upon the existing fourfold division of society the theory of four Varṇas: Chāturvarṇya. According to the *Cambridge History of India* the conception of Varṇa, literally meaning 'Colour', differentiating later into 'the four Varṇas', arose from the difference of class, which was partly a difference of race: of a superior white (the three higher Varṇas) and a dark-coloured aboriginal race. Originally there were only a white and a dark Varṇa. [3]) In the next period, the period of the Yajur-veda and the Brāhmaṇas we hear for the first time of four Varṇas, independently of race and colour. [4]))

---

[1]) *The Oxford History of India*, p. 36.

[2]) *Ṛig-veda* X : 90 : 11 14. Also: *Vājasaneyi-saṃhitā* of the *White Yajur-veda* (31 : 1—6) and *Atharvaveda* (19 : 6 : 1 sqq.) Colebrooke, *Miscellaneous Essays* Vol. I, pp. 167, 184. Muir, *Original Sanskrit Texts* Vol. I, p. 10.

[3]) *Cambridge History of India*, Vol. I, p. 54.

[4]) *Śatapatha-Br*., see *Vedic Index* II, p. 247.

It seems that *race* was taken as determining factor in the birth of the theory of Varṇa. Yet not in its anthropological sense, but as factor approximately determining the *degree of culture*. With regard to this in connection with the conception 'Ārya' we refer to the next Section. That in Varṇa *culture* was the momentous and determining factor, and not *race*, we shall try to show again and again.

In the Brāhmaṇas 'Varṇa' is mentioned as a Divinity. There is a curious passage: "To Varṇa, one who works for the sake of another, not for himself, (should be sacrificed)." [1]) The cultural implication of the passage is clear. It is evident that in Varṇa altruistic was exalted above egoistic conduct. The leading idea was the sociality of the individual. [2])

There is no need really to quote the later cosmogonical explanations of Varṇa and caste, since they all come to very much the same.[3]) For our purpose it is important that they have an allegorical sense.

Probably on account of them the view is sometimes expressed that the castes developed from a division of labour on a totemistic basis. [4])

In these allegorical and cosmogonical passages the Varṇas are given an *inner* origin, they spring from different organs or members of the body of the Divine Man, they have diifferent functions to perform in his organically divided body: human society. [5]) The Brāhmaṇas (the mouth) are the spiritual and social leaders and instructors. The Kshatriyas (the arms) represent power, they are meant to rule and protect. The Vaiśyas (the thighs) are those whose duty it is to be productive of food to sustain the body, the lower part of the body is the depository of food. The Śūdra's work is to serve the others. The feet are the support of the whole body and lead it where the mind directs. Thus it is the *inner* or *higher* origin of Varṇa which is stressed; the work in society ought to be and under

---

[1]) *Aitareya-Br.* of the *Black Yajur-veda* 40.

[2]) There is of course no question of human sacrifice, the passage is one of a great many similar ones, which have a very deep sense. (See R. C. Dutt, *A History of Civilization in Ancient India*, Vol. I, pp. 274—275).

[3]) *MBh. Vana-parvan 189* : 13; *Taittirīya-saṃhitā* VII : 1 : 1 : 4 sqq.; *Vishṇu-P.* I : 6 : 2—5; *Manu* I : 31; *Bhāg.-P.* XI : *17* : 13—14. etc.

[4]) *Propyläen Weltgeschichte*, Vol. III, p. 252.

[5]) The conception of the Purusha one may compare with the modern conception of 'group-soul', compare also the eleventh Chapter of the Gītā.

natural conditions *is* done according to the nature of every organ, as a natural result of its individual organic development, dependent upon its past function in the organic whole of society. [1]) Here we have the organic theory of society, as a "physio-psychic organism", as called by Professor Giddings, "a psychical organism essentially, but with a physical basis." [2]) And of course not only an *organism*, but an *organization* as well. [3])

In the Vāyu-purāṇa we are told that in the first period of man's history or the Kṛita-yuga there were no Varṇas, and that subsequently Brahmā the Creator established divisions among men according to their works, as quoted below. In the Rāmāyaṇa we find that in the Kṛita-yuga there were only Brahmans [4]) and that all people were of one Varṇa [5]). In the Bhāgavata we find similar information. [6])

The Vāyu-purāṇa says: "Those of them who were suited for command and prone to deeds of violence, he appointed to be Kshatriyas, from their protecting others. Those disinterested men who attended upon them, spoke the truth and declared the Veda aright were Brāhmaṇas. Those of them who formerly were feeble, engaged in the work of husbandmen, tillers of the earth, and industrious, were Vaiśyas, cultivators and providers of subsistence. Those who were cleansers and ran about on service, and had little vigour of strength, were called Śūdras." [7])

From this we conclude that the compilers of these verses took *work* as the basis of Varṇa, yet not as profession or occupation, as work for individual profit (which became a factor in the development of jāti), but *as social service resulting from individual inner development.* [8]) Especially for the two higher Varṇas this is very clear from this text, and even for the two lower Varṇas the stress is laid respectively on social service, and cleaning plus other services.

---

[1]) For simplicity's sake we have not always upheld in these pages the technical distinction of Professor Tonnies (*Gemeinschaft und Gesellschaft*) and others between 'community' and 'society'.

[2]) F. H. Giddings, *The Principles of Sociology*, p. 420.

[3]) See p. 152 and Part II Ch. IX E.

[4]) *Rām. Uttara-Kāṇḍa* 74 : 9—11.

[5]) *Uttara-kāṇḍa* 30 : 19.

[6]) *Bhāg.-P.* XI : 17 : 10—11. See also *Manu* I : 83.

[7]) Quoted from R. C. Dutt, *A History of Civilization in Ancient India*, Vol. I, p. 236.

[8]) In relation with caste: "Birth is difficult to be discriminated *until action is shown.*" See p. 114.

The same conclusion we can draw from the following passage in the Mahābhārata: "Red-limbed twice-born men who were fond of sensual pleasure, fiery, irascible, daring and forgetful of their sacramental duties, fell into the Varṇa ot the Kshatriyas. Yellow twice-born men, who derived their livelihood from cows and agriculture, and did no more practise sacramental duties, fell into the Varṇa of the Vaiśyas. Black twice-born men who were impure and addicted to violence and lying, and were covetous and subsisted by all kinds of work, fell into the Varṇa of Śūdras. Being thus separated by these their works, the twice-born men become of other Varṇas."[1])

In this passage *all* are called twice-born, which means they were initiated Āryas. And here too we find that the 'works' are primary, not as professional actions, but as actions of men as socializing individuals. Racial inclination and racial characteristics are here also recognized as being factors in the individual stage of cultural development. The compilers saw a correlation between the cultural standard and occupation, yet Dharma and social conduct come before all and open the door leading to other Varṇas. From this passage, as from many others, it is also clear that the caste system had not yet become rigid, people could in fact also raise or lower their caste, or social status, as will be described in Section D, and in Part II, Chapters II and IV.

And, as Dutt remarks [2]), the composers of the passage knew of the origin of the Varṇas from the members of the Creator, but they treated it as an allegory which it is.

In the Taittirīya-Brāhmaṇa we read: "The Brāhmaṇa-varṇa is sprung from the Devas ('gods', or superhuman beings); the Śūdra from the Asuras". [3]) Character and behaviour are primary as we see, the 'gods' were socializing powers, the Asuras anti-social or unsocial powers.

Also the predominance of character or quality over the professional factor is seen clearly from the following quotation from the Vishṇu-purāṇa: "When, true to his design, Brahmā became desirous to create the world, creatures in whom harmony and goodness (s a t t v a) prevailed sprang from his mouth; others in

[1]) *MBh. Śānti-parvan* 188 : 11—14*a*. See also the quotation from the MBh. on p. 72.

[2]) R C Dutt, *A History of Civilization in Ancient India*, Vol. I, p. 237.

[3]) *Taittirīya-Br.* I : 2 : 6, 7, quoted from Muir, *Original Sanskrit Texts* Vol. I, p. 21.

whom passion (rajas) predominated came from his breast; others in whom both passion and ignorant darkness (tamas) were strong proceeded from his thighs; others he created from his feet, whose chief characteristic was ignorant darkness. Of these was composed the system of the four Varṇas, Brāhmaṇas, Kshatriyas, Vaiśyas and Śūdras, who had respectively issued from his mouth, breast, thighs and feet." [1]) Here the symbolism is more perfect, there is no more a cutting up, but an issuing.

Conclusive is: "A man, whether he be a Brāhmaṇa, Kshatriya, Vaiśya or Śūdra, is such by nature, this is my opinion. By evil deed a twiceborn man falls from his position.... The Kshatriya or Vaiśya who lives in the condition of a Brāhmaṇa, by practising the duties of one, attains to Brahmanhood...." and so on, even to the last consequence: "by practising the following good works, a Śūdra becomes a Brāhmaṇa", and that by perfectly performing his Śūdra-duties of service and obedience! [2])

There is no need to quote any more passages, in the different chapters of Part II this and other points of view will be elaborated. The *word* 'Varṇa' means 'colour.' The usual opinion is that this colour is an indication of race, and this opinion gets some justification from ancient history. The Indo-Aryans were a white people and the people they found in India, were dark and mainly of two types, the one representing the high civilization of the Dravidians, the other uncivilized aboriginals. [3]) As we shall see in the Section about the conception *Ārya*, not *too* great an importance must be attached to the factor of race and blood, the personal degree of culture being influenced, but not determined by it, as we can make out from the ancient texts. And people could change their Varṇa in the early ages, but certainly not their race!

There is another view of Varṇa however which may also be substantiated by statements from the scriptures. It is that the colour is a symbol of the inherent qualities of nature, the guṇas, mentioned in passing in Chapter I Section D. The Sattva-guṇa

---

[1]) *Vishṇu-P.* I : *6* : 3—6.

[2]) *MBh. Anuśāsana-parvan* 143 : 6.

[2]) Vivekananda mentions that there are clear proofs about caste being based on qualification in the stories of Ajagara and of Uma and Maheśvara in the *MBh. Bhīshma-parvan*. We have not verified this. (*Complete Works* Vol. VI, p. 177).

[3]) For detailed information see G. S. Ghurye, *Caste and Race in India*, pp. 101—123.

is represented as being white, it stands for harmony, purity, goodness, equilibrium, light, wisdom. And since it was associated with the Brahmans, the Brahma-varṇa may have been called the Varṇa of *white* 'colour'. The Rajo-guṇa is represented as red, it stands for activity and passion, it was associated with the Kshatriya. [1]) Hence the Kshatriya-varṇa may have been called the red Varṇa. The third Varṇa, of the Vaiśyas was called the yellow Varṇa. Associated with it was a mixture of the two lower guṇas, black and red. The fourth Varṇa was quite tamasic, the persons belonging to it were black, like the tamo-guṇa. If one should like to explain this from racial colours it would be childish to expect four races, of white Aryans, of red people, of yellow Mongols, and of black aboriginals, to fit exactly into the position of the four Varṇas!

Besides taking the colours symbolically, some authors (like Dr. Bhagavan Das) consider them to indicate the colours radiated by the subtle bodies of man, in concord with and caused by his psychological make-up. This view is too metaphysical to concern us here, and has to be tested by psychology and parapsychology.

Against the racial theory of Varṇa is also an opinion that we find expressed in the Mahābhārata: "If the caste (Varṇa) of the four classes is distinguished by their colour (Varṇa), then a mixture of all the castes (Varṇa-saṃkara) is observable." [2]) Even then observable!

We must also remark that the white complexion was not always the most popular and the most admired one, Śrī-Kṛishṇa, the greatest Hindu Divine Incarnation and human hero, always being called the "dark-cloud-faced-one" or the "dusky-one" or the "dark-blue-one", and Rāma, the divine hero, usually being represented as dark or blue or green. [3]) These two were the ideal of all that was most beautiful in a man. In the Bhāgavata the beauty of Śuka, the "glorious son of Vyāsa", is described at length. He is said to be of dark complexion. [4]) And more examples could be adduced. On the other hand in women a fair colour was valued, and still is at the present time.

---

[1]) See quotation above from the *MBh. Śānti-parvan* 188 : 11—14*a*.

[2]) *MBh. Śānti-parvan* 188 : 6. For the sake of clearness we have for once translated 'Varṇa' by 'caste'.

[3]) The green colour, as found in the *Rām. Bāla-kāṇḍa* 1, may possibly indicate the occult radiation, as mentioned above.

[4]) *Bhāg.-P.* I : 19 : 28.

The following text is also significant, in that not the complexion is meant, but the colour of the inner man, whether symbolical or actual: "Six colours of living creatures are of principal importance; black, dusky, and blue which lies between them, then red is more tolerable, yellow is happiness and white is extreme happiness. White is perfect, being exempted from stain, sorrow and exhaustion.... the destination of the black colour is bad. When it has produced its results, it clings to hell." [1]

We have respectively considered five conceptions of Varṇa: racial, cultural, professional, symbolical and occult. The symbolical and the occult conceptions I am not in a position to judge. I could only bring them forward. Regarding the other three conceptions we have demonstrated that in Varṇa the cultural takes precedence of the racial and the professional elements. What we have been provisionally endeavouring to show is that the system of four Varṇas, the Chāturvarṇya, was conceived on the basis of degrees of culture and sociality. Social service was seen as the test of Varṇa, service as a natural outcome of the stage of individual cultural development. Varṇa was not based on profession or occupation, nor primarily and exclusively on race, the latter however sometimes predestinating to some extent the Varṇa of a person. From our inquiry we come to the principle: "A man's Varṇa shows itself according to his behaviour as a member of society." In Part II we shall recur to this, in Chapter V we shall study the hierarchical implications of Varṇa and of caste.

The theory of Varṇa is a social theory, it concerns the *vertical composition* and the *practical view* of *society*. We have to distinguish it clearly from the psychological theory which concerns the *horizontal composition* and the *spiritual view* of *humanity*. [2]

The norms of the theory of Varṇa, aspects of the basic norm — Dharma — are absolute, like the norms of ethics, logic, religion. They are partly directly realized, partly experienced. The norms of the ideal of Varṇa are autonomous. When the Brahmans posited them and they were sanctioned to some extent by the rulers, the norms became heteronomous norms of class and caste, or norms

[1]) *MBh. Śānti-parvan* 280 : 33—37.
[2]) See Part II Ch. VI.

of convention and common law. In the sanction lies the weakness. [1]

Many of the norms of science are considered as absolute (perhaps in spite of all relativity) and have no sanction but the natural consequences of disobedience or disregard. It is really the same with the norms of Varṇa.

To distinguish clearly the different kinds of norms as mentioned above, let us remember that Varṇa is both theory and ideal. This means that it represents fundamental laws of society, demonstrating the tendencies of individuals and groups in the social composition. In so far Varṇa represents laws of *social facts that are.* [2] Next it propagates them as *ideals* to be manifested in the social constitution. It presents the normal, the socializing tendencies as opposite the abnormal, separative tendencies that are at work in society. If posited as ideal, Varṇa presents *facts (as conceived) how they ought to be.* Concerning caste we might say that it represents facts as they are in the social constitution (and, in so far as they do not agree with Varṇa, as they ought *not* to be).

Ancient Indian sages conceived the Chāturvarṇya. Whether they saw the theory and ideal of Varṇa in its pure form as theory and ideal of natural class (many of the later writers surely did not) — whether I have been able to unearth and conceive it in its pure form, remains to be seen. More detailed and particular studies will be welcome to modify and clarify points which have possibly remained hazy or doubtful in these pages.

C. THE CONCEPTION 'ĀRYA'. As we have seen before, in the Ṛig-veda the Ārya-varṇa is contrasted with the Dāsa-varṇa. [3] The word Ārya occurs nine times in this connection. We read for instance: "He destroyed the Dasyus and protected the Ārya-varṇa." [4] And: "Distinguish between the Āryas and those who are Dasyus; chastizing those who observe no sacred rites, subject them to the sacrificer." [5] Professor Muir writes that by means of the word Ārya, we are able to connect the early Hindus with the early Persians. For the first Medes were

---

[1]) The extreme we find in the well-known saying of the French Revolution: "Be my brother, or I kill you."

[2]) See Part II Ch. IX E.

[3]) *Cambridge History of India,* Vol. I, pp. 54, 92. G. S. Ghurye, *Caste and Race in India,* p. 41.

[4]) *Rig-veda* III : 34 : 9.

[5]) *Ṛig-veda* I : 51 : 8.

called Arians in the Greek accounts. Later it was a word for the Persians in the most ancient Zoroastrian books. [1]) In Avestan Ārya is Airya.

Max Müller has traced the progress of the word 'Arya' all over the Aryan world, from *Irān* or Persia, to *Erin* or Ireland, and argues with considerable force that the word was invented in the primeval home of the Aryans in Central Asia, to indicate their partiality to cultivation, as distinguished from the nomadic habits of the Turanians, whose name indicates their rapid journies or the fleetness of their horse. [2]) Darius calls himself "an Aryan and of Aryan descent", in the Behistun inscription Ahuramazda is styled "the God of the Aryans." The Sassanian kings called themselves the kings of "Aryan and Unaryan Races." The Greek writers also frequently employed the term Aryan as a tribal designation. The word perhaps occurs in *Armenia* and *Albania*, and is found as *Iron* in the Caucasus, the native name of the Ostiaks, and on the banks of the Vistula as the name of a German tribe. The Westernmost limit of Aryan migration is *Ireland*.

As already mentioned the word was thought to come from a root meaning 'to cultivate' or 'to plough'. The agriculturists who were doubtless the most advanced in civilization of the race, adopted it as their tribal designation. Other tribes subsequently followed their example, and the term became the common name of a large number of heterogenious racial groups. As such it was later interpreted to mean 'honorable' or 'noble', and it is generally thought that the races and tribes who assumed it as their particular race name, prided themselves upon their forming a noble race. According to Muir the term has to be translated as 'respectable'. More recent Saṅskritists think that 'Ārya' originally meant 'kinsman'. Later, to distinguish the 'kinsmen' from the primitive aboriginals, the word gradually assumed the meaning of 'noble'. Derived and related words are 'to order' (German 'ordnen'), 'to arrange', the German 'Herr', a.o. [3])

Whatever the etymology of the word may have been, it is at least certain that its racial meaning changed into a cultural soon after the Aryans had settled in India. [4]) For when dark people

[1]) Muir, *Original Sanskrit Texts*, Vol. II, p. 291.
[2]) R. C. Dutt, *A History*, etc. Vol. I, p. 55.
[3]) See also p. 9.
[4]) See p. 83.

showed they could behave as Āryas they became Āryas. We shall revert to this below and in Part II.

The race theory has become very much complicated since it has been recognized that the Dravidians had a very high civilization when the Indo Aryans came to India, some authors even maintain that their culture was equal, if not superior to that of the Aryans. [1])

At any case in the first period of the Indo Aryans' stay in India, there were no rules prohibiting inter-marriage, and a great deal of race-admixture took place. [2]) The process of admixture continued throughout Indian history up to the present time. Bouglé collected some interesting instances to illustrate this. [3]) Anthropological research brought to light the greatest admixture in spite of the strictest rules prohibiting inter-marriage. [4]) Dr. D. R. Bhandarkar demonstrated that the higher castes cannot pride themselves on purity of blood. [5])

Already in ancient times men seem to have been well aware of the fact of continuous race-admixture. "All sorts of men are continually begetting children on all sorts of women." [6]) We refer also to the work of Dr. Ghurye. [7])

Originally the conceptions 'Ā r y a' and 'D v i j a' ('twice-born') were uniform, later when twice-born men had been degraded to Śūdras and outcast ranks and when non-Aryans had been admitted to the twice-born community, the words could no more be synonymous. [8])

Dr. Ketkar remarks that we must translate the word Ārya as found in the Dharma-śāstras not with the Vedic vocabulary or with the semi-developed vocabulary of the modern etymology, but that we should try to translate it in the sense current at the time of the Dharma-śāstras. Manu "never defined the term 'Ārya'.... What meaning he had in mind, the meaning which was accepted by the people of India for centuries before and after the period of our

---

[1]) G. Slater, *The Dravidian Element in Indian Culture.* F.E. Pargiter, *Ancient Indian Historical Tradition.* See also p. 120.

[2]) See Part II Ch. I C.

[3]) C. Bouglé, *Essais sur le Régime des Castes*, pp. 29—31.

[4]) W. Crooke, *The Tribes and Castes of the N. W. Provinces*, Vol. III, p. 27. Quoted by Bouglé.

[5]) D. R. Bhandarkar, *Foreign Elements in the Hindu Population* (*Ind. Ant.* Vol. XL.) See also p. 140.

[6]) *MBh. Vana-parvan* 180 : 34. See p. 114.

[7]) G. S. Ghurye, *Caste and Race in India*, pp. 101—123.

[8]) N. K. Dutt, *Origin and Growth of Caste in India*, Vol. I, p. 139.

writer — must be gathered from the uses of the word 'Ārya' in the text. For centuries till the arrival of European scholars on Indian soil, the people of India never meant by the word 'Ārya' that race of invaders who reduced the natives of the soil to servitude. The word indeed probably had such a meaning, but only for a short period antedating the concrete beginnings of civilization in India. Before the close of the period of the composition of the Ṛig-veda, the descendants of the invading tribes had forgotten where they came from, and thought themselves to be autochthonous and men of noble qualities and culture. The word 'Ārya' had received some sanctity, and had become rather a title to be applied to properly qualified people, than a word expressive of the *recently-born conception of race.* [1]) Occidental scholars who usually attach more importance to the study of the Vedas than to the later Sanskrit literature [2]), revived the long-forgotten Vedic meaning of the word, and made it once more current, although since the beginning of India's characteristic civilization (say from the close of the Ṛig-veda) until 1800 A.D. the word had a meaning entirely different." [3])

Dr. Ketkar demonstrates that the word 'Ārya' had become synonymous with character. [4]) "In the whole book (Manu) there is not a single expression which would indicate that our writer has any conception of what we may call race, and the readers of our text should take every care, not to put into the word 'Ārya' a meaning which modern philology has attached to the English word 'Aryan." He further remarks that the Dravidian princes who held their own against the Aryan invaders were by no means excluded from the title 'Ārya' and that the colour of the skin had long ceased to be a matter of importance. The attitude of Manu is further essentially the same as that of the composer of the Epic to whom 'Ārya' was also rather ethical than ethnic. "Thus an Ārya act was a noble act, whoever performed it, and an Ārya was a gentleman." [5]) Śūdras were of course "not representative gentlemen, though, theoretically, a good Śūdra might be so regarded, as a low-born man in this Western world might reluctantly be given the same title, if his virtue or heroism raised him above his caste level." [5])

The element of character and culture is evident in many passages

---

[1]) Italics are mine.
[2]) Here we have to remember that Dr. Ketkar wrote in 1909.
[3]) S. V. Ketkar, *History of Caste in India,* Vol. I, pp. 78—80.
[4]) *Op. cit.* pp. 81—82.
[5]) *Op. cit.* p. 82.

in the Dharma-śāstras. [1]) In Gautama we find: "If Āryas and non-Āryas interchange their occupations and conduct there is equality between them." [2]) Here the race factor is conclusively set aside by the cultural and professional factors.

For the Buddhists the word 'Ārya' awakened not the slightest racial associations. The Buddha preached the "Noble (ariya) eightfold Path".

The word Ārya thus has a long history. Originally meaning either 'cultivator' or 'kinsman', in a period of migration and strife it developed the sense of 'superior people'. From this the step to 'superior race' was only a small one. Later it denoted 'nobility', gradually losing its racial associations and more and more implicating 'nobility of character'. When its cultural and psychological meaning had been fully established for centuries, under Western influence a racial feature was again assigned to it.

In recent days the conception 'Aryan' has come again very much to the foreground, and it seems that here and there the separative racial conceptions or aspirations are winning upon the cultural inclinations. This is not the place to judge or to inquire into the causes of this social-psychological problem. From time to time in the world's history people seem to be at variance about the question race v. culture. [3])

As far as Ārya means nobility of character and an Ārya a gentleman, it forms part of the theory and ideal of Varṇa.

D. JĀTI, ORIGIN, AND DEFINITIONS OF CASTE. In this section we shall present conclusions and definitions of some of the leading authorities on caste, to serve as a basis for the different studies to follow. [4])

The Dharma-śāstras try to explain the Jātis as having come into existence from mixed marriages of the members of the four original classes. The *details* of these explanations are — as all scholars agree — highly fanciful later additions to the original doctrine. Yet are these explanations based on facts: of course have the Jātis developed out of the four classes of society in Vedic times.

Before inquiring into the origin of caste as distinguished from and

[1]) E.g. *Manu* VII: 211; VIII : 395; X : 57—58; *Gautama* IX: 68—74.

[2]) *Gautama* X : 67. Cf. *Manu* X : 73. See also p. 83.

[3]) E.g. see *Romans* 2 : 28—29.

[4]) For a detailed and all-inclusive picture of caste we refer to any good analysis and history of caste.

based upon Varṇa [1]), it will be well to analyse the conception 'caste' and to quote some definitions. These definitions are based on the caste system of India and applied to caste phenomena in other parts of the world. Bouglé in his analysis of caste mentions three characteristics, one or more of which are mentioned by the different scholars: 1. hereditary specialization; 2. hierarchic organization; 3. mutual exclusion [2]).

The second characteristic need not concern us in this place, since it is obviously a characteristic of Varṇa, and as such we shall discuss it in several Chapters of Part II. The other two characteristics however it will be well to consider now. According to some, economic factors have had a great influence to bear upon the origin of the hereditary caste system. [3]) The guilds of ancient India, on which the castes were founded, according to them, can only be compared to the guilds of mediaeval Europe. The guild system is, according to Dahlmann, a typically Indo-German phenomenon. He goes as far as calling a caste a guild which has become rigid. [4]) Bouglé remarks that, if this were true, every profession ought to correspond to a caste, whereas sometimes in one caste there are several professions represented. The problem of caste is not so simple. Yet it is true that sometimes a new profession leads to the creation of a new caste, but also other causes sometimes lead to the same effect. Some castes bear names of localities. Others again originate among the followers of some particular saint. [5]) We see many causes at work side by side. Yet the hypothesis of the professional basis of caste seems to hold true. The religious castes may have imitated the social organization of the economic castes, as was the case in Greece. [6]) Similarly the castes may have imitated the utilitarian organization of the guild castes. These guild castes required the attention of all the aspects of the individual life of its members. Only in the more recent phases of social structure in the past, due to the increased specialization, the different organizations require

[1]) See Section B of this Chapter, especially p. 54.

[2]) C. Bouglé, *Le régime des Castes*, p. 32.

[3]) Nesfield is the most dogmatic upholder of the occupational doctrine of caste.

[4]) J. Dahlmann, *Das altindische Volkstum in seiner Bedeutung für die Gesellschaftskunde*, pp. 113—116, 24, quoted by Bouglé.

[5]) Examples of these different categories, see Bouglé, *Op. cit.* p. 41.

[6]) Foucart, *Des associations religieuses chez les Grecs*, p. 50 sqq., quoted by Bouglé.

only a one-sided recognition and obedience from their members, leaving them free in the fields outside their pale. This applies to the State, the Church, the family, the club, the trade-union, the political party, etc.

The psychological make-up of individual man has become divided into many loosely connected compartments, and sometimes unity is failing altogether. In society specialization has lead to a social complexity which can and does easily lose its balance if the synthesizing factor is lost. Some recent nationalistic states are trying to focus again the attention of a great many of the different subdivisions of the psychology of their subjects on some national ideal or body of ideals, to the exclusion of other ideals. There is a healthy thought at the bottom of this course of action. The ultimate success of the endeavour depends however upon the purity, the nobility, and the all-inclusiveness of the leading ideal, upon the efficiency of the subsidiary ideals, and not in the last place upon the methods employed to materialize them. Here are hidden *many* perils.

The power which these states exercise over their subjects and to some extent over all those who take part in the 'participation mystique', perhaps somewhat approaches to the sway which the medieaval guilds or the Indian castes exercised over their members.

To return to the medieaval guilds, they have, as Bouglé writes, often been explained to contain remnants of the traditions of the ancient Roman *gens*. [1]) Bouglé concludes that thus the traditions of the ancient family religion, and not the requirements of industry, are responsible for the traits which make the guilds resemble the castes. Similarly in India the Varṇa traditions formed the model for the caste system.

(Bouglé continues that the three characteristics of caste are difficult to explain from the industrial evolution. [2]) The hereditary specialization is easiest to be accounted for. It is necessary that the skilled worker instructs his successor. But, as Bouglé writes, it is no proof that the *father* ought to be succeeded by the *son*. Here I venture to suggest that under the influence of Varṇa the son would strive to live up to the standard of the father and to imitate his

[1]) Casquet, *Institutions politiques de l'ancienne France*, Vol. II, p. 240—243; Waltzing, *Les corporations professionelles chez les Romains*. Vol. I, p. 329.

[2]) Bouglé, *Op. cit.* p. 45.

social conduct as faithfully as possible. To attain this end he might want to keep in the presence of his father as much as possible, and thus naturally he would succeed him in his profession or occupation.

As to the hierarchic element in the specialized groups, Bouglé also writes that the religious influence is very clear. And the mutual exclusion of the castes, why their members cannot marry outside their caste, why they cannot eat together, etc., cannot be explained at all from economic causes. [1]) The economic theory is not tenable. [2]) The true prototypes of the modern castes were the jātis of the Dharma-śāstras. A Jāti ('birth' or 'species' is the meaning) consists of a group of people descending from the same stock. The Jātis of Manu are the first true castes. As the leading sociologists agree, the theories of the Śāstras to account for the origin of the 'mixed castes' are fanciful and show the compromise of ideal and theory with social tendencies that could not be checked. Only by prohibiting inter-marriage of the castes something could be achieved.

Risley's theory that caste is a matter mainly relating to marriage has been generally accepted.

"The Hindu legislators made the castes exclusive, not so much by prescribing particular professions for each, as by prohibiting inter-marriage and interchange of hospitality on a footing of equality." Originally intermarriage was allowed in so far that a man of superior class could marry a girl of lower class, later it became prohibited altogether. [3]) We suggest that the main factor which brought this about was the fear of 'mixture of castes' (v a r ṇ a-s a ṃ k a r a), which, as we shall see later [4]) was a great danger. In this place we shall just mention it. Of course the danger was lying (and is lying still) in a mixture of the standards of the Varṇas, or rather in a tendency of equalizing society, and by that ignoring social facts of inequality.

This mixture was artificially prevented by the prohibition of intermarriage, etc. But, instead of working beneficially, it caused the crystallization of Hindu society. Another important factor adduced by some to explain the fear of intermarriage of the castes

---

[1]) Bouglé, *Op. cit.* p. 50.

[2]) Even the state-enforced division of work on hereditary principle by the Theodosian Code under the Roman Empire failed to generate caste. (N. K. Dutt, *Origin and Growth of Caste in India*, Vol. I, p. 25).

[3]) See J. N. Bhattacharya, *Hindu Castes and Sects*, p. 11.

[4]) See Part II Ch. VII.

is that the Brahmans saw with apprehension that the purity of the blood was endangered by too much class-admixture. But, as we saw above, race often predestined to some extent the cultural standard. If the standard had been kept up by the upper classes after intermarrying with the darker lower classes, there would have been no reason to make intermarriage difficult or to prevent it altogether in later times after it had extensively been the practise for a long time.

As regards physical beauty, the Indo-Aryans and the cultured Dravidians were equally handsome. While in the Ṛig-vedic age there had been hardly any or no artificial prohibitions of social intercourse, intermarriage or profession, and there had been no social barriers but the natural ones of culture, as soon as the various races and cultures began to be amalgamated into 'the Hindu people' and 'the Hindu culture', the caste regulations as we now know them, gradually came into being. It was a slow process.

The distinctions between the castes were by no means so rigid in the times of the Brāhmaṇas as during a later period. The Aitareya-brāhmaṇa mentions that one who was not recognized as a Brahman could be the performing priest and bring a sacrifice. [1] Still more remarkable is the passage in the same Brāhmaṇa, stating that when a Kshatriya eats at a sacrifice the portion assigned for the Brahmans, his progeny has the characteristics of a Brahman "ready to take gifts, thirsty after drinking Soma [2] and hungry of eating food, and ready to roam about everywhere according to pleasure." And "in the second or third generation he is then capable of entering completely the Brahmanship." [3] And when he eats the share of Vaiśyas his offspring will be born with the characteristics of the Vaiśyas, and in the second or third degree he will be fit for entering the caste of the Vaiśyas. [4]

In the beautiful legend of Satyakāma Jabāla, which we will quote elsewhere, we will see exemplified the fact that in those early days truth and character opened out a path to the highest honor and the highest caste. And there are more examples. [5]

Brahmans, Kshatriyas and Vaiśyas were all able to sacrifice, and

[1] *Aitareya-Br.* I : 16 and II : 17.
[2] Soma is the drink used at sacrifices by the Brāhmaṇas.
[3] *Aitareya-Br.* VII : 29.
[4] R. C. Dutt; *A History of Civilization in Ancient India*, Vol. I, p 241
[5] See Part II Ch. IV.

therefore the distinctions between these classes were small [1]), and the supremacy of the Brahman was almost mininal yet. In one passage we have stated even that a Brahman may be of uncertain birth, but that he only is a true Brahman who is born of the Brahman of the sacrifice; wherefore even a Rājanya [2]) or a Vaiśya should be addressed as Brahman "since who is born of the sacrifice is born of the Brahman and hence a Brahman." [3])

In early times there must have been four classes somewhat corresponding to the four Varṇas, besides there must have existed in out of the way places tribes and races that had not yet amalgamated with Hindu society. These later developed into new castes, and the Śāstras tried to place them somewhere in the theoretical system.

Dr. Bhattacharya mentions the following causes which have been operating in later times in forming new subdivisions which also developed into castes:

1. By migration to different parts of the country.
2. By different sections being devoted to the practice of distinct professions.
3. By any section being elevated above or degraded below the level of the others.
4. By quarrels between the different sections of the same caste as to their relative status.
5. By becoming the followers of one of the modern religious teachers.
6. By the multiplication of the illegitimate progeny of religious mendicants. [4])

Sir Herbert Risley mentions in addition to those also castes of a national type, "which cherish tradition, of bygone sovereignty and seem to preserve traces of an organization considerably more elaborate than that of an ordinary tribe." Examples are the Newars of Nepal and the Mahratta-Kunbis. Also he mentions castes formed by changes of custom. Established usage has been neglected in that case and new ceremonial practices adopted. As examples he mentions some castes a section of which has attained a higher rank by prohibiting the remarriage of widows, and other sections which

[1]) *Śatapatha-Br.* III · 1, 9. Dutt, *Op. Cit.* p. 246.
[2]) Kshatriya.
[3]) *Śatapatha-Br.* III · 2, 1, 40, see Dutt, *Op. cit.* p. 246.
[4]) J. N. Bhattacharya, *Hindu Castes and Sects*, p. 13.

lost connections with their castes by again admitting remarriage of widows. [1])

We have to restrict ourselves to this short introductory to caste, and leave out the problems of gotra (gens), which though sociologically very interesting and important, have no direct bearing on the questions with which we are concerned.

To conclude it will be well to give a few opinions and definitions of caste which do not need comment, which in a way complement one another showing various aspects of caste. Mr. Shama Shastri in his *Evolution of Caste* describes it as follows: "Caste means a social exclusiveness with reference to diet and marriage." He goes as far as to say that "Birth and rituals are secondary." The *Oxford History of India* states: "A caste may be defined as a group of families internally united by peculiar rules for the observance of ceremonial purity, especially in the matters of diet and marriage." "Race has little concern with caste,.... and the members may believe or disbelieve any creed or doctrine, religious or philosophical, without affecting their caste position." [2]) "Each caste has its own Dharma, in addition to the common rules of morality as accepted by the Hindus generally, and considered to be the Dharma of mankind." Risley defines caste in *The Tribes and Castes of Bengal* as " a collection of families or groups of families bearing a common name; claiming common descent from a mythical ancestor, human or divine; professing to follow the same hereditary calling; and regarded by those who are competent to give opinion as forming a single homogeneous community. The name generally denotes or is associated with a specific occupation. A caste is almost invariably endogamous in the sense that a member of the large circle denoted by the common name may not marry outside that circle, but within the circle there are usually a number of smaller circles each of which is also endogamous." These smaller circles are really also castes. The occupational element in this definition is one-sided, as we have seen. Bouglé defines Caste in his *Essais sur le Régime des Castes*: "A society is subjected to this system if it is divided in a large number of groups, hereditarily specialized, hierarchically instituted, mutually opposed, — if it tolerates in principle no new people, no bastards, no mutual changes of profession, — if it opposes mixture of blood, the gaining of a higher social scale, and a change of

[1]) H. Risley, *The People of India*, pp. 70—92, quoted by N. K. Dutt.
[2]) This is not quite correct, see p. 159.

occupation." This definition has the merit of looking at the caste system as a whole. But changes of profession are sometimes allowed. And a higher social scale is sometimes attained by a caste as a whole. If Bouglé applies it to the members of a caste individually, it should be remarked that under the influence of Western ideas wealthy persons certainly stand higher in the social scale than the poorer people of the same caste. And sections of a caste can attain a higher standard within their caste and develop into a new caste. Mr. A. L. Kroeber defines Caste in the *Encyclopaedia of the Social Sciences* as "an endogamous and hereditary subdivision of an ethnic unit, occupying a position of superior or inferior rank of social esteem, in comparison with other such subdivisions."

Weighing the different elements of the definitions, and leaving out those which are not *essential*, though perhaps *usual in India*, we come to the following definition:

A society subjected to a caste-system consists of a number of subdivisions or castes which are exclusively endogamous, which show a strong tendency to be socially exclusive, which perpetuate themselves hereditarily, which are hierarchically superposed on a basis of standard supposedly cultural, and which by the working of these four tendencies within the social field of their own delimitations may split up into more and more castes indefinitely.

E. THE DUTIES OF THE VARNAS.

In the Mahābhārata the duties of the Varṇas are enumerated as follows: "He who is pure, consecrated by the natal and other sacraments, who has completely studied the Veda, lives in the practice of the six works, performs perfectly the rites of purification, who eats the remains of oblations, is attached to his religious teacher, is constant in religious observances, and devoted to truth, — is called a Brāhmaṇa. He in whom are seen truth, liberality, inoffensiveness, harmlessness, modesty, compassion and asceticism, is declared to be a Brāhmaṇa. He who practises the duty arising out of the office of ruler, who is addicted to the study of the Veda, and who delights in giving and receiving, — is called a Kshatriya. He who readily occupies himself with trade and cattlebreeding, who is devoted to agriculture and acquisition, who is pure, and is perfect in the study of the Veda, — is denominated a Vaiśya. He who is habitually addicted to all kinds of food, performs all kinds of work, who is unclean, who has abandoned the Veda, and does not practise pure observances, — is traditionally called a Śūdra. And if this were not to be found in a Śūdra, and if this were to be found in a Ḍvija, (twice-born), then a Śūdra would be no Śūdra, and a Brāhmaṇa no Brāhmaṇa." [1])

In the Bhagavad-gītā, that main bible of the Hindus, the duties of the different Varṇas are described similarly, in a beautiful form, "*according to the qualities born of their own natures.*"

"Of Brāhmaṇas, Kshatriyas, Vaiśyas and Śūdras, O Parantapa, the duties have been distributed according to the qualities born of their own natures. Serenity, self-restraint, austerity, purity, forgiveness and also uprightness, wisdom, knowledge, positive faith, are the Brahman's duty born of his own nature. Prowess, splendour, firmness, dexterity, fearlessness, generosity, the nature of a ruler, are the Kshatriya's duty, born of his own nature. Agriculture, cattlebreeding and trade are the Vaiśya's duty, born of his own nature. Action of the nature of service is the Śūdra's duty, born of his own nature." [2])

There is no need to quote the manifold enumerations of the duties of the Varṇas as found in the Dharma-śāstras; they do not widely differ in character from the two given above, which present the philosophical and ideal view unalloyed, whereas the Dharma-śāstras often show traces of compromising between theory and ideal on the one hand and actual conditions on the other hand. For instance in Manu we read that "To the Brahmans the Lord *assigned* teaching and studying, sacrificing etc....., the Kshatriya he *commanded*.... etc." [3]) The same applies to the theories of the origin of the 'mixed castes'.

In a late Purāṇa, the Bhāgavata, the ideal of Varṇa is held up anew to a society that had become split up into many castes. It is curious that the tendency appears in it to stress the horizontal view of humanity (the spiritual) instead of the customary vertical conception (the social). [4]) The four Varṇas are — as a reaction to mediaeval Indian conditions of caste — presented here almost as

---

[1]) *MBh. Śānti-parvan* 189 : 2—8.

[2]) *Gītā* XVIII : 41—44. Similar enumerations: *Bhāg.-P.* VII : *11* : 14—15: *Vishṇu-P.* III : *9*. See also the quotation from the *Vāyu-P.* p. 55.

[3]) *Manu* I : 98—91; The duties of the Varṇas are also mentioned by *Gautama* IX : 68—74; *Parāśara* I : 34—64; *Saṅkha* I : 1—5; *Yājñ.* I : 118—121; *Vasishṭha* II : 12—16; *Vishṇu* I : 8; *Hārita* I : 17—32 and II : 1—15; *Atri* I : 13—15. Also *Artha-śāstra* I : *3* : 4—7.

[4]) See Part II Ch. VI.

co-equal and as containing socializing tendencies almost to the same degree. [1]) And the anti-social elements were placed outside the pale of the Varṇas in a fifth group, which was a new development. "Absence of piety, lying, stealing, want of faith, quarrelsomeness without cause, violent passion of love and anger and inordinate thirst — these form the nature of those that are beyond the pale of the four Varṇas." [2]) All this may be explained as an attempt by the social idealists and leaders of the time to give a higher status in Hindu society to the Śūdra castes. Their stimulating power was very strong, and much was accomplished. [3])

Apart from the various duties of the different Varṇas, other duties were brought forward as the common duty of all the Varṇas, of all men. [4])

When the castes had become hereditary, the theory of reincarnation came to the foreground (in a way taking the place of the theory of Varṇa) to explain the possibility of rising to higher castes in subsequent lives.

To conclude we feel tempted to quote the words of a Hindu writer, who in a few words sums up the social theory as part of the greater plan: "The physical basis of life referred to by artha and kāma is to be sublimated in accordance with the principles of dharma. And dharma or social righteousness includes two aspects: āśrama or the duties flowing from the stage of life, youth, manhood or old age; and varṇa or the duties flowing from one's position in society as determined by karma (action) and guṇa (character). Dharma is the principle of synthesis linking the individual and society, time and eternity, for it is the bridge that leads to moksha or absolute freedom of self-realization. The principle of dharma envisages the whole process of the education of the spirit from the 'minimum' morality of bodily control to realization of the ātman or sarvātma bhāva (all-self-ness), mediated in the central phase by social contribution." [5])

[1]) *Bhāg.-P.* XI : *17* : 17—19.
[2]) *Bhāg.-P.* XI : *17* : 20.
[3]) See p. 97.
[4]) See e.g. *Manu* X : 63; IV : 246; *Gaut.* VIII : 23; *Yājñ.* I : 122; III : 65; *Vishṇu* II : 7—8; *Atri* I : 34—41; *Usanā* I : 32, 33, 40 etc.; *Vishṇu-P.* III : 8; *Bhāg.-P.* XI : *10* : 6—7 and XI : *19* : 33—37.
[5]) M. A. Venkata Rao, in *The Aryan Path*, Vol. IV, p. 789.

F. APPENDIX: THE ĀŚRAMAS. Analogous to the theory of the four Varṇas is the Hindu theory of the four Āśramas or orders of life, which is on the whole of greater interest to the psychologist than to the sociologist. Yet it has also fargoing social implications, as will be seen in several of the following chapters.

Human life is represented in the Āśrama system as consisting of four consecutive stages, the first three falling within the pale of class and caste and as such we shall not specially consider them. Ordinarily men do not pass beyond the second or for the most the third stage. The first stage is Brahmacharya, the stage of the student. It is the stage of the young man. The second is Gārhasthya, the stage of the householder. It is the stage of manhood. The third is Vānaprastha. The Vānaprastha retires to the woods and spends his time with meditation and sacrifice, he represents the stage of the older people, when the care of the children no longer takes up their time. The fourth stage is that of the Sannyāsin or mendicant, of the man who has given up his all to God or Truth, not only his possessions in the world, his wife and relations, but also the social distinctions of caste and the practices and ceremonies of religion. The Sannyāsins, recruited from all castes, form a group resembling a caste, but only superficially, for it shows none of the characteristics of a caste. [1])

The Dharma-śāstras abound with enumerations of the various duties and of descriptions of the social field of action of the four orders of life.

The Brahmachārin or student of the Veda or Revelation, originally any young man of the higher castes corresponding to the three higher Varṇas, later mostly only Brahman, lives with his Guru or spiritual preceptor, who accepts him as pupil on the day of his initiation, when he is invested with the 'holy thread' and becomes 'twice-born', he must study the sacred literature, serve his Guru, lead a life of continence and learn his duties as a member of society and his duties in the greater cosmic world, as conceived by the sages.

After being dismissed by his teacher he enters into the order of the householder (Gṛihastha), which is by some Śāstras proclaimed as the most important, since it is the most social. He takes with

[1]) Caste is defined on p. 71. Regarding the class of Sannyāsins, see p. 158.

lawful ceremonies a wife, he maintains a house and possessions and must discharge his duties to the world to the best of his power. His house is the refuge of the wandering Brahman and of the Sannyāsin. Hospitality is the principal duty of the householder and the poor depend upon him for their maintenance.

When his children get married and no more specially want his attention, he retires, probably with his wife, to a quiet place in the country to lead a more introverted life. This order is that of the Vānaprastha.

The fourth order is that of the Sannyāsin, who foregoes the three objects of life: Artha, Kāma and Dharma, to concentrate on Moksha alone. [1]) "Regarding all with an equal eye, he must be friend to all living beings. And being devoted, he must not injure any living creature, human or brute, either in act, word or thought, and renounce all attachments." [2]) He lives by begging food at a time when people have finished eating, and he is continually roaming. Women can also enter this fourth order of life, in fact as well as in theory.

The idea at the background of this scheme and of the summary of duties is of course that if some one does not live according to it, he is no true Sannyāsin or Brahmachārin, etc.

The Śāstras differ as to whether a man is allowed to pass over one or more of the orders of life or stages on the Path of Unfoldment. The oldest view is that the duties of all four stages have to be performed consecutively and that the lessons — social and spiritual — of the lower orders have to be experienced and learnt before passing to the higher ones.

The later view is that under exceptional circumstances people may pass from the first to the fourth stage. But under no condition are people allowed to take up again the life and duties of a previous Āśrama, since this would mean a step back on the Path.

This system of Āśrama is no mere theory, and the duties mentioned for the four orders of life are not merely hollow precepts.

Compared to the divergence between the ideal of Varṇa and the practice of caste, one may say that the Āśrama system has on the whole been applied and followed rather faithfully; perhaps not so much in the consummate social realization of the various *virtues*

[1]) See p. 26. The Sannyāsin is *theoretically* supposed to have at one time or another perfected the other three objects of life.

[2]) *Vishṇu-P.* III : 9.

of the four grades as according to the intention and spirit of the *fourfold division* of man's life. The weakness of the Āśrama system lies in that it was conceived only for persons high in the cultural hierarchy. The fourfold division and systematization is practical and serviceable, but the standards vary according to the hierarchic place (Varṇa) of a person. [1])

[1]) Cf. p. 176.

PART II

Chapter I

The universal and international element in Varṇa

A. PROPOSITION. The theory of Varṇa in its wider sense was a theory not applying to Hindu society exclusively, but to human society generally. In other words, 'Varṇa' contains a universal element. It is a theory of natural class. This universality manifested itself as a kind of international law in the scriptures and in Indian history.

As an ideal Varṇa was intended mainly for the Hindu people, but in addition to this there was a tendency to uphold it as an international ideal.

Consequently it was possible in ancient times that foreigners were taken into the castes or classes corresponding in some degree to the Varṇas, even into the Brahman fold, if they lived according to its rules.

The division into *four* classes presents the simplest all-inclusive division of society into groups with special functions in the organic whole. We shall specially consider the number four and its universality. We shall also consider the connection of caste and race.

B. THE UNIVERSALITY OF FOUR VARṆAS. Directly related to the four Varṇas were without doubt the four classes of the Iranians: 1. Āthravan (corresponding to Brāhmaṇa), 2. Rathaēštar (corresponding to Kshatriya), 3. Vāstrya fšuyant (corresponding to Vaiśya), 4. Hūiti (corresponding to Śūdra).

The division of society into *four* classes is found in many ancient cultures [1]), and this can easily be explained by regarding the all-

[1]) H. Kern, *Indische Theorieën over de Standenverdeeling*, p. 10 (*Verspreide Geschriften* XIII).

inclusiveness of the functions of the four groups of men in the organic unity:

1. Persons concerned with the guidance, the education of their fellowmen in the highest sense, involving the psychological unfoldment (the priest, the teacher, the psycho-analyst, the medical man, etc.); 2. persons with a regulative Dharma (persons with legislative, executive (and judicial) powers, the business-magnate, the military man, the policeman, etc.); 3. persons with a distributive task (in business, trafic, intercourse); 4. persons with a productive task (in agriculture, industry, industrial arts). [1]) If we consider these four groups, we realize that they include all possible specialists. We shall recur to them below. [2])

Sometimes in the theory of Varṇa the productive and distributive functions are both assigned to the Vaiśya, and the function of the Śūdra is considered to be the service of the higher Varṇas. This service, apart from domestic service, would be rendered almost exclusively in the productive field: agriculture and industry. Hence the difference is not so great, and the number of *four* Varṇas is as reasonable.

Abul Fazl in the wonderful Introduction to his Āīn-i-Akbarī, perhaps inspired by Hindu teachings, also divides society into four classes. He does not mention them in the hierarchical order, like the Hindus. "By means of the warmth of the ray of unanimity and concord, a multitude of people become fused into one body, and the people of the world may be divided into four classes: 1. **Warriors,** who in the political body have the nature of fire. Their flames, directed by understanding, consume the straw and rubbish of rebellion and strife, but kindle also the lamp of rest in this world of disturbances. 2. **Artificers and merchants,** who hold the place of air. From their labours and travels, God's gifts become universal, and the breeze of contentment nourishes the rose-tree of life. 3. **The learned,** such as the philosopher, the physician, the arithmetician, the geometrician, the astronomer, who resemble water. From their pen and their wisdom, a river rises in the drought of the world, and the garden of the creation receives from their irrigating powers a peculiar freshness. 4. **Husbandmen and labourers,** who may be compared to earth. By their exertions, the staple of life is brought

---

[1]) Also art: "to serve the twice-born is the religious work of the Śūdra, and industrial arts are his secular work." (*Atri* I : 15).

[2]) Regarding the number 4 see also pp. 26—28.

to perfection, and strength and happiness flow from their work. It is therefore obligatory for a king to put each of these in its proper place, and by uniting personal ability with a due respect for others, to cause the world to flourish. ....the grand political body maintains its equilibrium by the above four ranks of men." [1]) As we shall see later, Abul Fazl's views present the pure Varṇa doctrine. [2])

Abul Fazl may perhaps have borrowed some ideas from Plato. Plato also brought forward a doctrine of four classes. If he compared the State with the Soul, his pupil Aristotle saw an analogy between the State and the human body. The state as conceived by both of them consists of four classes, which somewhat correspond to the four Varṇas. The two lowest classes were often taken together as one. [3])

An interesting modern doctrine of four classes is presented by Adam Müller. His classes also correspond somewhat to the Varṇas. They are: 1. **The clergy,** incl. the **teaching classes,** he calls this the '*Lehrstand*'. 2. **The nobility,** the '*Wehrstand*', consisting of landed proprietors and military men. 3. The class of those occupied in **business, trafic and intercourse.** This is the '*Verkehrstand*'. 4. The class of those occupied in **industry and productive labour.** This is the '*Nährstand*'. [4]) It is clear that these classes are based upon the traditional classes of the German Reich.

The pure types of the four Varṇas, as we mentioned them above, have to be generally realized and appreciated again. (1. Spiritual and psychological, 2. Ruling and regulating, 3. Distributive, 4. Productive). At present they are hardly manifested in the social constitution at all. Neither the priest, nor the teacher, nor the doctor of these days, is an exclusive performer of the Dharma of the highest Varṇa. The modern representative of the highest Varṇa will have to be priest, teacher and psychologist at the same time. He will have to be a guide, but not a master.

The second and third groups also largely overlap in their functions in modern society. Here it is interesting to notice that many econo-

[1]) *Ain-i-Akbari,* by Abul Fazl 'Allami, transl. H. Blochmann, Vol. I: p. V.

[2]) It is also interesting that the analogy of the four elements is called to aid. It corresponds only partly to our analogy in Part I Ch. I.

[3]) See *Encyclopaedia of Religion and Ethics,* Vol. X, p. 552.

[4]) A. Müller, *Von der Notwendigkeit einer theologischen Grundlage der gesamten Staatswissenschaften und der Staatswirtschaft insbesondere,* p. 18.

mists and politicians of recent days advocate a capitalism and industrialism controlled to some extent by the State or rather by some international body. This means a clearer demarcation between the functions of groups 2 and 3.

The four Varṇas, on the racial basis which we have mentioned before, were originally pictured as given above: spiritual and psychological; ruling and regulating; distributive; productive. They formed of course the natural social composition of all races and were universal and international. In Chapter IV of Part II of the Vishṇu-purāṇa we are repeatedly told that the four Varṇas, called by other names, consist in other parts of the world. The impression of universality we also gain from the Bhāgavata [1]) and from the Gītā. [2]) When considering Dharma we mentioned its international or universal aspect [3]) and need not recur to this. [4])

If the Dharma of the Hindus is mainly found in the Dharma-śāstras, which hardly show the universal note, the universal Dharma, and the general doctrine of class are found in the more purely religious and philosophical works: the Brāhmaṇas, the Purāṇas and the Bhagavad-gītā. The Epics are a mixture of the two, universal and Hindu Dharma. Dr. Ketkar also points to the universality of the theory of Varṇa, and goes as far as to stress that there was really no 'Hindu-dharma', but Mānava-dharma, Dharma of Man. [5]).

C. FOREIGNERS AND CASTE. As Professor N.K. Dutt writes: "The Indian religion and social system were cosmopolitan and not national, the prevailing conception being that there is only one eternal religion, Brahmanism, the other religions of the world being only varieties or corruptions of the same, and that all the peoples of the world form one community divided into four Varṇas." [6]) In accordance with this conception it was sometimes possible in ancient times that foreigners were adopted into the social system of the Indians. As Dutt remarks, in early times there was no such bitter religious difference as we now find between Hindus and Mohamedans or Christians. "Similarly, the difference of race was unknown. There may have been

[1]) *Bhāg.-P.* VII : *11*.
[2]) *Gītā* XVIII : 41—71.
[3]) See p. 16.
[4]) Cf. pp. 41, 46 and 47.
[5]) S. V. Ketkar, *An Essay on Hinduism*, p. 29 and 11—13.
[6]) *Origin and Growth of Caste in India*, Vol. I, p. 32.

some racial struggle between the Aryan and the Dāsa in the Vedic age, but by the time of Manu all memories of that struggle had been lost. The word Ārya is not used in the literature of the time to denote a particular race, but is generally applied to those who practised the Vedic rites, or were honourable. There were no acknowledged differences between an Indian and a Chinese or a Greek as human beings, and if the latter consented to respect the Brahmans and practise Brahmanical rites he might be given a place in the society and called an Ārya." [1]) The factor of language was of no account. [2]) Always quoting Dutt: "Under these circumstances it was not unnatural for Manu and other sacred writers to regard the whole mankind as belonging to one community and to determine the social status of the various tribes and nations according to their conduct and respect for the Vedic rites." "This gives a clue to the success of Hinduism in keeping a firm hold upon the heterogeneous elements of the Indian population and its wonderful power of absorbing alien races and cultures, though apparently it is not a proselytising religion. The Brahmans would not regard any foreign religion as antagonistic to their own. They would say to the foreigners that their religions were only varieties of the one eternal religion, and that they belonged to one or other of the four Varṇas into which the whole manking was supposed to be divided. Those who would not care anything for Brahmanical usages were called Mlēchchhas or Dasyus and were let alone. But those who felt any the least respect for the Brahmanical institutions were told that their status in society, that is, the estimation in which they would be regarded by the Brahmans, would depend entirely upon the greater or less strictness with which they followed the teachings of the Śāstras. No force was applied or even necessary. Unconsciously and imperceptibly the alien barbarians would be tempted by the unfailing bait of higher social status to give up their old practices and conform more and more to the Brahmanical usages." [3])

The foreign warriors like the China (Chinese), Yavana (Ionians or Greeks), Śaka (Scythians) were by the Śāstras considered to have

---

[1]) Dr. Ketkar writes: "Had the Chinese only respected Brāhmaṇas our writer (Manu) would have perfectly been willing to call them Kshatriyas and therefore Āryas." (S. V. Ketkar, *History of Caste in India*, Vol. I, p. 81).

[2]) See *Manu* X : 45. See also S. V. Ketkar, *Op. cit.* pp. 78—81.

[3]) N. K. Dutt, *Op. cit.* pp. 13—15.

been Kshatriyas, afterwards degraded to a lower status, because they did not conform to the Indian standards of life and ceremony.[1]) They were called Vrātyas, and could become fully recognised by the Vrātyastoma rite. If they did live up to the Indian requirements they became fully recognised Kshatriyas. The stories which we find about their origin [2]) are highly fanciful and show the disregard of the Brahmans for racial distinctions. Dutt writes: "The stories, however fanciful, of the origin of some classes of Brahmans, apart from the anthropometric evidences lend colour to the supposition that non-Aryans (in the racial sense) did not fail to gain admission even into the Brahman fold." [3]) He proceeds to substantiate this view by quoting many scriptures and traditions and by the evidence of anthropometric researches.

From the North and the East, Tibetans, Burmese, Ahoms and Mongolians came to India in great numbers, established short-lived kingships and were in the long run entirely absorbed by the Hindus. From the West came Phoenicians, Egyptians, Arabs, Jews, Greeks and Alexandrian Romans, Abyssinians and Persians, who made trade settlements on the coast and who became Indians in the course of time. Completely Indianised groups still in some way betraying their origin are for instance the Ben-i-Israel and the Naviyat Arabs of Konkan, the Abyssinians of Janjira, and the Nestorian Christians of Malabar.

The ancient Ṛishis made whole tribes into Kshatriyas and Brahmans. How the integration of the Śakas (Scythians), Yavanas (Greeks) and the like was to take place, we gather from the Mahābhārata — if they behaved like Hindus, they became Hindus and were treated as such. [4]) [5])

In the centres of learning like Nalanda and Taxila there were opportunities for Chinese, Greeks and Iranians to meet and study, promoting a spirit of internationalism. How quickly the process of Indianisation took place is illustrated by the pillar of Besnagar,

[1]) *Manu* X : 43—44.

[2]) *Gautama* for instance mentions that "sons begotten on a Śūdra woman by a Brāhmaṇa, Kshatriya, Vaiśya or a Śūdra are respectively designated as Pāraśavas, Yavanas, Karaṇas and Śūdras." (IV : 21)

[3]) N. K. Dutt, *Op. cit.* p. 135.

[4]) *MBh. Sānti-parvan* 64—65.

[5]) The different groups of Phoenicians, Persians, Parthians, Scythians, Ionians, Pahlavis, etc. are mentioned: *Ṛig-veda* I : 33 : 3, 83 : 1, *Atharva-veda* III : 15; *Vāyu-P.* 88, 122, etc. Quoted from Aksaya Kumari Devi, *The Fundamental of Hindu Sociology*, p. 7.

erected by the Yavana ambassador Heliodorus, the son of Dion of Taxila, to the honour of Kṛishṇa Vāsudeva, about 150 B.C. Heliodorus is styled a "follower of Vishṇu". [1])

From Megasthenes and from the Artha-śāstra we gather that foreign travellers in India were well looked after by law and regulation. [2])

D. CASTE AND RACE OUTSIDE INDIA. If in '*Varṇa*' there is a universal and international note, in *caste* on the contrary the factor of race may be of great moment. We have seen this in connection with the conception 'Ārya', and we shall notice it again in the historical Chapter to follow. Here we shall only adduce instances of caste and caste-feelings outside of India.

As examples of isolated castes not forming part of a caste system may be brought forward the Jews and the Gypsies in Europe. In South Africa a regular caste system is evolving, there are no less than five castes: blacks, whites (South-Africans consisting of English and Boers), Cape-coloured, Indians, and Malays. We tend to believe that on the whole the racial feeling is heavily outweighing the sense of Varṇa. In North America conditions are very much the same, as seems to be the case in all countries where people of Anglo-Saxon race are living side by side with other races and are forming an influential group. The Spanish race is equally caste-separative and fanatic about purity of race, as may be noticed in the Spanish South American states.

On the other hand the racial feeling and the tendency to caste formation are shown far less by the Dutch in the Dutch East Indies and in the West Indies, and hardly at all by the Portuguese in Brasil, where a mixture of the white and black races is even considered an advantage. [3]) On this point Brasil presents a complete contrast to the other states of South America originally colonized by the Spanish.

E. CONCLUSIONS. We have seen in this Chapter that the theory of Varṇa is fundamentally a universal theory

---

[1]) *Cambridge History of India*, Vol I p. 558.

[2]) See B. C. J. Timmer, *Megasthenes en de Indische Maatschappij*, pp. 210—211.

[3]) K. Edschmid, *Glanz und Elend Süd-Amerikas*, pp. 422, 442—3, 449—451.

of class. Consequently a kind of international law of class is found in the scriptures and in Indian history. Foreigners could sometimes be admitted into the higher ranks of Indian society on a basis of equality if they undertook to live according to the standard of those ranks. The condition was: if equal social behaviour, equal rights and an equal social status.

Society was generally divided into four fundamental classes. This represents the simplest all-inclusive division into groups with special functions in the organic whole of society. Consequently many theories of class picture society on the basis of four fundamental classes in all.

We also noticed that if in 'Varṇa' there is a universal and international note, in caste on the contrary the race-factor may be of great moment.

Chapter II

The Social Process — Life and Form

A. **PROPOSITION.** In this Chapter, after pointing to the fact (Section B) that the texts are not always reliable, we shall pass in bird's eye view the different periods of history in India. We shall distinguish two aspects of Dharma, the one more or less corresponding to Varṇa and the other to caste. We want to demonstrate that in alternate periods, which we shall for briefness' sake call 'periods of life' and 'periods of form', the corresponding aspects of Dharma predominated. We shall consider one by one the different 'periods of form' in which various 'social evils' evolved, which were artificial developments. Next we shall consider the different 'periods of life'. We shall see that as a reaction to the tendency towards social crystallization and caste-separatism we find again and again in Indian History the promulgation of Dharma in its first aspects by the great teachers, some of whom were social reformers pre-eminently. This new Dharma always had far reaching social effects. In these 'periods of life' social evolution tended to follow its natural course after having restored the natural social equilibrium, being the social application and natural outcome of the renewed realization of Dharma in its first aspect.

Then we shall summarily watch the birth and development of various 'social evils', phenomena of social crystallization, noting their sensible and excusable origin. Dharma was invariably degraded from its first aspect to the second, from the ideal it became a system of compromise, from moral norm it became convention and law. The substitution of the principle of virtue and valour by the principle of birth has been the main factor in the process of social crystallization and caste-separatism. *True* Brahmans conceived the theory of Varṇa and advocated it as the natural law of the evolution of society and as an ideal, the Brahmans as caste upholders partly caused, and contributed to the 'evils' of caste. After noting the difference between the North and the South of India concerning the points studied we shall finally try to formulate the basic law of social process, a simple law of action and reaction, of life and form.

Vivekananda wrote: "What little good you see in the present caste clings to it from the original caste (read: class as based on Varṇa), which was the most glorious social institution. Buddha tried to re-establish caste in its original form. At every period of India's awakening there have always been great efforts made to break down caste." [1]).

B. QUESTIONABLENESS OF TEXTS. One of the greatest difficulties that we have to put up with in the study of caste, especially from the point of view that we have taken in this book, is the fact that the original scriptures have been altered and tampered with by Brahmans of later days. Unless we have clear proof of changes we can only rely on our common sense.

For instance Manu, in spite of its great reputation, is not really very ancient in its present form. The original Manu, a book of aphorisms, has not yet been recovered. What is now known as the book of Manu is a composition wholly in verse, based upon the original Manu, which was extremely ancient. For this reason this book has a great number of dates attributed to it, ranging between 1200 B.C. and the fourteenth century A.D. [2]) This later Manu code was the product of a special school, like there were so many in the centuries before and after Christ, and its compilers derived their inspiration and their material from the ancient Mānava-sūtra, the scripture of the gens of the Mānavas or 'the scripture of man'. And the Brahmans of these later schools often changed the texts according to the requirements of the times or their own pleasure. They left out undesirable dictums, like for instance the well-known verse of Parāśara sanctioning remarriage of women under certain circumstances, which verse occurred in Manu, as was known to the

[1]) *Complete Works*, Vol. V, p. 128.
[2]) See J. H. Nelson, *Scientific Study of Hindu Law*, p. 37.
[3]) N. K. Dutt, *Origin and Growth of Caste in India*, Vol. I, p. 127.

author of Vīramitrodaya, but has dropped out of the modern Manu. [3])

Below, in connection with the practice of suttee, we shall give an example of a seemingly unscrupulous tampering with an old text, by which a harmless practice was turned into a death warrant of many.

How such changes came about we may see perhaps from the following instance where two readings of a text are used side by side. It presents the transitional stage. Eventually that reading that does not suit the spirit of the time gets replaced by the other. "The duties of a Kshatriya are three, viz. studying, sacrificing for himself, and giving alms. His own special duty is also to protect his subjects according to spiritual injunctions; let him gain his livelihood thereby." [1]) '*According to spiritual injunctions*' is Śāstrena, the other reading is Sastrena, meaning: '*with his weapons*' [2]). Though in fact both readings turn down to very much the same, since the Kshatriya's duty is to protect his community, the two readings present two different mentalities, and show how easily texts were varied.

There has been hardly any tendency however to interpret texts into something more favourable than the original compilers meant or change them to something more humanistic than they intended. If we find verses which are idealistic and logical and express lofty sentiments they can in most cases be proved to be ancient.

Later texts sometimes show signs of compromise, as we shall see.

If in later times of revival and struggle to break loose from the prison house of social traditions and conventions people were in need of new slogans and fresh ideals, they either dug out ancient texts which fitted into the needs of the times or expressed their thoughts and feelings in an entirely new form. The first was the course followed by the more conservative reformers and it never presented great difficulties, whereas the latter was even easier and came naturally to the mystics who cared not a straw for anything but their ideal. And the mystics were the greatest social reformers in India.

As to the social aspects studied in this treatise apologetic tendencies have not appeared in India to any extent, except perhaps in

1) *Vasishtha* II : 15—17.
2) M. N. Dutt, *The Dharma Śāstra*, Vol. II, p. 755.

modern times as a reaction to one-sided and ill-informed Western criticism.

In recent times ancient texts have been misused again to keep the Untouchables out of the Temples. [1])

C. IDEALS AND ACTUAL CONDITIONS, THE CYCLIC PROCESS.

In our analysis of Dharma we have seen that Dharma has two aspects which are essentially opposed. We have seen that the ethical, the religious, the mystical and the ideal aspects of Dharma are really aspects of what we might call the 'first aspect of Dharma'. Dharma, economic, political, racial, professional, etc., appertains to the 'second aspect'.

It is the same contrast which the Western philosophers of law have grappled with in their distinctions of 'divine law' and 'human law', of 'natural law' and 'positive law', of absolute and empirical law, and so on.

Since our main object in this treatise is not philosophical but sociological we shall not try to compare the dual aspect of Dharma with the dual aspects as mentioned above, or endeavour to decide where they cover one another and agree and where they do not, but we shall accept the dual nature of Dharma as a psychological and sociological fact and factor.

The same essential distinction is found between the theory and ideal of Varṇa and the practice and reality of caste. The 'first aspect of Dharma' accounted for the birth of the theory and ideal of Varṇa. The 'second aspect of Dharma' created caste in India.

This philosophical and sociological contrast is however no contrast if we consider the matter in the light of social psychology. For both Varṇa and caste were and are part and parcel of the psychological property of the Indian (and in principle of all mankind). In his mind, conscious or subsonscious, both conceptions are interwoven and form for the most two degrees in a catena, but no factual opposites. We are thinking here of the Social Mind and the Social Unconscious.

In accordance with the latest theories of Psychology we may say that when caste and the 'second aspect' of Dharma began to predominate in man's mind and in social life, the 'first aspect' and Varṇa receded to the background, and the different aspects of the

[1]) E.g. see: S. N. Suta, *An unjustifiable double standard*, in *Vedanta Kesari* Vol. XIX, pp. 352—360.

'first aspect' reverted to the Social Unconscious. This process went on till social conditions became too rigid and impossible, and till the 'first aspect' had to come to the foreground again, that is to say, take its place in the conscious life of the race and adjust the balance, first in the psychological life of the people, next in society.

In the history of India we watch the predominance of either the first or the second aspect of Dharma.

According to Hindu theory, in the Golden Age, i.e. in the 'beginning', the 'first aspect' was predominant (not to say that it held undivided sway). Though highly efficient in its social implications it was probably not yet *mentally* realized. I have shown in Chapter I, Part I, that it was mystically or *intuitively* realized. This would explain also its efficiency as a highly socializing power. [1])

Mental realization however came about only when its contrast, the 'second aspect', had been known and experienced. Only then times were ripe for a realization of the dual nature of law. Needless to say that this knowledge and experience have been accumulating through the ages up to the present hour.

Then we watch the growth of the laws, conventions, traditions and religious rituals in the ages that followed — the first historical ages.

Follows the period when the form-side developed at the expense of the life-side. Religious rituals became elaborate and complicated, their inner meaning was slowly obscured. Ceremonies and conventions slowly turned into superstitions. Laws and political usages were followed after the letter instead of according to the spirit.

In India the period after the Ṛig-vedic Age corresponds to this stage.

As a reaction to this inevitably Life itself as living realization of the divine unity and of the social unity, manifesting first in a leader and in a few chosen ones, who call it out of the collective unconscious of the people, attacks the old stale forms of religion and society, puts up new ideals and standards and begins either to revolutionize the existing forms or to create new ones in a new field. [2]) In religion it is the period of the struggle of the prophet and the mystic against the despotic priest, in society it is — at least at first — the period of the horizontal view of humanity (equality — brotherhood) trying

[1]) See pp. 43, 126 and 143.
[2]) See p. 123.

Buddha, indeed, brought forward again the Varṇa (v a n n ā) doctrine in its pure form. Of interest is the implication of the import of Dhamma as primarily norm or standard. In the words of Mrs. Rhys Davids: "Khattiyas might be distinguished as originally administrators of justice; Brahmins, as originally followers of religious, pure, or righteous lives. But the *dhamma* of the other two classes was indisputably their proficiency in certain secular unmoral arts and crafts. Hence, whereas Dhamma may imply righteousness, justice, truth, virtue, law, its most fundamental meaning is more general, being "that on account of which" — be it righteousness, or some *un*moral proficiency — a distinction is assigned, in other words a rule, test, standard or norm." [1])

Again and again Buddha stressed in his teachings that the true Brahman is not he who is born in the Brahman caste, but he who behaves as a Brahman. [2]) In the older Anthologies of the Buddhist canon, the Tri-piṭaka, the truly worthy, good man is over and over again called Brāhmaṇa. [3])

The priests of other religions and of other periods seem to have periodically shown the same tendencies as the Brahmans. [4]) Here we cannot resist the temptation of quoting from the Zoroastrian books "There is many a one, O holy Zarathushtra, said Ahura Mazda, who wears a wrong Paitidāva, and who has not girded his loins with the Religion; when such a man says I am an Āthravan, he lies, do not call him an Āthravan, O holy Zarathushtra!" [5]) "Him thou shalt call an Āthravan who throughout the night sits up and demands of the holy wisdom (i.e. studies the Law and learns from those who know it), which makes man free from anxiety and wide of heart, and easy of conscience at the head of the Chinvaṭ bridge, and which makes him reach that world, that holy world, that excellent world of Paradise." [6]) If the names did not point to Zoroastrianism these lines might equally well have applied to the teachers of other religions.

Buddha came in a period of form-culture and crystallization. If in the previous periods of form the stress had been lying on the religious forms, now the tendency is even deeper and the stress is

---

[1]) Mrs. Rhys Davids, *Buddhism*, (1st Ed.) p. 239.
[2]) See p. 119.
[3]) *Dhammapada*, *Sutta-nipāta*.
[4]) See pp. 17, 113—118.
[5]) *Fargard* XVIII : 1 (*S.B.E.* Vol. IV).
[6]) *Fargard* XVIII : 6 (14).

lying predominantly on the social forms. Caste had become a social pest. Buddha's influence was directly social by propagating the spiritual equality of men, by opening up the (exoteric) spiritual path to all, desrespective of caste or sex, by disowning the authority of the Brahmans by their merely being born in that caste, by reforming the caste system among his followers. "Within the order caste disappeared, and many low castes were admitted as monks." [1]) It was the external system of Hinduism in religion and caste that was found wanting by the early Buddhists, not the internal system of spiritual values. Buddha was not an opponent in philosophical matters, but a reformer. [2]) Also his minor reforms — like his prohibition to slaughter animals for sacrifice and his food-reform — were important.

Yet his social influence outside of his own movement may not be overrated. As Professor N. K. Dutt remarks, few would nowadays agree with Rhys Davids in his statement in *Buddhist India* that "it is no more accurate to speak of caste at the Buddha's time in India than it would be to speak of it as an established institution, at the same time, in Italy or Greece." [3]) Fick warns against this overestimation. [4]) Caste continued to exist in very much the same way in Hindu society and it took hundreds of years before changes were noticeable due to Buddhist influence.

The reason is that Buddha's doctrine was meant for the individual seeker as a way out of his troubles by entering an inner course of truth, not so much by trying to reform his outer worldly conditions, but by accepting them as they were and meeting them with a pacified spirit. It may be a wiser course than that of so many other reformers who were so intent on changing the outer structure of society that they neglected the happiness of their followers. And as such the treatment was worse than the ailment.

Yet we must not ignore that most historians lay stress on Buddha's importance as a social reformer, and that he came because the Śūdras were not admitted to the old Hindu scriptures and ceremonies. [5]) People like Upāli and Sunīta, a barber and a sweeper,

---

[1]) E. J. Thomas, *The Life of Buddha*, p. 128.

[2]) Mrs. Rhys Davids, *The Relations between Early Buddhism and Brahmanism*, in *Indian Historical Quarterly*, Vol. X, p. 282.

[3]) N. K. Dutt, *Origin and growth of Caste in India*, Vol. I, p. 256.

[4]) R. Fick, *Die soziale Gliederung im Nordöstlichen Indien zu Buddha's Zeit*, pp. 20, 215.

[5]) R. C. Dutt, *A History of Civilization in Ancient India*, Vol. II, p. 306.

rose to honour and fame in Buddhism. In the days before Buddhism they would have remained mere Śūdras. The rise of Buddhism represented no doubt a mass movement against the growing Brahmanical tyranny. [1]) A very important feature of the social-psychological teaching of Buddha is that he revived the pure theory and the sense of Varṇa.

The great Buddhist Emperor Aśoka abolished caste as far as he could. [2])

Biologically anti-social may be considered Buddha's withdrawing of the noblest elements of humanity from the married state to monkhood. The spiritual-social gain may have outweighed the biological sacrifice in the first centuries of Buddhism, who can judge? But in the long run society went from one extreme to the other. Lower caste people went over by thousands to the lazy and sheltered life of monkhood as it developed, something against which the Dharmaśāstras with their graduated scale of Dharma had always watched. And the army of idle monks and nuns was one of the causes of the disappearance of Buddhism from India. Persecution and violence did the rest. [3])

Yet Buddhism had stimulated the internal forces of Hinduism by its noble doctrine and by the example of its earlier adherents. The Brahmans had adopted many good points from Buddhism in theology and philosophy. When Buddhism had finished its task in India, it vanished from the stage. The final union of Brahmanism and Buddhism (if one may so call it) resulting in a simplified Hindu theology, a popular symbolic ritual, a most exalted ethic and great ideals of humanity (as embodied in the Rāmāyaṇa and the Mahābhārata) had taken place by the year 800 A.D. The ancient Vedic religion had been modified by Buddha's influence and the Vedāntic doctrine of the Upanishads had taken its place. We may compare the process to the inner purification of the Roman Catholic Church after the Reformation and the Protestant criticism.

Jainism, a movement a little older than Buddhism, presented similar doctrines.

In the 8th to 10th centuries A.D. there were great political upheavals in India and an opportunity was presented, as it was presented before in early Buddhist times, of admitting the Śūdras

---

1) N. K. Dutt, *Op. cit.* p. 151.
2) R. C. Dutt, *Op. cit.* Vol. II, p. 306.
3) *Ibid.* p. 307.

to the benefits of higher and socially respectable Hinduism. The opportunity was lost again. It was the time of Śaṅkara and of the Bhāgavata-purāṇa [1]).

To Śaṅkarāchārya, born probably in 788 A.D., it fell to inaugurate a new 'period of life', to re-establish the One godhead and truth as against the doctrines of the many sects that existed, to supply the growing need for light and life, and to make the Vedānta Philosophy the basis of all the nobler movements of Hinduism. His attitude to form, formality and formalism is typically expressed in one of his hymns: "I am neither castes, nor the rule of caste, society and custom, nor for me are concentration, meditation, Yoga and other practices [2]); for, all this illusion of 'I' and 'Mine' is rooted in the not-self and is therefore dispelled by the knowledge of the self. I am therefore the secondless, uncontradictable, attributeless Bliss (Śiva)." [3])

The result of Śaṅkara's tours of reformation and religious purification were that the abominations of the Śāktas, Gāṇapatyas, Kāpālikas, Bhairavas and other sects received a severe check and many centres of immoral and unholy rites were purified altogether.

But the tide again turned the other way. Religion was once more objectified and dogmatized, caste prospered as never before.

Professor Rangacharya writes "The development of thought in Indian civilization made it necessary that the old Vedic religion of ritualism should be superseded by another religion, which had more of real life in it, and was more capable of satisfying the religious needs and aspirations of the human heart, irrespective of all considerations of race, caste and social status. Nevertheless this new religion could not be altogether new. In fact the progress of religion is so effected in the history of all civilizations that no new religion can be absolutely or unmixedly new. When a new institution or a new idea has to be introduced among a people for their immediate benefit, it invariably happens that this new institution or new idea becomes implanted upon something that is really old...." [4])

Mohammedanism began to spread in India and made converts among the lower castes by the million, securing them a higher

[1]) See p. 73.
[2]) As over-systematized and dogmatized.
[3]) S. Venkataramanan, *Select Works of Śrī Śaṅkarāchārya*, p. 27.
[4]) M. Rangacharya, *Rāmānuja and Vaishṇavism*, in: *Three Great Āchāryas*, p. 173.

status in society. The Emperor Akbar encouraged inter-caste and inter-racial marriage, also by his personal example.

The Vaishṇava Reformation, of which Rāmānuja may be called a forerunner, brought the renewed propagation of equality and brotherhood and the realization of One Religion and Truth at the back of the sects of Hinduism and the Mohammedan faith. Great social ideals were advocated and proclaimed by the great saints that lived between 1200 and 1600 and which can roughly be said to fall into two or three classes.

I. Those who fell within the pale of orthodox Hinduism, like Rāmānuja, Rāmānanda, Mādhava, Jñāneśvar, Chaitanya, Vallabha and many others. They continued the line of liberal and protestant saints and philosophers begun with Śaṅkara in the 8th century.

II. Those who stood outside orthodox Hinduism and had both Hinduism and Mohammedanism as their background and as their field of influence, like Kabir (a disciple of Rāmānanda), Dadu, Raidās, Nāmdev and hundreds of others, many of which were Śūdras and Untouchables.

III. In a third class we may put Nānak and the other Gurus of the Sikhs, who formed a side-branch from Hinduism, a religious and social community which grew ultimately into a nation.

Mādhava of orthodox Hinduism gave to women the right to study the Vedas.

The Brahman Rāmānuja tried to improve the condition of the Untouchables. It was for the first time in the history of Hinduism. He secured for them the privilege of visiting the temple one day in the year. [1])

Great saints sprang from the Untouchable classes and lived right in the centres of orthodoxy like Nanda in Chidambaram, Ravi Dās in Oudh, the ancient Ayodhyā, Chokamela in Mahārāshṭra and many others. The number of Śūdra saints was legion. These on the whole upheld the theory of Varṇa and the principles of caste, only freeing the low caste population from the Brahmanic domination in spiritual matters. [2]) There was one movement which proclaimed a wholesale revolt against caste. It proved to be an unsuccessful attempt, since the followers of this sect were con-

[1]) G. S. Ghurye, *Caste and Race in India*, p. 95.
[2]) *Ibid.*

temptuously treated and bitterly hated by all castes, and it even gave rise to a new caste, of the Mānbhāvas. [1])

In this period fell also the birth of vernacular literature. The many gods of earlier ages became merged in the One God or Truth. Even Buddha had become an Avatāra (the ninth) of Hinduism. [2]) The hymns of the time abound with vehement censure and rejection of formalism in religion and in caste. It is hardly necessary to give examples. The cry for free primary education is a revised edition of the universal religious education after Buddha's time.

Careers of glory and heroism were once more open to lower caste people and to the illiterate. The horizontal ideal of humanity was much on the foreground. In short, the philosophers and saints which lived between 1200 and 1400 witnessed one of the greatest religious movements in India, a movement with far-reaching social effects, since the Śūdras' position was greatly improved and caste suffered many defeats.

After 1400 the social aspect of life had become more or less balanced, 'life' and 'form' were somewhat in equilibrium. The great saints that lived after that time — Ekanāth, Tukārām, Rāmdās, and others — accepted the social system as it had become at the time. They criticized no more the Brahman caste as such, but the Brahman hypocrites and impostors. Most of the preachers upheld Varṇa and Āśrama, and the Brahmans were on the whole content. The evils of caste were condemned, not in concrete cases, but abstractly. The distinctions and ideals of Varṇa were advocated and the vertical theory of society put before the people. Caste did no more hamper so severely the religious life and the last saints of that age had no need to be social fighters, they were in the first place spiritual awakeners.

In the same 'period of life' the Sikh community came into being. It was in the course of time to grow into a nation. Its founder, Guru Nānak (1469—1539), severely condemned the artificial caste system. "It is mere nonsense to observe caste and feel pride over grand

[1]) *Ibid.*

[2]) Buddha is first mentioned as Avatāra (divine incarnation) in the 12th century. But an inscription has been found in a cave near Madras of the 7th century. (*Memoirs of the Archaeological Survey of India, No 26*, Rao Bahadur H. Krishna Sastri, *Two Statues of Pallava Kings and five Pallava Inscriptions in a Rock Temple at Mahabalipuram*, p. 5). The story of Buddha's misleading teachings, as found in some Purāṇas, is a later interpolation.

names." [1]) There was not to be a priestly class: "Whoever worships Him is honourable." [2]) Any man of his sect could perform ceremonies, address prayers, lead in congregations, perform rites of baptism and marriage for their children. The history of the Sikhs is a remarkable example of the social consequences of spiritual teaching. It would lead us too far to go into details, which can be found in any book of Indian history. The first Gurus and leaders of the Sikhs propagated ideals of love and harmlessness to the last consequences of "turning the other cheek", and the Sikhs brought these into practice to an admirable extent. But after a time they were so ill-treated and persecuted so ruthlessly that it looked as if their community would in the long run cease to exist altogether. For that reason the later Gurus began to propagate ideals of manliness and strength, somewhat like the chivalrous ideals of the crusaders. The Sikhs, faithfully putting into practice the teachings of their leaders, held their own and developed into great fighters, the repute of which they are holding up to the present day.

After this Reformation the tide was to turn once more to rigidity of laws and priestly regulations, to Brahman corruption and to social sectarianism. After 1700 form began to predominate, the competition between the Brahman and the non-Brahman began anew with all the concomitant evils.

But in the middle of the last century the first notes were heard of rebirth, of renewed social idealism, of the propagation of unity and brotherhood, of a great urge to reform existing religious and social evils. And we may say that in spite of the vehement struggles of orthodoxy the spiritual and social powers of a Maharshi Devendranath Tagore, the father of the great poet, a Dayananda, a Ramakrishna, a Vivekananda, a Mahatma Gandhi, only to mention a few of the beacon lights, are slowly gaining the upper hand.

If in former periods of revival problems had arisen mainly about the status of the Śūdra, in the present period the status of the Untouchables forms a subject of contention between the enlightened and idealistic section of Hindu society and orthodoxy. In former ages the Untouchables had been much despised. In the Mātaṇga Jātaka we read for instance how 16000 Brahmans lost their caste because they, though unknowingly, had partaken of food which had been polluted by contact with the leavings of a Chaṇḍāla's

[1]) *Śrī Rāg* I.
[2]) *Japti.*

meal! But in those times Chaṇḍālas and Nishādas etc. were on the whole as yet but savages that did not mix much with Hindus. [1]) In recent times however many have socially come to the light of day, possessing a certain education.

If in the two former 'periods of life' many lower caste people had become Buddhist monks and Mohammedans to improve their social status, in recent times many Untouchables have become Christians for the same reason. Apart from the moral and spiritual benefit of the new religion this phenomenon of wholesale conversion works as a warning, an example and an eye-opener to the upholders of the older established religion and social system. If the present time in India cannot yet rightly be called a 'period of life', yet it surely is on the way of becoming one. The so-called 'pagan renaissance' in Bengal brought forth the great poet Michael Madhusudan Dutt. The Brahmo Samāj, a religious movement to reform Hinduism and to combine the best elements of Hinduism, Islam and Christianity, spread from Bengal to some other provinces. Ram Mohun Roy, Devendranath Tagore, Kesav Chandra Sen were its pioneers and leaders. When the Brahmos began to lose their solidarity the Ārya Samāj was founded to renew Hinduism internally. The saint Ramakrishna followed in the footsteps of the mediaeval saints. At times he broke all possible caste-rules, as also his great disciple Vivekananda. If Ramakrishna's merit was that he put into motion great forces to the religious awakening of the Hindus, Vivekananda's merit was as much a social one. The Ramakrishna Movement and the Ramakrishna Mission carry on the work of their inspirers, a work of spiritual awakening, education and social service. Many movements, often hardly organized at all as a sect, inspired by leaders of the mystic and prophet type, do similar religious and social work. To mention only a few of their founders: Swami Dayananda, Swami Rama Tirtha, Sri Abaninda Ghose and the Christian Sadhu Sundar Singh. Side by side with the religious awakening and the religious-social movements we may mention the political awakening, which began in the middle of the 19th century. Organized political activity began in 1885 when the National Congress was founded. In India politics go together to some extent with religion, ethics and social idealism, as Mr. Gandhi illustrates in his own life and work.

[1]) Sometimes the Chaṇḍālas lived in special suburbs, the Nishādas were nomad tribes.

And in so far as this is the truth, politics may be reckoned to form part of the 'life' of the period.

As to caste, Mr. Gandhi and others are continually criticizing its evils and fighting for the admission of the Untouchables — there are 27 millions in India — to the important temples. Much has been achieved already, but there still remains a stupendous task to be done. Various social evils — criticized so severely in Miss Mayo's *Mother India*, book of fame (or ill-fame) — are being vigorously opposed. We shall mention the origin and development of some of them below.

Having considered the various manifestations of 'life' in the different 'periods of life' of Indian History, we shall now inquire into the 'periods of form'. At the beginning of such a period we notice that the element of compromise is growing, the friction between Dharma in its first aspect and social facts becomes less noticeable and soon stops altogether. Perhaps its task has been greatly achieved. Dharma grows into a set of adjusted rules and finally into accepted laws and conventions — which yet for a time fulfil their social purpose. Dharma has fallen into the hands of the Brahman as privileged priest and of the Brahman as lawyer and caste-preserver.

In other parts of the world the process is fundamentally similar, only instead of the Brahman one must substitute other associations of persons. But perhaps nowhere else there were such religious and social extremes as in India — this perhaps being the reason that the process may be followed so distinctly in the history of Indian culture.

Of the first more important 'period of form' the elaborate ritual, the complicated later Vedic Sacrifices are typical phenomena. Because they are mainly religious and theological, and have not yet social consequences of any depth, we shall not quote any examples. Mighty and often monstrous ceremonies had developed out of the simple Vedic sacrifices, like the Aśvamedha-ceremony out of the simple horse-sacrifice. [1])

For the later important 'period of form' we can take many samples of the systematized, dogmatized, priest-ridden Dharma from the Dharma-śāstras. The fourth book of Manu, containing an

[1]) R. C. Dutt, *A History of Civilization in Ancient India*, Vol. I, p. 67.

infinite variety of rules for householders, is typical. Another example of this kind is for instance the description of the sacrificial food the ancestors will be satisfied with, contained in Manu III: 266—274. "The ancestors of men are satisfied for one month with sesamun grains, rice, barley, *māsha* beans, water, roots and fruits, which have been given according to the prescribed rule, (267). Two months with fish, three months with the meat of gazelles, four with mutton, and five indeed with the flesh of birds, (268) Six months with the flesh of kids, seven months with that of the spotted deer.... (269)". And so on for 8, 9, 10, 11 months, one year, twelve years. Till at last food is mentioned that serves for endless time: "All kinds of food eaten by hermits in the forest serve for endless time (272). Whatever food, mixed with honey, one gives on the thirteenth lunar day in the rainy season under the asterism of Maghā, that also procures endless satisfaction (273)." If originally there may have been some symbolical meaning (astrological in 273?) in the long run these rules became matters of form and superstition.

Or: "The foolish man who, after having eaten a Śrāddha-dinner, gives the leavings to a Śūdra, falls headlong into the Kālasūtra hell." [1])

The other Dharma-śāstras abound with similar examples. We may specially mention Parāśara. As to the rules invented by the Brahmans for their own glorification, etc., we refer also to the analysis of Dharma (12) in Part I Chapter 1, Section C.

The Dharma-śāstras are a curious mixture of 'life' and 'form', of the noblest and purest thoughts of humanity and the grossest superstition.

Before the time of Śaṅkara 'form' was ruling supreme. The many sects all based their faith on the Vedas, their special scripture consisted of particular texts or passages from the Vedas, interpreted in a special way. They were at that time very intolerant of each other, only in the common fight against Buddhism they were at one. Many of the practices were abominable. Caste had grown into a social evil once more.

A few centuries later form again began to predominate. As Professor Rangacharya writes, the influence of the priests became so markedly preponderant that the gods almost began to disappear

[1]) *Manu* III : 249.

from the vision of the sacrificers. The letter of the law was all-important. When somebody asked to a priest: "Who is Indra?", the reply was: "Dont ask who he is. He may be anything or nothing. He is simply that thing the name of which is here in this formula inflected in the dative case." All thought bearing upon the vital questions of godhood disappeared, what happened to be left behind was nothing more than mere form overloaded with numerous complicated and unattractive details involving much useless expenditure of time, wealth and labour. Naturally the common human heart would be prone to rebel against such a religion, writes Rangacharya. There can be no real life of any kind in an over-encrusted and fossilized shell of religion. [1])

Remains the last 'period of form' which has left India the social evils many of which it still has to overcome. Form has predominated since about 1700.

It will be interesting to follow summarily the birth and the development of some of the 'social evils'. Various factors will be seen to be significant. All the time we must mark the two social forces: on the one hand idealism, 'life', with its social consequences, on the other hand class-interest, formalism and conservatism.

To begin with a practice which has been made punishable by law during the Viceroyalty of Bentinck in 1829, **suttee,** the "self-immolation of widows". No ancient regulations can be found enjoining or encouraging it. The references of the ancient texts to widows (about which below) show that the practice was unknown.

The Mahābhārata and the Rāmāyaṇa both recognize the existence of suttee, but only the former gives a case of a royal widow burning herself with her husband. As Professor Washburn Hopkins writes, it is perhaps the extension of a royal custom as in the epic which has made the rule general so that later law and practice recommend it for all. [2])

The codes do not sanction suttee till late, the provisions for widows show that they were not expected to die with their husbands though they probably lived miserable lives. The line in the Vishṇu-saṃhitā is often regarded as a later interpolation. [3])

[1]) M. Rangacharya, *Rāmānuja and Vaishṇavism*, in: *Three Great Āchāryas*, p. 176.

[2]) *Cambridge History of India*, Vol. I, p. 292.

[3]) *Vishṇu* XXV : 14 : "It is a duty of a wife to live a life of perfect chastity after the death of her lord, or to follow him on the funeral pile."

The Greek writers mentioned suttee. Onesicritus spoke of it as specially a custom of the Kshatriyas. [1] Aristoboulus was told that a widow sometimes followed her husband to the pyre of her own desire, and that those who refused to do so lived under great contempt. In the year 316 B.C. the leader of an Indian contingent which had gone to fight under Eumenes in Irān was killed in battle. There was immediately a competition between his two wives as to which was to be the s a t ī (suttee). The generals decided when the question was brought before them that it was to be the younger, the elder being with child. The elder woman then went away lamenting as if tidings of great disaster had been brought her, the younger departed, exultant at her victory, to the pyre. [2]

But if in those times the widows still had comparative freedom of choice, the only pressure brought to bear upon them being the weight of local public opinion, which may develop from a harmless admiration into a pitiless tyrannic force, in later ages the practice was authorized and even enjoined by the priesthood. Max Müller called it "the most flagrant instance of what can be done by an unscrupulous priesthood! Thousands of lives sacrificed on the authority of a passage, mistranslated and misapplied". The Ṛig-vedic line in question, referring to a procession of women at a funeral ceremony, runs: "May these women not suffer the pangs of widowhood. May they who have good and desirable husbands, enter their houses with collyrium and butter. Let these women, without shedding tears, and without sorrow, first proceed to the house, wearing valuable ornaments." This perfectly harmless line was turned into something entirely different by the changing of one word, of one letter: *Agre* was altered into *Agne,* which is Fire. [3] This forgery is of quite modern date. [4]

One of the social curses of India, especially also of modern times, is the prohibition of the **remarriage of widows.** In the early periods of Indian history widow marriage was not prohibited, an there was probably sanction for it. In the Ṛig-veda we find: "Rise up, woman, thou art lying by one whose life is gone, come to the

---

[1] H. Zimmer, *Altindisches Leben,* p. 331; this writer mentions that suttee existed among the princely class.

[2] *Cambridge History of India,* Vol. I, p. 414—415.

[3] R. C. Dutt, *A History of Civilization in Ancient India,* Vol. I, pp. 110—111.

[4] Fitzedward Hall traces it to Raghunandana (1500 A.D.) see *Cambridge History of India.* Vol. I, p. 108.

world of the living, away from thy husband, and become the wife of him who holds thy hand, and is willing to marry thee." [1]) Mr. R. C. Dutt, who quotes this passage, mentions that the translation is based on Sāyana's rendering of the passage in the Taittirīya-āraṇyaka, and that there can be no doubt as to its correctness, because the word *didhishu* has only one meaning in Sanskrit, viz. the second husband of a woman. [2]) Other scholars however have expressed doubt about this interpretation.

Men belonging to one caste sometimes married widows of another caste without any scruple, as can be gathered from a passage in the Atharva-veda. [3])

In the period when the Dharma-śāstras were compiled, the remarriage of widows was disapproved. It was put in the same class as inter-caste marriage, which shows that it was still in existence, though the Brahmans desired its abolition. The son from the second marriage of a widow is of a degraded class and must not be invited to a Śrāddha. [4]) Vasishṭha gives some forms of marriage, which, being less valid than other forms, entitle to a second marriage. [5]) And he continues that the wife of a Brahman who has gone to a foreign country shall wait five years before remarrying, and if he had no children, four years, the wife of a Kshatriya who has children, five years, and who has no children, three years, as to the Vaiśya, it is respectively four and two years, and as to the Śūdra, it is three and one year. Kauṭilya adds that if the husband is a Brahman, studying abroad, she shall wait twelve years if she has children and ten if she none. And he continues to state a great variety of rules for different cases. [6])

The later lawgivers prescribed a very hard life for widows. This was done by merely inserting the widows in a list of persons intended to follow those rules. Such tampering with the texts was often indulged in by the later compilers of the Dharma-śāstras. They may have made the life of the widows so miserable that Suttee may have been a godsent liberation to many of them without much encouragement.

In modern times the life of the Hindu widow is still a wretched

[1]) *Ṛig-veda* X : 18 : 8.
[2]) R. C. Dutt, *A History of Civilization in Ancient India*, Vol. I, p. 109.
[3]) *Atharva-veda* V : 17 : 8; R. C. Dutt, *Op. cit.* Vol. I, p. 260.
[4]) *Gautama* XV : 18.
[5]) *Vasishṭha* XV : 73—78.
[6]) *Artha-śāstra* III : 158—159.

one. Slaves of their relations, often almost outcasts, compelled to live an ascetic life they may be entirely unfit for, in simple dress with hair cut short, working for their married female relations and their children, they can on the whole wait for no other happiness than that of religion. In the last twenty years many of them have emancipated themselves by becoming nurses and teachers, often thus severing all connections with their relatives. But of course they are few compared to the great number in all. The rules of the various castes differ greatly, they vary from our above description to those of other castes that have readmitted the marriage of widows.

The sinking of the status of the widow will go parellel to a large extent with the sinking of **the status of womanhood.** In Ṛig-vedic India there were women Ṛishis, the wives participated in the ceremonies with their husbands. [1]) They were highly honoured and respected, and could even perform the function of a priest at a sacrifice. [2])

Mr. R. C. Dutt writes about the position of women in Ancient India: "We have seen that the absolute seclusion of women was unknown in ancient India. Hindu women held an honoured place from the dawn of Hindu civilization four thousand years ago; they inherited and possessed property; they took a share in sacrifices and religious duties; they attended great assemblies on state occasions; they openly frequented public thoroughfares, according to their needs, every day of their life; they often distinguished themselves in science and the learning of their times; and they even had their legitimate influence on politics and administration. And although they have never mixed so freely in the society of men as women do in modern Europe, yet absolute seclusion and restraint are not Hindu customs, they were unknown in India till Mahommedan times; and are to this day unknown in parts of India like the Mahārāshṭra, where the rule of the Moslems was brief. No ancient nation held their women in higher honour than the Hindus, but the Hindus have been misjudged and wronged by writers unacquainted with their literature, and who received their notions of the women of the East from Turkish and Arab customs." [3]) And he proves these statements with quotations from the Brāhmaṇa literature.

[1]) *Ṛig-veda* I : 83 : 3; VIII : 31 : 5; from N. K. Dutt, *Origin and growth of caste in India*, Vol. I, p. 78.

[2]) V : 28; *Ibid*

[3]) R. C. Dutt, *Op. cit.* Vol. I, pp. 256—257.

He concludes: "....never in the most polished days of Greece or Rome were women held in higher regard in those countries than they were in India three thousand years ago." [1]

The Ṛig-veda gives side by side the most contradictory opinions and information of practices. We find sayings as from a modern novel: "With women there can be no lasting friendship; hearts of women are like those of hyenas." [2] Or: "The mind of woman brooks no discipline, her intellect hath little weight, Indra himself hath said." [3] Or: "Many women select their husbands for their wealth."[4] But far more frequent are the remarks like this: ".... a wife is home and dwelling.... Thy joy is in thy home, thy gracious consort." [5] And side by side with instances of polygamy and moral laxness, monogamy was held up as an ideal. [6]

The trouble started with the notion that she was ceremonially impure. [7] In many of the ceremonies the priest was to take her place at the side of the husband. [8]

By the contact with the matriarchal Dravidians of the South the position of woman became higher, and the mother became socially pre-eminent by the time of the Sūtra period. The Dharma-śāstras say that the father, the mother and the Guru are to be respected most. The Guru usually comes foremost, but we read in Gautama: "A teacher is the foremost of all preceptors or superiors; according to others a mother is the highest of them all." [9] Vasishṭha spoke in the same spirit: "The father is a hundred times more venerable than the spiritual preceptor, and the mother a thousand times more than the father." [10] And: "A father, who has committed a crime causing loss of caste, must be cast off. But a mother does not become an outcast for her son." [11]

It is curious that these two tendencies are found all the time working in opposite directions: the tendency towards the depression

1) *Ibid.* p. 260. See also N. K. Dutt, *Origin and Growth of Caste in India*, Vol. I, pp. 77—78.
2) *Ṛig-veda* X : 95 : 15; from N. K. Dutt, *Op. cit.* Vol. I, p. 76.
3) VIII : 33 : 17; *Ibid.*
4) X : 27 : 12.
5) III : 53; from N. K. Dutt, *Op. cit.*
6) I 124 : 7; IV : 3 : 2; X : 71 : 4, *Ibid.*
7) *Śatapatha-Br.* XIV : *1* : 1 : 31.
8) *Śatapatha-Br.* I : *1* : 4 . 13.
9) *Gautama* II : 51.
10) *Vasishṭha* XIII : 48.
11) XIII : 47.

of the female status, according to some an Aryan tendency; and on the other hand the worship of the mother, which is sometimes seen as an influence originally foreign. [1]) We cannot accept the supposition that it was an Aryan tendency so easily. There was a religious tendency of the Aryan classes to regard her as inferior, there was an equally strong social tendency to honour her as mother. The sinking of her status probably began with the loss of the vision of true womanhood, next came the idea of the moral insufficiency [2]) and of the ceremonial impurity of woman. [3]) Step by step she was pushed back to a more subordinate position in society, till Moslem influence condemned them to seclusion. In every consecutive 'period of form' another step was done into this direction. Yet within the confines of the home she always held a supreme position.

A noble view we find in Āpastamba: "If he has a wife who is willing and able to perform her share of the religious duties, and who bears sons, he shall not take a second. If a wife is deficient in one of these two [qualities], he shall take another, but before he kindles the fires of the Agnihotra." [4]) From this we see that the Dharma of a woman was seen as: 1st, the spiritual community with the man; 2nd, the founding of a family.

In case of barrenness the husband could abandon the wife [5]) and the wife was justified to marry again, when the husband was impotent as also when he was insane, outcasted or had died. [6]) To what extent these injunctions were really followed is hard to say.

Other verses showing the attitude to women we find in Manu: "Women must be honoured and adorned by their fathers, brothers, husbands, and brothers-in-law, who desire (their own) welfare. Where women are honoured, there the gods are pleased; but where they are not honoured no sacred rite yields rewards. Where the female relations live in grief, the family soon wholly perishes; but that family where they are not unhappy ever prospers. . . . ." [7]) And in this spirit the Māṇava-śāstra continues.

[1]) See N. K. Dutt, *Op. cit.* p. 238.

[2]) The Śāstras show in many places very little faith in the nature of woman.

[3]) *Śatapatha-Br.* XIV : *I* : 1 : 31.

[4]) *Āp.* II : 5 : 11 : 12—13.

[5]) *Baudhāyana* II : 2 : 4 : 6.

[6]) *Vasishṭha* XVII.

[7]) *Manu* III : 55—57.

That Purdah was not the practice yet as it was later, but also that its possibility was sometimes considered and that it may have been tried, we make out from the lines in Manu which show a combination of wisdom with common sense: "No man can completely guard women by force; but they can be guarded by the employment of the following expedients: Let the husband employ his wife in the collection and expenditure of his wealth, in keeping everything clean, in the fulfilment of religious duties, in the preparation of his food, and in looking after the household utensils. Women, confined in the house under trustworthy and obedient servants, are not well guarded; but those who of their own accord keep guard over themselves, are well guarded." [1]

If the compiler in the ninth book of Manu is well aware of the faults of women [2], on the other hand he also compares them to goddesses of fortune [3], he says that the husband owes to his wife a second birth [4], and that "the due performance of religious rites, faithful service, highest conjugal happiness and heavenly bliss.... depend on one's wife alone" [5].

Under Mohammedan influence the confinement of the women to their houses developed to the extent as found at present. Even so Hinduism has at all times since then continued to bring forth great woman mystics, poets and Yoginis, which shows that woman has had comparative freedom. In districts where Mohammedan rule and influence was only short-timed, she kept her old freedom. At any case, if perhaps in society her movements have been hampered, in the home she always had and still has a certain pre-eminence.

Child marriage seems to have been unknown in ancient India of Ṛig-vedic times, it was probably still unknown in the Epic period, and there are numerous allusions to the marriage of girls at a proper age. The marriage of young girls probably came into vogue gradually in the Rationalistic period. That it was not yet settled in that period we infer from the contradictory rules on that subject. In Vasishṭha we see that child-widows were allowed to marry again in that period, if they had been married young. We find also traces of an age-limit of three years after puberty. After

[1]) *Manu* IX : 10—12.
IX : 2, 5, 13, 15, 17, etc.
X : 26.
: 8.
: 28

that a religious (superstitious) motive is given for child-marriage to prevent sin falling upon the father [1]), clearly a later development.

Modern authorities consider as the greatest immorality not the sexual intercourse of children at a tender age (since usually after the marriage or betrothal ceremony the children go back to their parents till they have reached the age of puberty), but the prohibition of remarriage of the girl if her boy-husband has died, thus dooming the girl to the life of widowhood. Due to the continuous endeavours of Hindu reformers, who called to aid the English lawgiver, child-marriage has now been practically abolished.

Another 'social evil' which we shall only mention in passing since it is not so directly contained in the field covered by this study, is the problem of **food**. Here also we watch how originally quite sensible hygienic and religious rules were crystallized into social injunctions and blown up in the course of time under the influence of the caste spirit into anti-social enormities of separativeness. So much so that the body of food injunctions has become one of the most important attributes of caste in India.

We have already mentioned the problem of the **Sannyāsin.** We have seen that in Buddhist times many lower caste people sought to raise their status by becoming Buddhist monks. At the present time many lower caste people try to raise their status within the fold of Hinduism by becoming Sannyāsins. The original purpose of the fourth Āśrama is not fulfilled in that case, for these people become Sannyāsins not from any spiritual motives, but from motives of gain: food, subsistence and social consideration. And so it has come that a great army of beggars is parasitizing India and bringing the fourth Āśrama into disrespute. Of course there are brilliant exceptions in true Sannyāsins and intellectual monks.

Remain the more direct problems of caste. **Untouchability** is another example of a 'social evil' which seems to have been entirely unknown in Ṛig-vedic times. The Dāsas, as painted in the Ṛig-veda in the darkest colour by the conquering Aryans, cannot be shown to have a low state of culture or dirty fashions of living which might cause feelings of abhorrence. [2]) A Brahman Ṛishi is even found to associate himself with a Dāsa king and celebrate his

[1]) *Vasishṭha* XVII : 67—68.
[2]) N. K. Dutt, *The Aryanisation of India* Ch. V.

generosity. [1]) There was no 'untouchability' between the Aryans and the Dāsas.

The earliest mention of the Chaṇḍālas and Nishādas is found in the Yajur-veda [2]), where they are represented as savage races who lived in a repulsively dirty fashion and subsisted from hunting and fishing when they were first encountered by the Aryans. They were of dirty habits and low culture and belonged to a Pre-Dravidian stock, probably Munda-Monkhmer race, who had remained unabsorbed by the Dradivians, and had been treated as pariahs even by the latter. The spirit of contempt was taken over by the Aryans. [3]) From this we see that Untouchability in its original form was natural and excusable. In Epic days it had not yet become general custom. This we gather from the story that Rāma when he went into exile with Sītā and Lakshmaṇa visited his friend Guha, the Chief of the Nishādas, and embraced him heartily at the meeting.

As soon as Untouchability became part and parcel of public opinion and of social custom, and, instead of being left to the feelings of the persons concerned, was handed over to objectivity, it tended to become a social pest.

Untouchability, as other extremes of caste-separatism, has developed to its worst form in the South of India. We have already noticed its South Indian origin. We have also to remember that the Aryan element in the South was far smaller than in the North. The Aryans had to take their stand against admixture of blood and the influence of the Southern civilization. To the difference between caste in North and South-India we shall refer below [4]). We have already seen how Rāmānuja and others broke a lance for the Untouchables. Since the standard of culture of many groups of Untouchables has steadily risen in the course of time, their problem has grown in proportion. Nobody cares to propagate the spiritual equality of dirty and uncultured savages to cultured people, but if many of these savages in the course of time have individually developed a higher degree of culture, the question of their equality arises in accordance with the theory of Varṇa, for: according to

[1]) *Ṛig-veda* VIII : 46 : 32; from N. K. Dutt, *Origin and Growth of Caste in India*, Vol. I, p. 62.

[2]) N. K. Dutt, *Op. cit.* p. 105.

[3]) *Ibid.*, p. 106. The Dravidians were at first classed as Śūdras, and the aboriginal tribes as 'fifth Varṇa' (*Nirukta* III : 8, *Bṛihaddevata* VII : 69)

[4]) See p. 120.

the standard of individual behaviour people can be assigned to their group of peers.

It is not here the place to mention all that is being done at the present time for the social betterment of the Untouchables or Depressed Classes, '*Harijans*' as they are called by the followers of Gandhi. Enough to say that much is being done, Mr. Gandhi of course coming in the foremost place. He adopted a girl of an untouchable caste as a member of his family, eating and working in her presence and breaking all the time all possible caste-rules of separativeness. His influence has penetrated into the strongholds of orthodoxy.

Apart from the campaign to get the standard of the Untouchables raised in Hindu-society, much work is also done to bring them education and culture. Mr. A. V. Thakur of the Servants of India Society, Poona, has worked for more than twenty years amongst the Bhils of Southern Rajputana, and many are now doing the same work elsewhere.

Having followed the position of the people on the lowest rung of the ladder of Hindu society — in truth on the lowest rung, or only in the imagination of the people — we shall now follow those on the topmost rung, the **Brahmans.**

Hinduism owes to true Brahmans the blessings of the theory and the ideal of Varṇa, and to the Brahmans as caste-upholders many of the diseases of caste.

In Ṛig-vedic society there were no temples (as far as one knows) and every householder was his own priest. Step by step we may watch in Indian history the development of a priestly profession, a priestly class and finally a priestly caste.

How the two tendencies — of birth and conduct — began to be at variance we may see from an interesting dialogue in the Mahābhārata. We can make out that there are already then strong upholders of the theory of birth. "The Smṛiti declares.... that he is a Brāhmaṇa, in whom truth, liberality, patience, virtue, innocence, asceticism, and compassion are seen.... The qualities characteristic of a Śūdra do not exist in a Brāhmaṇa (nor vice versa). Were it otherwise the Śūdra would not be a Śūdra, nor the Brāhmaṇa a Brāhmaṇa. The person in whom this regulated practice is perceived is declared to be a Brāhmaṇa; and the man in whom it is absent, should be designated as a Śūdra...." [1]) Then the other

[1]) Cf. the quotation on p. 72.

remarks: "If a man is regarded by you as being a Brāhmaṇa only in consequence of his conduct, then birth is vain until action is shown. Yudhishṭhira replied: ....birth is difficult to be discriminated in the present condition of humanity, on account of the confusion of all Varṇas. All sorts of men are continually begetting children on all sorts of women." [1]) Birth could not yet possibly be upheld as a deciding factor on account of the great number of mixed marriages. Yet both tendencies were seen to be at work, and birth plus endogamy slowly gained the upper hand. That all people who behaved as Brahmans could become Brahmans, as was possible in early times [2]), soon became impossible when endogamy had become the rule. But then the Dharma-śāstras try to put the ideal of true Brahmanhood before the caste-Brahmans. These idealistic lines sometimes stand side by side with lines of the other class, meant to secure and affirm the supreme position of the Brahman-caste in society. Of both we shall give examples. [3])

Lines of the second category are to be found for instance in Gautama XII, where punishments are given for the three lower Varṇas if they have in some way sinned against the supremacy of the Brahmans. Such teachings and injunctions show that the Varṇa theory which is to be found in the Dharma-śāstras is not at all the pure Varṇa theory, but only a compromise between Varṇa and caste. Lines as the following, which are understandable as a symbolic attitude in the case of true Varṇa, cease to form a part of the Varṇa theory as soon as they are given in the form of an obligation: "A Brāhmaṇa should treat a Śūdra, even if of full eighty years, as his own child, but a member of a superior caste, although younger in years than a Śūdra, should be bowed down by the latter." [4])

It is curious how sometimes a good Brahman is considered to be one who performs his ceremonial and scriptural duties rather than one who has a noble character. This shows the predominance of 'form' over 'life' in the Dharma-śāstras. "A Brāhmaṇa without the Gāyatrī-Mantra is more degraded than a Śūdra. Brāhmaṇas, who know the supreme Brahmā and are devoted to the Gāyatrī, are the foremost in honour and sanctity. The person of a wicked Brāhmaṇa

[1]) *MBh. Vana-parvan* 180 : 21—34.
[2]) See Ch. IV Section B.
[3]) See also the analysis of Dharma, Part I Ch. I C.
[4]) *Gautama* VI.

is more worshipful than that of a Śūdra, who has controlled his senses. Who will milch a docile she-ass in preference to a vicious cow?" [1]) This comparison affords a typical example of how the inadequacy of symbolism can be misused for personal purposes, in this case of class.

The following, also perhaps acceptable in the case of real Varṇa, becomes ridiculous if taken in a dogmatic sense and if applying to a caste: "Riding in the chariot of scriptures, and wielding the swords of Vedas in their hands, Brāhmaṇas, whatever they may speak even in jest, is Dharma." [2]) "The blessing of a Brāhmaṇa ranks equal with the merit of all pieties combined." [3]) "The word of a Brāhmaṇa is the word of a god. A Brāhmaṇa is a moving pantheon" [4]). And so on. The following is also true in the case of true Varṇa, but loses its value if put in the form of heteronomous norms: "The three Varṇas shall remain under a Brāhmaṇas control. The Brāhmaṇa shall declare their duties and the king shall carry them into practice...." What follows is a privilege which — according to circumstances — may or may not be in accordance with the theory of Varṇa: "The Brāhmaṇa saves (one) from misfortune. Therefore the Brāhmaṇa shall not be made to pay taxes." [5]) If a man is a true Brāhmaṇa, he will probably have few possessions and put all his spiritual and mental faculties at the service of his fellowmen. It would be unjust to make him pay taxes. If however a man is only a Brāhmaṇa in name, lacks the character of a Brāhmaṇa and subsists like a Vaiśya householder, or if a man is a true Brāhmaṇa who in some way acquired material riches, it would be unjust to other members of the community *not* to let him pay taxes. Priests in other countries were often exempt from paying taxes, sometimes as a privilege which they had taken to themselves or exacted from the rulers, and sometimes as a self-evident grant to them by the rulers. The latter which is quite in accordance with the theory of Varṇa was undoubtedly historically older. A typical example is furnished by a law of Genghis Khan, who ruled the greater part of Asia. Priests of the different religions in his empire (Buddhists, Mohammedans, Shamans, Nestorian Christians, etc)

[1]) *Parāśara* VIII · 31—32.
[2]) *Parāśara* VIII : 33.
[3]) *Parāśara* VI : 51.
[4]) *Parāśara* VI : 61. Parāśara is one of the younger Dharma-śāstras.
[5]) *Vasishṭha* I.

were all exempt from taxes. "Leaders of a religion, preachers, monks, persons who are dedicated to religious practice, the criers of mosques, physicians and those who bathe the bodies of the dead are to be freed from public charges." [1]) In India the exemption from taxes and other privileges of the priests were undoubtedly originally sensible injunctions in accordance with Varṇa. When they became class or caste privileges they turned into social evils.

The class struggle slowly gained on the sense of Varṇa, and the wisdom of Varṇa was used in a dogmatic form for the purposes of caste.

To enforce their position the Brahmans established, besides the corporal punishments which we have already mentioned, also terrible theories of punishments in different hell states or of rebirth in animal bodies or in deformed or diseased human bodies. [2]) These theories were all later day inventions.

On the other hand the theory of reincarnation offered to the people of lower caste the possibility of attaining to the Brahman caste in subsequent incarnations. In this way the old maxim of conduct and character was saved to some extent, though the consequences of action in society were transferred from actual life to a hazy and theoretical future state.

Yet the share of the Brahmans in the evolution of caste must not be overrated. They have been compared to the Jesuits in Western society. [3]) It is not possible to explain a system as complicated as the caste-system as an invention of a few, as Bouglé remarks quite sensibly. Many factors have co-operated in the evolution of caste, as we have seen before. Yet we cannot but believe that if the Brahmans had lived up to the Varṇastandard of the Brahman which would have meant also that they had kept up a graduated standard of sociality, worked for the sense of Varṇa and the realization of Varṇa in the social mind, and maintained a healthy self-criticism, caste could never have come into existence.

The sphere of influence of the Brahmans, originally purely religious and ceremonial, slowly passed more and more from the spiritual to the social. Instead of the 'Varṇa-Brahmans' who tried

---

[1]) H. Lamb, *Genghis Khan*, p. 214.

[2]) See e.g. *Gautama* XX, *Vasishṭha* XVIII, *Manu* XII : 54—78, *Yājñ*. III : 206—225, *Vishṇu* XLIV.

[3]) L. von Schröder, *Indiens Literatur und Cultur*, quoted by Bouglé, *Essais sur le Régime des Castes*, p. 35; Sherring, *Natural History of Caste*, quoted by Senart, *Les Castes dans l'Inde*, p. 178.

to help man to understand his place in the cosmic world and to make clear to him the relations between man mutually, and between man and the divine powers, the caste-Brahmans began more and more to turn their attention to laying down rules of conduct, laws determining the duties of the castes.

The Brahmanical schools did not start with any idea of making law. They began with religious hymnology, devotional exercises, ritual and theological speculation. Only later some of the schools began to lay down rules of conduct, how a man should behave, what he should do, what would happen to him if he did not, and by what acts, if he lapsed, he could restore himself to uprightness. Gradually there arose in the schools the conviction that for the purpose of regulating conduct by uniform rules, the best course was to call to aid the rulers, and thus the king was called in to help the Brahman and to be consecrated by him. The beginning of this alliance with the king was the beginning of true civil law, as Sir Henry Maine remarked, who described the above process. [1]) He continued that something very similar would have happened in the legal history of Western Europe if the Canonists had gained a complete ascendency over Common Lawyers and Civilians. The system which they would have established might be expected to give great importance to the purgation of crimes by penance. This in fact occurred, he says, the preference of the ecclesiastical system with its penances over the secular system with its cruel punishments, had much to do, as may be seen from the legendary stories, with the popularity of St. Thomas (Becket). Then they would have invoked the aid of the secular ruler in the case of graver sin, to secure the proper expiation, and the severer punishments would have been entrusted more and more to the secular arm, till in the long run, if the sole advisers of the European king had been ecclesiastics, a system would have been constructed with proper sanction enforced by the Courts. This system of civil and criminal law would have been deeply tinged with ecclesiastical ideas, like Hindu law.

As it is, Sir Henry Maine was quite right in remarking: "On the whole, the impression left on the mind by the study of these books is, that a more awful tyranny never existed than this which proceeded from the union of physical, intellectual, and spiritual ascendency." [2])

---

1) H. S. Maine, *Early Law and Custom*, p. 44.
2) *Op. cit.* p. 47.

The Brahmans were supreme, they held the keys of heaven and hell, of life and death, they had to be looked upon as gods.

They had become moral preachers and legal advisers and the pure religious leadership of the early Brahmans had largely passed out of their hands. Religion had slowly been breaking its ceremonial fetters. The sages themselves noticed that ritual was passing out and that prayer (Japam) was taking its place, as we can gather from the well-known line in the Vishṇu-purāṇa: "That which one obtained through meditation in the Satya-yuga, through sacrifice in the Tretā and through worship in the Dwāpara, may be attained in the Kali-yuga by reciting the names of the Lord". True religion has no need of priests with rules and dogmas but of holy men with inspiration.

No wonder the Brahmans lost the heart of the people when they encouraged class contempt like this: "(The Brahman) shall not ordinarily give the residue of his food to a person who is not a Brahman. When he gives it to such a one, he shall cleanse his teeth and give the food after having placed in it [the dirt from his teeth.]" [1]) And when they propagated ideas of this kind: "He who in anger raises his arm against a Brahman, will be banished from heaven for a hundred years; if he strikes, for a thousand years." [2]) Yet the value of such passages must not be overestimated, in the majority of cases they represent the views of the priests of what their own powers should be rather than what they actually were. [3])

On the other hand we find in the Dharma-śāstras remains of the pure original Varṇa theory or attempts to put the ancient ideal once more before the caste-Brahmans. As for instance: "Brāhmaṇas, who are ignorant of the Vedas, and Gāyatrī and Sandhyā, and those who do not cast any oblation in the sacrificial fire and live by agriculture, are only Brāhmaṇas in name." [4]) Yet here the form aspect is stressed, and not the grade of spirituality of the Brahman, as is more the case in the following line: "A Brāhmaṇa reaches the highest goal by muttering prayers only; (whether) he perform other (rites) or neglects them, he who befriends (all creatures) is declared

[1]) *Āp.* I : 11 : 31 : 24.

[2]) *Gautama* XXI : 17—20. Both quotations from N. K. Dutt, *Origin and Growth of Caste in India*, Vol. I, p. 150.

[3]) See *Vedic Index* II. 256—257.

[4]) *Parāśara* VIII : 11. Cf. the Zoroastrian quotation on p. 94.

(to be) a (true) Brāhmaṇa." [1]) In the following line character is preferred to birth: "The panegyrists, the flatterers, cheats, those who act harshly, and those who are avaricious, — those five Brāhmaṇas should never be adored, even if they are equal to Bṛihaspati in learning." [2]) And sometimes practical virtue is exalted above the performance of ritual practices: "The Brāhmaṇas, by a thousand sacrifices, do not attain to that piety which the kings do by protecting their subjects." [3])

The pure conception of a Brahman according to the Varṇa theory is to be found in the Epics and in the Purāṇas. It is of the following type: "Serenity, control of the senses, austerity, purity, forgiveness and also uprightness, knowledge, realization, belief in the higher life, are the *karmans* of the Brāhmaṇa, born of their own nature." [4]) We shall dwell upon this elsewhere.

Buddha and the great reformers tried to revive this conception. As for instance: "A man does not become a Brāhmaṇa by his platted hair, by his family, or by birth; in whom there is truth and righteousness, he is blessed, he is a Brāhmaṇa." "He who is thoughtful, blameless, settled, dutiful, without passions, and who has attained the highest end, him I call indeed a Brāhmaṇa." [5]) The whole twentyeighth Chapter of the Dhammapada continues in this line.

Not long ago Dayananda, the founder of the Ārya-samāj, Vivekananda and others taught in the same spirit, as indeed all the awakeners of former and of recent times did. It would lead us too far to give more quotations. [6])

Leaving the Brahmans, let us consider for a moment the castes claiming to correspond to the three lower Varṇas (leaving out the conception of the mixed castes). There is no need to say much about the **Kshatriya-castes.** On the whole they held their own in the process of the ages, since their worldly protection was always important and the Brahmans needed their co-operation. As to the **Vaiśya-castes,** they have been slowly sinking in status and the **Śūdra-castes** have slowly improved theirs, all this since, let us say,

[1]) *Manu* II : 87. "Befriends all creatures" implies "does not offer animal sacrifices". See G. Bühler, *S.B.E.* Vol. XXV, p. 46.

[2]) *Atri* 379.

[3]) *Atri* 29.

[4]) *Gītā* XVIII : 42. See also pp. 130—131.

[5]) *Dhammapada* XXVI . 393 and 386.

[6]) See Part II Ch. XC.

800 B.C. The Vaiśya-castes, of all Aryan groups representing the least cultured, tended to get mixed most with people of dark race. The Śūdras by their ever greater admixture with Indo-Aryans, slowly ascended the social ladder. Recent archaeological researches in the Indus valley show that the Indo-Aryan people that came from the North found in India a civilization equal if not superior to their own, side by side with tribes of uncultured aboriginals.

It is extremely difficult to find a formula that will cover all these questions of race in connection with the evolution of caste and the conception of Varṇa, and we feel it beyond us to try it with any conviction, deeming it wise to wait till more is known about the pre-Aryan civilizations. Only it seems to be certain that the pre-Aryan culture was absorbed wholesale by the culture of the conquerors, this being the origin of the 'Hindu culture' [1]), and we may perhaps assume that the leading elements of these ancient cultures were originally largely recognized as having their place among the Brāhmaṇas. The undeveloped, uncivilized aboriginals which were despised by the older civilization were naturally equally or more despised by the newcomers. The present untouchable castes developed from those groups: Pulkasas, Chaṇḍālas, Nishādas, Dasyu-groups, etc. "It seems", to quote Dr. Ghurye, "that the Vedic Dāsa, by constant association and slow assimilation, had been partially turned into the Śūdra and partially into the Nishāda, while the refractory and incorrigible elements were despised and styled Paulkasa and Chaṇḍāla". [2])

The authors of the Dharma-śastras wanted to keep to the fourfold division of society. A 'fifth Varṇa' was rejected and these groups were placed among the mixed castes. [3]) It was a hopeless effort to bring about conformity between theory and actuality, and it entailed ridiculous explanations.

Another fact which is evident is the difference between the North and the South of India in matters of caste. Caste has developed its most tyrannical and separative aspects in the Dravidian South,

[1]) For instance the Atharva-veda shows signs of compromise between Indo-Aryan and non-Aryan rites. See further *Cambridge History of India* Vol. I, p. 233. S. V. Viswanatha, *Racial Synthesis in Hindu Culture*, p. 207.

[2]) G S. Ghurye, *Caste and Race in India*, p. 48.

[3]) *Manu* X: 8—45.

probably because the elements of caste already existed there [1]), and because the differences of social and religious conceptions were much greater than in the North, where the dark races (with the exception of the civilized nation) on the whole consisted of uncultured aboriginals which were altogether not cultured enough to mix with the fairer race in the earliest times. [2]) Consequently the clash of ideas in the North was far less intense. On the whole the Varṇa-spirit tended to be more influential in the North, whereas the caste-spirit was stronger in the South. We find the Hindu laws and institutions in their purest form, very much in the state in which they were before the Brahman expositors took them in hand, in the Punjab, which country was the earliest seat of the Aryans on their descent from their original home into the plains of India. The laws and institutions of this province have been the subject of an exhaustive official enquiry [3]). Sir Henry Sumner Maine writes about this: "The traces of the religious ideas which profoundly influenced the development of what is known as Hindu law are here extremely slight; and few things can be more instructive to the legal archaeologist than the comparison of the Punjab rules with those worked out in Brahmanical schools far to the south-east. This Punjab Hindu law exhibits in fact some singularly close resemblances to the most ancient Roman law." [4]) Instead of Maine's 'traces of religious ideas' we should like to put 'traces of priestcraft', viz. a varnish of priestly dogmas, which backed the development of caste.

D. CONCLUSIONS. We have seen in this Chapter that Hindu History, as a reaction to the tendency to social crystallization and caste-separatism, from time to time shows consecutively a renewed realization, promulgation and social application of Dharma. This 'new' Dharma always caused a breaking up of the most rigid manifestations of the social constitution and worked towards the realization of a social constitution more in harmony with the social composition. After having more or less restored the social equilibrium the new Dharma in its turn gradually

[1]) See G. Slater, *The Dravidian Element in Indian Culture*, pp. 53—150. See also p. 112.

[2]) For the same reason as that the Europeans in Australia did not mix with the Australian aborigines.

[3]) Ed. C. L. Tupper, *Punjab Customary Law.*

[4]) H. S. Maine, *Dissertations on Early Law and Custom*, p. 8.

became old and stale and form-ridden. Caste interest as opposed to the true sense of Varṇa played a large part in this process of forming society along such artificial lines.

In this connection two periods may be distinguished which alternate. Social practice (custom and law) and social need, always at variance, periodically clashed completely. Social need in the higher sense, that is to say, the nobler and socializing instincts of humanity, periodically gained the upper hand. There was a cyclic rebirth of Dharma.

If the ideal and the sense of Varṇa came into prominence during a 'period of life', side by side with the mystical ideal of humanity and the emotional experience of brotherhood [1]), and if they stood for conduct and example, in a 'period of form' feelings and injunctions of caste, as disseminated, advocated and enforced by caste-Brahmans and upheld by the lower castes [2]), were on the foreground.

Apart from this, is it possible to discover an evolutionary tendency in the consecutive 'periods of form' and 'periods of life'? Yes, it may be noticed that step by step the vital centre of gravity was gradually transferred from the more religious to the social aspects of life. If in the earlier periods the great problems of 'life' and 'form' (as far as we know) were lying mostly in the religious field, we notice later a moving of the centre of gravity via the mental and the emotional life to the social. If in earlier 'periods of form' religious ceremonies and texts often tended to suffocate true religion and were privileges of certain groups, in more recent times social customs and laws tend to obstruct a healthy social intercourse, and there is comparatively more freedom of religious belief and practice.

When we were considering various social evils of Hinduism of the 19th and 20th centuries, we noticed how they were lacking in the earliest ages of Indian History, how they originated in one or other of the 'periods of form' and slowly developed in the subsequent 'periods of form' to their present shape. They were based on sensible hygienic (food-problem, untouchability) or excusable (if somewhat delusive) moral or spiritual (suttee, widow-problem, childmarriage) conceptions which, when they were posited as heteronomous social norms and became general custom, gave birth to anti-social ten-

[1]) See Ch. VI.
[2]) See p. 182.

dencies of the first magnitude. Sometimes old texts were tampered with to give a surer foundation to these practices.

E. AFTERTHOUGHTS. In Chapters to follow we shall recur to the group-spirit, the realization of brotherhood, the manifestation of the widest circle of the 'consciousness of kind' of Giddings.

A great many national as well as world movements may be traced to the fundamental source which wells up from the mind of man. Confining ourselves to more recent times, we mention only a few: the great revival of which Rousseau was one of the first prophets, the idealistic impulses of Liberalism, Socialism, Communism, the 'back-to-nature' movements of Youth, like the German 'Wandervogel' movement, the numerous efforts to found ideal communities, and the movements of religious revival, far too many to enumerate. Many of these movements failed before their time, either because the vision had not been clear enough, or because the leaders were side-tracked by personal motives, or because the emotional impulse overruled the mental. [1])

As history has demonstrated, in the case of the great religions the periods following upon the life of the founders or of the great prophets or seers who gave a powerful stimulance are the most spiritual. This means that the vision is clearer and that the ideal can be put into practice more efficiently in the beginning than in later times. Slowly degenerations are creeping in, and spirit and form of the religion become disconnected. This process is going on till conditions become unbearable to the most serious of its priests or adherents. These become seekers, searching for the Supreme and Eternal Truth or God. They find encouragement in ancient texts and traditions and in the stories about Great Ones that lived in the past. [2]) They get flashes of illumination, and at last the vision is vouchsafed to them. Others become inspired by them, and then follows an outburst of religious idealism and fervour which is bound to start a movement of reform — according to the nature of the form-side of the religion, either inside its organization, or outside as a green branch. This process may be followed in all the great religions of the world. Some 'green branches' (like the religion of Akhen-Aten in ancient Egypt) were suffocated by the mother-

---

1) See p. 157.
2) See p. 97.

tree, but on the whole they have proven viable, probably because their inspiration was Life itself, and because the religions they were the reactions to had become mere concoctions of forms and formulas.

The same process we can follow in politics. The first periods (but not the time of adjustment) after the institution of an entirely different form of government manifest usually its most efficient functioning. Later degenerations are setting in, necessitating after a time a change to a new system. But here the process cannot be seen as clearly as in the case of religion, because a tendency is usually shown to change the forms of social and political life before the thoughts and desires of the people have been adjusted. This is a mistake just as ridiculous, though not as obvious, as that one should try to change the ceremonies of a religion, hoping that thereby its adherents would become more religious! The change of form must of course be the natural outcome of a change of inner attitude. Man must first think and then act, not only individually, but also collectively.

We can follow the phenomena of the rebirth of Life — religious, philosophical, social, political, biological, surely also artistic — through all the ancient civilizations up to the present time. From time to time, owing to routine and consequent loss of vision, leading to crystallization of the forms and anti-social or egoistic conduct, inner dissatisfaction springs up, at first only conscious in a few. Its consequence is seeking and self-purification leading to a new outburst of idealism, showing its fruits in some movement of reform — in either or all the fields mentioned, for one cannot draw a hard and fast line of demarcation between them.

The Hindu scriptures contain some interesting verses also pointing to this process, from the spiritual angle. Śrī-Kṛishṇa spoke the well-known words to Arjuna: "Whensoever, O Bharata, there is decay of Dharma, and Adharma is in the ascendant, I Myself come forth. I am born from age to age for the protection of the good, for the destruction of evil, and for the sake of firmly re-establishing Dharma"[1]).

Mrs. Rhys Davids writes that "this is never lost sight of in the Pāli books: — that the Buddha is expressing not only his own convictions, the fruit of intense effort and self-communing, but also something that was, and had in the infinite past been, and would ever be, objectively and constantly valid and true for any and every human society, nay, something that was cosmic law,

[1]) *Gītā* IV : 7—8.

eternal, necessary, *omnipresent*, whether discerned or not. And the function and hall-mark of a Buddha was not to devise, or create a new Dhamma, but to rediscover, recreate and revive that ancient Dhamma (norm) [1]. His was to bring about its renascence as a cult in the lives, and apply it to the special needs, of his own age and its posterity. This, in words ascribed to him, is how the Buddha viewed his mission:

"As a man, brethren, wandering in the forest, in the mountain jungle, might see an ancient path, an ancient road, trodden by men of an earlier age; and following it, might discover an ancient township, an ancient palace, the habitation of men of an earlier age, surrounded by park and grove and lotus-pool and walls, a delightful spot; and that man were to go back, and announce to the king or his minister: Behold, sir, and learn what I have seen! And, having told him, he were to invite the king to rebuild that city, and that city were to become anon flourishing and populous and wealthy *once more*: — Even so, brethren, have I seen an ancient Road, trodden by Buddhas of a bygone age.... the which having followed, I understand life, and its coming to be and its passing away. And thus understanding, I have declared the same to the fraternity and to the laity, so that the holy life flourishes and is spread abroad once more, well propagated among men." [2])

We find in the above mentioned process a cyclic course of sleep and renascence, presenting far more cheerful thoughts than the pessimistic theory of Spengler.

This process applies only to the cultural fields, since it deals with the life-side of man's manifestation. It does not seem to apply to the scientific field. For the greater part of the scientific achievements concerns the form-side of man's manifestation, they serve to extend his physical instrument, his body. In so far as science brought into existence productive machines and means of transportation and communication (and agressive machines) it served to extend the body of man — productive, distributive and destructive — from the hands of the primitive up to the complicated system of the modern economic world.

[1]) In the Revised Edition of 1934 Mrs. Rh. D. has discarded her translation of Dhamma as 'Norm', leaving the word untranslated. See p. 10.
[2]) Mrs. Rhys Davids, *Buddhism*, (1st Edition) pp. 33—34, quotation: *Sutta-piṭaka, Saṃyutta-nikāya*, 'The City'.

And as such man's task is just — as it has been from the beginning and will be till the end, it is but logical — to learn to use his 'hands' as his soul, inspiring practical brotherhood, directs. Or in other words, that part of the population which corresponds to the three lower Varṇas must be guided by the highest Varṇa.

In contrast to the process described above, it seems that the scientific knowledge of the plain material field, of the province of form and physical energy, has been increasing throughout the ages, and that scientific application, in the extension of the 'hands' of man has never been so advanced as at the present time, in spite of the fact that the ancients possessed remarkable knowledge.

If it seems that the 'scientific' knowledge of man has been increasing, periodically but steadily, it also appears as if the general spirituality and sociality of man has slowly decreased, in spite of the periods of renascence and revival. Man of the ancient past (who lived in the 'Golden Age', and in the Garden of Eden) had to learn to master the material world. By its contact he slowly lost the natural sociality of the anthropogenic stage of his history, his natural wisdom and spirituality were veiled. [1])

His goal in the far-off future will surely be twofold: to be a perfect controller of his own inner, and to be a master of external nature. And as such his goal is really only one: the perfect harmonization of 'spirit' and 'matter', of 'life' and 'form'.

Culture depends upon the capacity to apply the ideals practically. If the ideal is merely intellectually grasped or emotionally experienced, imperfections of character will prevent an efficient social realization, but if in addition it is spiritually realized, it will overrule all shortcomings of character, for such is its nature, and it will be applied efficiently.

Two things must be seen clearly: on the one hand the ideal, on the other hand the terrible conditions that prevail everywhere on earth. If a man has no idealism, he is helpless, and cannot improve the least little thing. If he does nothing but dream over the ideal, and build Utopias, he is equally helpless. He must reach high, but stand firmly on earth. The first thing wanted at all times is to see clearly the next step he has to take to the ideal. [2])

[1]) See pp. 10, 43 and 143.

[2]) Sometimes there is a tendency to skip a number of steps which will always have to be made up later with greater pains. No greater progress can be made than man is mentally ripe for, individually and collectively.

Chapter III

Duty and Right — Conscience and Punishment

A. PROPOSITION. In the theory of Varṇa as expressive of Dharma we find the social duty of the individual always on the foreground and never his personal rights, and in accordance with this it contains the principle: the higher Varṇa, the more exacting duties and the stricter education. This principle was lost sight of to some extent in caste, when the tendency appeared to lay more stress on privilege than on duty.

Also we find that in the doctrine of Varṇa there is expressed that on the whole the morally strong man, manifesting socializing powers, has to be guided by and left to his sense of duty and his conscience, whereas the morally weak man, with anti-social tendencies, has to be made to feel the weight of punishment for anti-social acts.

Some thoughts and conceptions arise in connection with the above which we shall also consider in this Chapter.

B. DUTY AND RIGHT. In the Varṇa theory social duty and not right is always on the foreground, as we clearly see from those scriptures in which the Varṇa theory is presented in its purest form. [1])

The theory is preserved in an approximately pure form in the Dharma-śāstras and in the Artha-śāstra side by side with the caste laws. Only instead of the pure Varṇa idea, that of the four Varṇas "the duties are distributed according to the Guṇas (qualities) born of their own nature" [2]) we find in a few of the Dharma-śāstras: The Lord *assigned* to the Brāhmaṇa certain duties

---

[1]) *Gītā* XVIII : 41—46; *Bhāg.-P.* VII : *11* : 8—24; *Vishnu-P* III 8, etc.

[2]) *Gītā* XVIII : 41.

and *commanded* the Kshatriya to do certain things, etc. [1]) Harita, Atri, Parāśara, Yājñavalkya, Vishṇu, Baudhāyana and Vasishṭha express it simply by stating that a Brahman's duty *is* such and such, etc.

The more the Varṇa theory was overlaid with caste rules the more of course the human rights were described and laid down. These rights are to a great extent rights of the specific groups of people forming the castes, and only to some extent individual rights. In these scriptures the transition from the Varṇa theory to caste law is usually marked by sentences like: "The observance of one's own duty leads one to Svarga and infinite bliss. When it is violated, the world will come to an end owing to confusion of Varṇas and duties. Hence the king shall never allow people to swerve from their duties, for whoever upholds his own duty, ever adhering to the customs of the Āryas, and following the rules of Varṇa and order of religious life, will surely be happy both here and here-after." [2]) Here is clearly shown the same mistake that was often made by ancient law-makers. Instead of keeping a clear distinction between the autonomous norms of social ethics and religion, and the heteronomous norms of government, the first were bereft of their power in the consciousness of the people, by becoming overshadowed by and by being to a large extent merged into the second. Also the essential difference between Varṇa and caste was lost sight of, the social theory and the social ideal became confused with the actual conditions of the social constitution.

If the social leaders of the past laid more stress on duty, "the modern tendency is to lay more stress on the rights than on the duties of the individual, on the contrary. "Right and duty are the obverse and the reverse aspects of the same thing, Dharma", to quote a modern Hindu writer. [3]) The latter statement is founded upon the assumption that every duty creates a right, or is balanced by a right, with which I do not agree, neither with the statement that every right creates a duty or is balanced by a duty. Some wealthy individual may consider it his duty to look after the cares of a poor orphan he happens to come across, whilst the orphan may not consider it his right at all to be looked after by the wealthy man. And a right cannot create a duty, but only a legal liability. To what extent

---

1) *Manu* I : 87—91.
2) *Artha-śāstra* I : 3 : 13—14.
3) Bhagavan Das, *Kṛshṇa,* p. 96.

and whether at all a legal liability contains an ethical obligation which was not there a priori, is still an open question.

C. NOBLESSE OBLIGE. In the theory of Varṇa the principle is found that the higher the individuals' Varṇa and place in the natural hierarchy of society, the more exacting are his duties. Noblesse oblige!

The Mārkaṇḍeya-purāṇa pronounces that a Brahman should do nothing for the sake of enjoyment. The Dharma-śāstras lay down a severe rule of life for the Brahman, and an easier rule proportionally for the lower Varṇas, the easiest for the Śūdra. Understanding this, Nietzsche has praised the institution of caste (read: Varṇa), for he thought it right that life should grow colder towards the summit. [1] [2]

In modern times more than ever there is a general tendency of men of all classes to strive to the summit, because the summit has become identical in the social mind, and consequently also largely in society, with power, pleasure and fame. When the natural hierarchy, or in other words, the graduated scale of Varṇa as expressive of Dharma, will again come forward in the social consciousness, people will no more feel to such an unnatural and unhealthy degree this desire to climb the social ladder, but tend to be more satisfied with their own place and work and natural advance, realizing the increase of social responsibility and the decrease of personal enjoyments of life with the ascension of every rung of the social ladder.

The higher Varṇa, the more freedom in spiritual sense, in that the individual becomes master of himself and consequently is able to influence his fate to a certain degree (whereas the man of lower Varṇa is more or less at the mercy of his desires and of his conditions of life) [3], but also: the higher Varṇa, the less freedom in the social sense. But a freedom sacrificed voluntarily.

Āpastamba warns against the temptations of 'the summit', even for those who perform their duties: "He shall not fulfil his sacred duties merely in order to acquire these worldly objects (as

[1]) Ananda Coomaraswamy, *The Dance of Śiva*, p. 121.
[2]) Cf *St. Matthew* 20 : 26—28, *St. Mark* 10 : 42—45, 9 : 35, and *St. Luke* 12 : 48, 22 : 26—27.
[3]) See p. 45.

fame, gain and honour). For when they ought to bring rewards, (duties thus fulfilled) become fruitless." [1]

To return to the Varṇas. Chapters III, IV and V of Manu are almost entirely concerned with the duties of the Brāhmaṇa and with the thousand and one taboos making his life very complicated. If the details often appear somewhat ridiculous to a modern mind, yet we notice that most of the taboos had a sensible basis, ethical, biological, hygienic, religious or philosophical. The great amount of taboos probably indicates a gallant but perhaps rather hopeless endeavour on the part of the law-givers to keep the standard of the Brahman caste high. The same applies to the other Dharma-śāstras.[2] As Gautama puts it: "There are two persons in this world whose lives are perpetual vows. The one is the king, the other is a Brāhmaṇa." [3] The king's duties too are described in detail in the Dharma-śāstras. [4] The Artha-śāstra gives a Chapter on the life of the saintly king [5] and is almost entirely concerned with the regulation of the life and the duties of government officials, with very practical recommandations and Macchiavellian hints.

About the lower castes we hear comparatively very little in the Śāstras, apart from enumerations of penances and punishments for crimes and offences. The prohibition of the occupation of the higher castes for people of the lower castes indicates the caste crystallization and confusion of theory with practice. Out of the early theory of Varṇa grew the Dharma-śāstras, meant to give guidance to the higher castes in their social dealings.

If above we have given the regulations applying to caste, it will be well to conclude with an example from the purer theory of Varṇa, referring also to our quotations elsewhere. "Piety, truthfulness, penance and self-restraint, freedom from animosity, modesty, endurance, freedom from censoriousness, liberality, sacred learning, courage, forgiveness, — these are the twelve great observances of a Brāhmaṇa. ....Self-restraint, abandonment, freedom from delusion, on these immortality depends. These are possessed by those talented Brāhmaṇas to whom the Brahman (Truth) is the principal thing." [6] This scripture of Sanatsujāta continues with sublime

1) *Āp.* I : 7 : 20 : 1—2.
2) *Gautama* V—X; *Śaṅkha* XIII; *Yājñ.* I : 98—115; etc.
3) *Gautama* VIII : 1.
4) *Vishṇu* III; *Manu* VII; *Gautama* XI; etc.
5) I · 7.
6) *Sanatsujātīya* V : 5—7.

teachings about the Brāhmaṇa. "The Brāhmaṇa has as much interest in all beings, as a big reservoir of water, to which waters flow from all sides. I alone am your mother, father and I too am the son. . . ." [1] Notice the positive social attitude.

From Chapter III it stands forth clearly: the true Brāhmaṇa is he who knows Brahman and lives according to his realization, swerves not from Brahman. In the introduction to his translation of the Sanatsujātīya, Mr. Telang writes: "The true Brahman is he who is attached to the Brahman. Perhaps this marks some little advance beyond the more general doctrine of the Gītā, but it is still very far short of the petrified doctrine, if I may so call it, of the later law-givers. The Brāhmaṇa has not yet degenerated into the mere receiver of fees and presents, but is still in possession of the truth." [2] In other words, ideal and reality still approached each other closely. The word Brāhmaṇa was derived from brahman, as also brāhma, magic incantation (thus meaning: 'the knower of magic', that is to say, the knower of the secret of world-order), which word was the root word for Brāhma and Brahmā. Significant is the verse in the Vishṇu-saṃhitā: "The Brāhma-energy of a Brāhmaṇa is extinguished by accepting such gifts." [3]

As mentioned before, after the Brahman caste had long developed along the line of privilege and power, the ideal of the true Brahman was brought forward again periodically.

Ambiguous is the verse from the Mahābhārata: "The Brāhmaṇa becomes the lord of all beings upon this earth for the purpose of protecting the treasure of Dharma." [4] If lordship is interpreted in the sense of the true Brāhmaṇa, it is all right, if in the sense of the lower Varṇas or of caste, it is against the natural course of things.

In accordance with the fact that more has to be expected from persons of higher Varṇa than from those of lower Varṇa, it is natural to expect the view that their education should be much stricter and much more austere and all-embracing, of course with the stress on character. Because it is to be expected that *generally* children will belong to the same Varṇa as the parents. [5] The extensive teachings on Brahmacharya are typical of this conception. It would lead us

---

[1]) VI : 23—24.
[2]) *S. B. E.* Vol. VIII p. 147.
[3]) *Vishṇu* LVII : 7. (Unsuitable gifts of a kind mentioned before).
[4]) *MBh. Śānti-parvan* 72 : 6.
[5]) This was turned into the terrible dogma that children did belong and ought to stay in the same caste as the parents.

too far to quote from them. Another classic example is the severe discipline, moral as well as physical, to which the young Incas were subjected in Peru. The noblest and fittest was meant to be the future ruling Inca. [1]) A more modern example is supplied by the severe education as described by Grand Duke Alexander of Russia to have fallen to his lot and that of his brothers. [2]) The education, if good, provides the test: to which Varṇa does a man belong? In the case of the Incas there was a consciously applied test. In the case of the Grand Duke there was an almost outrageous endeavour to make somebody fit artificially into a special position.

The initiation tests of primitive peoples are largely rudiments of Varṇa-tests. A relatively pure example of a Varṇa test is presented by the conditions on which the chivalrous warriors of early mediaeval times might rise to knighthood. Here, like in India, the hereditary succession spoilt the efficiency of the test and confused natural class and artificial caste.

D. CONSCIENCE AND PUNISHMENT. The appeal to conscience is often made in the Śāstras, as in Manu: "The Soul itself is the witness of the Soul, and the Soul is the refuge of the Soul; despise not thy own Soul, the supreme witness of men. The wicked, indeed, say in their hearts, "Nobody sees us"; but the gods see them and the man within their own breasts," which is addressed by the judge to the witnesses before a trial. [3]) [4])

In the doctrine of Varṇa we may find the conception that people which manifest highly socializing forces have to be guided by their sense of duty and their conscience, and that people which manifest no socializing tendencies, but are anti-social, have to be made to feel the weight of punishment. If society may safely rely on the former, she must take her measures against the latter. To put it in a few words: the higher natural classes mainly regulated by duty and karman, the lower natural classes mainly by law and a heteronomous sanction.

If these thoughts are not expressed in any formula, they are yet voiced by the great amount of verses in the Śāstras which aim at stimulating the social feelings and the consciousness of responsibility

---

[1]) W. H. Presscott, *Conquest of Peru*, pp. 11—14.
[2]) *Once a Grand Duke*, Ch. II.
[3]) *Manu* VIII : 84—85.
[4]) See also pp. **24** and **35**.

of the Brahman and the rulers [1]), and by the great amount of severe penances and punishments meant for the lower Varṇas or castes, which punishments are proportionally less for the higher Varṇas or castes. [2]) Punishments especially for Brahman evil-doers are often expected to await them after death in various hell-states or in future lives. [3]) And, of course, if the party injured belongs to a higher Varṇa, the sin is the greater, and the punishment accordingly.

Punishment is recognized to be an important matter in the Śāstras: "If punishment is properly inflicted after due consideration, it makes all people happy; but inflicted without consideration, it destroys everything." [4]) And: "The whole world is kept in order by punishment, for a guileless man is hard to find; through fear of punishment the whole world yields the enjoyment which it owes." [5]) And even the gods "give the enjoyments due from them only, if they are tormented by the fear of punishment" [6]), which shows clearly that 'punishment' has also to be taken in the wider sense of *karman*, and not only in our sense of the word.

"All Varṇas would be corrupted by intermixture, all barriers would be broken through, and all men would rage (against each other) in consequence of mistakes with respect to punishment." [7]) But how difficult to gauge it is! "Punishment possesses a very bright lustre, and is hard to be administered by men with unimproved minds, it strikes down the king who swerves from his duty." [8]) These verses fall into the same class as the sublime verses about justice. [9])

Typical for a different attitude towards the various classes is how the judge is to address the witnesses before a trial: "Let him examine a Brāhmaṇa beginning with "Speak", a Kshatriya beginning with "Speak the truth", a Vaiśya admonishing him by mentioning his kine, grain and gold, a Śūdra threatening him with the guilt of every crime that causes loss of caste, saying "Whatever

[1]) *Manu* III—V, VII, XI; IV : 245, XI : 98; *Vishnu* III; *Gautama* XI; etc., etc.

[2]) *Manu* XI, VIII : 267, 268, 270, 272, 277, 279; *Yājñ.* II : 209; etc.

[3]) *Manu* IV : 190, 197; *Vishṇu* XLIII—XLV; etc.

[4]) *Manu* VII : 19.

[5]) *Manu* VII · 22.

[6]) *Manu* VII : 23.

[7]) *Manu* VII : 24.

[8]) *Manu* VII : 28.

[9]) *Manu* VIII : 12—17. Compare also *Yājñ.* I : 354—359.

places (of torment) are assigned (by the sages) to the slayer of a Brāhmaṇa, to the murderer of women and children, to him who betrays a friend, and to an ungrateful man, those shall be thy portion, if thou speakest falsely." [1])

The conception that evil-doers the higher in the social scale ought to be punished the more severely, because their sin is the greater, as advocated by the great and wise Shogun Jeyasu (1542—1616), I have also found in the Hindu books, if only in one instance — for theft. [2]) [3]) If it may be a wise and just rule for a people of hereditary classes and offices, if we look at it more closely however we see that it can have no place in the pure theory of natural class, since, if a man from a higher Varṇa commits a crime, the very fact proves that he never belonged to that Varṇa at all, or, if one likes, that he degrades himself to a lower Varṇa, and has to be punished according to the standard of that lower Varṇa. Something might perhaps be said in favour of a punishment for the pretention of belonging to a higher Varṇa. [4])

Punishment is in the Dharma-śāstras sometimes meant to be retaliating [5]), sometimes awarded as a warning example [6]), and sometimes with a motive to reform. [7])

Sometimes the Dharma-śāstras prescribe very severe punishments side by side with milder ones, as is the case with adultery. Dr. Ketkar writes that the more lenient punishment was applied and that the intention was "to make the offender feel that he is really suffering a very mild punishment in proportion to what he really deserves." [8])

There were also ordeals or divine tests (d i v y a) for serious crimes differing for the different classes. [9]) They form a curious blending of the realization of the working of divine justice or karman with the urge to punish or prevent crime. [10]) A form of ordeal has survived

[1]) *Manu* VIII : 88—89.

[2]) *Manu* VIII : 336—338. With religious penances however it is often the case. E.g. *Parāśara* XI : 42.

[3]) Cf. *St. Luke* 12 : 47—48.

[4]) The Dharma-śāstras state punishments for low caste people for posing as high caste.

[5]) E.g. *Yājñ.* I : 359.

[6]) E.g. *Manu* VIII : 334, or, as quoted above: VII : 22.

[7]) E.g. *Yājñ.* I : 361.

[8]) S. V. Ketkar, *History of Caste in India*, Vol. I p. 149.

[9]) *Yājñ.* II : 97—115; *Vishṇu* IX—XIV.

[10]) See J. Jolly, *Recht und Sitte*, p. 144.

even to the present day in some low castes in Madras as a test of the justice of a claim. After a short ceremony in the village temple both parties have to plunge their hands into boiling butter. [1]

In the lower stages of development people are led by the class and Āśrama rules and regulations, like children are guided by their parents. When they are 'grown up' they see their own Dharma. In the religious literature we find the remark that one has to rise above rules [2], yet rules are always to be respected, even by the perfect [3] [4].

It is significant that in the higher castes the sanction of the caste rules is on the whole vested in the public opinion within the caste, whereas in the lower castes it is largely in the hands of the caste-headman or of the caste-council. [5]

E. MAIN CONCLUSIONS. We have seen that in the theory of Varṇa as expressive of Dharma, stress is always laid on duty and never on right. In accordance with this we find the principle: the higher Varṇa, the more exacting duties and the stricter education. And also the conception that society may rely to some extent upon the sense of duty, the sense of cosmic equilibrium (*karman*) and the conscience of the people higher up in the natural social scale, but must take its measures against the anti-social elements lower down in the natural social scale.

---

1) L. S. S. O'Malley, *India's Social Heritage*, pp. 25—26.
2) *Bhāg.-P.* XI : *12* : 14—15, etc.
3) *Nārada-sūtra* 61.
4) Cf. I *Timothy* 1 : 8—10.
5) L. S. S. O'Malley, *Op. cit.* pp. 24—25.

Chapter IV

The openness of the Varṇas and the artificial seclusion of the Castes

A. PROPOSITION. It is interesting to put side by side the natural openness of the Varṇas and the artificial fenced-in state of the castes.

In connection with this we shall consider in this Chapter how caste was born from the class conditions in ancient India which must have somewhat corresponded to conditions as presented by the theory of Varṇa, and how caste in practice drifted away more and more from its theoretical and idealistic foundation. *Why* this happened we have dwelt upon elsewhere.

B. BIRTH OF CASTE AND THE DEVELOPMENT OF SECLUSION. It is the basis of the theory of natural class or Varṇa that there are no artificial or man-made bounds between the different rangs in the natural social hierarchy. Every man belongs to a certain Varṇa in accordance with his character, social behaviour and function in the organic whole (which three factors are inextricably connected), and as he unfolds and grows he may himself raise his status to a higher Varṇa which may result in his becoming acknowledged by the members of that Varṇa as living according to their standard.

Many of the Aryan invaders of India had to take wives of the dark race and in the early Vedic ages the various classes mingled and intermarried freely. Let us recapitulate the process of birth of Varṇa and caste as described in Part I Chapter II. Originally there were only two Varṇas, a fair and a dark one. But soon the conception of three higher Varṇas must have developed from the classes into which the fair-coloured people became divided. Here we see that

the theory of Varṇa was based upon actual conditions in early Ṛig-vedic days. But when classes began to develop into castes and sub-castes, Varṇa became theory and ideal. Yet for a long time it remained possible for people of lower classes (we may not yet call them castes proper because of this) to pass into higher classes, individually and in groups. Quite in accordance with the theory of Varṇa one would expect mostly Kshatriyas to become Brahmans (since on the whole the classes would still correspond to the theoretical Varṇas). Professor N. K. Dutt proves that in the Ṛig-vedic period "persons of exceptional abilities might be admitted to the priestly class from other classes, especially the Kshatriya class", of which he proceeds to state many instances from the Vedas, the Brāhmaṇas and the Purāṇas. [1]) But even in later times occasionally the doors seem to have been open into the Brahman class, and even for Śūdras (Then the classes corresponded ever less and less to the Varṇas). As Sir Henry Sumner Maine wrote about the school of Dharma: "as it went on from generation to generation, it was recruited partly by voluntary adherence and partly by hereditary descent. The double process is clearly reflected in the text of one of our oldest authorities, Āpastamba. The student desirous of being initiated into sacred learning is to go to a man "in whose family it is hereditary, who himself possesses it, and who is devout in following Dharma." [2]) On the other hand, the pupil is directed to consider the teachers of his teacher as his ancestors." [3]) [4]) The recruiting by voluntary adherence was clearly the original practice, and the recruiting merely from the Brahman caste was a later development. But in the two rules quoted by Maine I find no contradistinction and take them as evidence that originally everybody who was morally and mentally developed could be taught by Brahmans and be raised to their standard. There is no statement to the effect that the pupil's ancestors must be Brahmans, and the admonition to the pupil that he should consider the teachers of his teacher as his ancestors probably indicates that he might have been of lower birth.

[1]) *Origin and Growth of Caste in India,* Vol. I pp. 46—50.
The classic example of a raising to Brahmanhood is that of Janaka. We shall not adduce the case of Viśvāmitra, for it does not exactly prove that the raising to Brahmanhood was an easy matter. (*Rām. Bālakāṇḍa* LI—LXV).

[2]) *Āp.* I : *1* : 1 : 11.

[3]) *Āp.* I : *1* · 7 : 12.

[4]) H. S. Maine, *Early Law and Custom,* p. 13.

In the following story from the Chhāndogya-upanishad we find a young boy from uncertain parentage who becomes a Brahman due to the nobility of his character. [1]

"Satyakāma, the son of Jabālā, addressed his mother and said: "I wish to become a Brahmachārin [2], mother. Of what family am I?" She said to him: "I do not know, my child, of what family thou art. In my youth when I had to move about much as a servant, I conceived thee. I do not know of what family thou art, I am Jabālā by name, thou art Satyakāma, say thou art Satyakāma Jābāla." He, going to Gautama Haridrumata, said to him: "I wish to become a Brahmachārin with you, Sir. May I come to you, Sir?" He said to him: "Of what family are you, my friend?" He replied: "I do not know, Sir, of what family I am. I asked my mother, and she answered — "In my youth when I had to move about much as a servant, I conceived thee. I do not know of what family thou art. I am Jabālā by name, thou art Satyakāma." — Therefore I am Satyakāma Jābāla, Sir." He said to him: "No one but a true Brāhmaṇa would thus speak out. Go and fetch fuel, friend, I shall initiate you. You have not swerved from the truth." I have quoted this story from the *History of Civilization in Ancient India*, by Mr. R. C. Dutt [3], who continues: "And this truthloving young man was initiated, and according to the custom of the times, went out to tend his teacher's cattle. In time he learnt the great truths which nature, and even the brute creation, teach those whose minds are open to instruction. Yes, he learned truths from the bull of the herd that he was tending, from the fire that he had lighted, and from a flamingo and a divebird which flew near him, when in the evening he had penned his cows and laid wood on the evening fire, and sat behind it. The young student then came back to his teacher, and his teacher at once said: "Friend, you shine like one who knows Brahman, who then has taught you?" "Not men" was the young student's answer. And the truth which the young student had learnt (though clothed in the fanciful and somewhat grotesque style of the period) was that the four quarters, and the earth, the sky, the heaven and the ocean, and the sun, the moon, lightning, and the fire, and the organs and mind of living beings, yea the whole universe was Brahman or God."

[1] *Chhānd.-Up.* IV : *4* : 1—5.
[2] Religious student.
[3] Vol. I, p. 242—244.

Mr. R. C. Dutt mentions another legend in the same Upanishad in which we find a Brahman imparting knowledge to a Śūdra, accepting presents from him, and taking his daughter for a wife. [1]) This implies that even Śūdras could be raised to a higher standard. In the Mahābhārata a story is related of a Śūdra who becomes an ascetic and performs sacrifices. [2])

The mother of the great Ṛishi Nārada (in his last life) was a maid-servant, the father was unknown. [3]) The mother of Vyāsa was a fisherman's daughter. [4])

In the Aitareya-brāhmaṇa we are told of Kavasha, son of Ilūsha, whom the other sages expelled from a sacrificial session, saying: "how should the son of a slave-girl, who is no Brāhmaṇa, remain among us and become initiated?" But Kavasha "knew the gods and the gods knew him", and he was admitted as a Brahman to the sacrifice. [5])

Even as late as in Manu we find mentioned that the son of Gādhi (*i.e.* Viśvāmitra) gained the rank of a Brāhmaṇa by *humility*. [6])

And Manu, even in his caste laws, mentions a rise in successive generations: "If a female of the caste sprung from a Brāhmaṇa and a Śūdra female, bear children to one of the highest caste, the inferior tribe attains the highest caste within the seventh generation. Thus a Śūdra attains to the rank of a Brāhmaṇa. . . ." [7])

That there was contention between the Varṇa principle of virtuous conduct and the hereditary principle of caste we gather from a sentence like: "He who was begotten by an Ārya on a non-Ārya female, may become like to an Ārya by his virtues; he whom an Ārya mother bore to an non-Ārya father is and remains unlike to an Ārya." [8])

There was still a sense of Varṇa: "Behaviour unworthy of an Ārya, harshness, cruelty, and habitual neglect of the prescribed duties betray in this world a man of impure origin (who has the appearance of an Ārya)." [9]) And yet in the verse that follows the

---

1) *Chhānd.-Up.* IV : 2.

2) *Anuśāsana-parvan* 10, from: N. K. Dutt, *Origin and Growth of Caste in India*, Vol. I p. 170.

3) *Bhāg.-P.* I : 5 : 23.

4) *MBh.-Adi-parvan* 105.

5) *Aitareya-Br.* II : 19, see R. C. Dutt, *Op. cit.* p. 242.

6) *Manu* VII : 42.

7) *Manu* X : 64—65. Cf. *Gautama* IV : 21.

8) *Manu* X : 67.

9) *Manu* X : 58.

hereditary factor has again gained the upper hand: "A base-born man either resembles in character his father, or his mother, or both; he can never conceal his real nature."

When in later times the Brahman caste had become thoroughly rigid, the only possibility to get a Brahmanlike standard was by the foundation of a new caste.

But even in much later times exceptions have been made. I must think here of the mediaeval pariah (!) saint Nanda, who was admitted as a Brahman because on a certain night all the 3000 Brahmans of Chidambaram dreamt that they had to initiate him as such, as the legend reports.

Typical of the renewed great sense of Varṇa as expressed by the thought of the time in the Bhāgavata-purāṇa, is that Kṛishṇa, who was a Kshatriya by birth, was called "the Perfect Brahman, hard to find!" [1])

In the course of the ages the process of fusion of the races had gone on. We have dwelt upon this elsewhere.

Mahānandin was the founder of a Śūdra dynasty through his marriage with a Śūdra woman about 350 B.C. [2]) It is remarkable that the Nandas, as well as the other two great dynasties of empire builders, the Mauryas and the Guptas, were originally of low origin [3]).

But apart from kings, whom one might expect to rise easily in the social scale, also soldiers were sometimes recruited from the lower classes. Kauṭilya, Megasthenes and others mention such regiments. If they did not become Kshatriyas in the orthodox sense, yet they were socially recognized as such. The Rājputs, while claiming Kshatriya origin, really descended (apart from foreign Chiefs, also) partly from prominent members of aboriginal tribes. [4])

If it was possible, though difficult in later times, to climb to a higher social status, it was equally possible to be degraded to a lower. The instances given by the Dharma-śāstras are in most cases perhaps serious warnings as an outcome of the sense of Varṇa, rather than degradations that actually took place [5]).

[1]) *Bhāg.-P.* VII : *15* : 76, 79.

[2]) *Camb. Hist. of India,* Vol. I, p. 313.

[3]) *Ibid.* p. 223; *Camb. Shorter History of India* pp. 88, 19, 32.

[4]) C. Bouglé (quoting Lyall and Crooke) *Essais sur le Régime des Castes,* p. 31.

[5]) From Brahman to Śūdra or outcast: *Manu* X : 43, 92; IV : 245; VIII : 102; XI : 98; *Baudhāyana* II : *1* : 2; *Vasishṭha* III : 1—3; I : 20; *Āp.* I : *7* : 21; *Gautama* XXI : 1. From Kshatriya to Śūdra: *Manu* X : 43.

In this Chapter we have not considered the trade and profession of the different classes and castes. In times of distress and under unusual conditions the castes are permitted in the Dharma-śāstras to take to the occupation of other castes (with certain limitations). This too may perhaps have led sometimes to a higher status (or to a lower) in the course of time, and the people concerned must have had cause to forget their lower origin as quickly as possible.

Also by means of the Vrātyastoma Sacrifice many lower class people, under the orthodox pretext of being degenerated Aryans, must have entered the ranks of the Aryans.

Recently a hypothetical Brahmanhood was conferred upon a son of Mr. Gandhi by a 'purification ceremony', after his marriage with a Brahman lady, in itself a revolutionary event. Mr. Gandhi belongs to a merchant caste.

C. CONCLUSIONS. In this Chapter we have followed the application of the principle of theoretical openness of the Varṇas in the actual class system. For a very long time there remained a possibility for people of lower class to be admitted to a higher class as a result of their character and social behaviour, till at last caste had become an entirely rigid and separative institution, which means that the principle of hereditary succession had gained complete ascendancy over the principle of the openness of Varṇa. Yet even then there were sometimes back-doors into a higher caste in exceptional cases.

Chapter V

Hierarchy

A. PROPOSITION. In this Chapter we propose to look into the nature of the social hierarchy and consider its implications. We want to put side by side the natural social hierarchy (as the basis of the theory of Varṇa) and the artificial social hierarchy, in particular as it has been built up in the Indian caste system. We shall point out that the *word* hierarchy has become rather unpopular in modern times on account of its power associations (and on account of the ideals of equality which we shall consider in the next Chapter), and also that the sense of Varṇa has been largely lost by modern man, and that it would be to the advantage of society if it came forward again out of the social-subconscious to the light of day, the natural phenomenon of hierarchy being again realized and appreciated.

In these pages we take the word 'Hierarchy' not in its older sense as 'a reign of priests', but in its more modern and wider sense as the whole of the different ranks of groups and individuals in society. If one would preserve also the meaning of 'a reign of' (like in monarchy, oligarchy, etc.), it could be given as implying a co-management of social affairs by the different social ranks in proportion to their social function and sociality.

B. HIERARCHIC COMPOSITION AND HIERARCHIC CONSTITUTION. As the Commentator on the 8th verse of the 189th Adhyāya of the Śānti-parvan of the Mahābhārata remarks: "righteousness, and not birth, is the cause of the division into Varṇas." [1]) This fundamental idea of Varṇa we have treated elsewhere. [2])

[1]) J. Muir, *Original Sanskrit Texts*, Vol. I p. 142.
[2]) See Part I Ch. II B.

The Varṇas do not correspond to the four social classes of general sociology: 1. *the social*, as represented by the natural aristocracy; 2. *the non-social*, as represented by those who cling to narrow individualism, and only ask to be left alone, to lead their own life; 3. *the pseudo-social*, as represented by the congenital and habitual paupers; and 4. *the anti-social*, as represented by the instinctual and habitual criminals. The second class, the non-social, is considered to be the original, the primordial class, out of wich the other three classes generated. [1])

The Varṇa theory takes the lower three classes into one, and considers the anti-social to be the extreme form of the non-social, the non-soçial a modified anti-social class. And it is indeed impossible to draw a hard and fast line between them, if one considers them well and remembers that certain acts which are not criminal in the ordinary sense of the word may be incomparably more anti-social than a single act of manslaughter even with malice aforethought. Let us mention as an example the moral crimes of the placing on the market of arms of war (not even to speak of the manufacture of poison gas), and the mere possession of shares of such manufacturing companies.

In contradistinction to the conception that the different social classes evolved from the non-social, the Hindu theory holds that they evolved from the highest class. The Śāstras speak of the existence of only one Varṇa in the original Golden Age of man. This may, like golden age legends and paradise myths all over the world, point to the vague remembrance of the anthropogenic stage in the evolution of man, when human society still possessed the natural sociality (like that manifested by animal herds) which was pictured by Wilhelm Wundt and other scholars.

The four Varṇas represent four degrees of sociality from the most highly social to the extreme non-social (incl. pseudo-social and anti-social) in addition to the functional principle which is inextricably interwoven with the principle of sociality.

Yet the definitely anti-social was at times felt by the Hindus to be an unnatural and abnormal phenomenon of the social constitution, and as such not really in its place in the fourth Varṇa (since *Varṇa* concerns the social *composition*). From this we may perhaps explain the fact that at times the scriptures mention a fifth

F. H. Giddings, *Principles of Sociology*, p. 126—127.

class, to which all criminal and socially impure elements were consigned. [1]) If not in its place in the theory of natural class as applying to a society which is still relatively natural, the positing of this 'fifth Varṇa' may perhaps be justified for the constitution of modern society. The analogy of the human body is illuminating. For the normal physical body the different organs may be put into several categories, the function of some organs being more important than that of others which might perhaps even be missed. Some organ may perhaps be less healthy than others, and perform imperfectly their function in the organic whole, yet the body may yet be relatively healthy. But when the body develops some cancerous tumour, it can no more be classed among the cases of normal health, neither can the tumour be classed among the organs of the body, though it has the appearance of an organ. Another class of organs has then to be recognized, of anti-organic, anti-social tendency. [2])

To revert to society. People belonging to this class — and they will not be many — will not ordinarily fall into the fourth social class as mentioned above, the anti-social class. Such people will be cases for the psycho-analyst rather than for the judge, they will be found rather in the upper than in the lower classes. But when the ancient Indian sociologists posited this fifth class, they meant no such anti-social class, but one somewhat more in the usual sense of a class comprising criminals and irresponsible primitives.

In the natural hierarchy everyone indicates his own place by his social conduct, by the degree or kind of his sociality. The natural hierarchy is not a dream and a mere ideal, neither is it only a theory, the natural hierarchy is a fact in society, it is always there, but at times in history it may not be consciously realized. Varṇas exist, but man has largely lost the capacity to recognize them, because the population classes of the social constitution: in India the castes, in the West the economic classes, obsess the social mind.

Yet here and there we find indications that the sense of Varṇa has not been entirely lost by the public. India is always ready to recognize and bow to the 'holy man'. The West is always ready to

[1]) *Bhāg.-P.* XI : *17* : 20; etc.

[2]) If affirming the organic theory of society care has to be taken not to take the conception 'organic' in too biological a sense. The word has to be taken in a wider sense, comprising the common characteristics of both the biological and the sociological organism and organization. See Ch. IX E.

respect the 'true gentleman'. The conception and ideal of the 'born leader' which is coming to the foreground more and more, is also significant. We do not mean to say that there have not always been individuals who had the sense of Varṇa; of course there were many at all times who were conscious of standards of Varṇa to a certain degree of clarity.

In a healthy and harmonious society the population classes correspond to the Varṇas. In early Ṛig-vedic India this may have been approximated, and the Varṇas may have corresponded to some extent to the four classes of Brāhmaṇas, Rājanyas, Viś, and Sūdras.

If in the natural hierarchy people determine and betray their place in the scale according to their degree of sociality and function, in the artificial hierarchy of the social constitution of the modern state, either in the East or in the West, not the degree of sociality but the amount of power wielded by the individual decides his place in relation to that of others in the scale. The art of the power may differ widely between different groups. In the West the power is largely economical (money is crystallized power), predominating even over the power of the Church. In India it is the power of caste, largely the product of the power of Brahmans and of the ruling classes.

In the West the social mind is obsessed by the idea of economical power, and in India by the idea of caste power. The orthodox Brahmans are afraid of nothing but an attack on their position in relation to the lower castes and untouchables, on their social and religious privileges.

If the social mind did not attach its seal to the economic power in Western society, and to the power of caste in India, these different kinds of power could never tyrannize society as they do by obstructing the freedom of the individuals. A reviving sense of Varṇa only may free the social mind of its obsession, then the natural hierarchy must again emerge out of the social subconscious into the light of recognition, and in proportion to this the tyranny of power will be weakened.

If a hierarchy be founded upon some principle of force, it is not a natural hierarchy. If some individual or group of individuals (a priest, a ruler, a familyfather, a meeting) or an abstract power (a law, a state, a Church, a caste, a society, public opinion) irreversably decides a person's profession, behaviour or Dharma, it denotes an unnatural constitution of the social group in question. In the social constitution corresponding to the natural hierarchy there can only be freedom of choice. This does not mean that even if the hierarchies correspond, force will not be applied to the definitely anti-social elements by the proper Varṇa of ruling and regulating people. As to the other rules of law, if the two hierarchies correspond, the Varṇas will naturally obey the laws of the Varṇa of rulers, even as they will naturally follow and respect the highest Varṇa.

The yoke of power of one or more population classes or groups, when the two hierarchies did not correspond, has been the main source of suffering to other population classes or groups. History provides us with a profusion of examples up to the present day.

Largely because of the power association the word hierarchy has become rather unpopular. The unpopularity grew by the propagation of the ideals of equality and brotherhood (which were a reaction to it) which we shall consider in the next Chapter.

Desire of power together with jealousy of the power of others were the main factors in the development of caste: caste privilege, caste separatism. But for the desire of power caste could never have become as it is.

Yet it will not do to condemn a caste system a priori as something anti-social. Caste has more than once served its purpose in history. To give an example here which has interest in connection with the conception of an organic hierarchy, Megasthenes writes: "If the Indians are at war with one another, it is not customary for them to touch those who are tilling the land, but the one group may be engaged in battle, ... the other is peacefully engaged in plowing, or reaping, or pruning, or mowing nearby." [1]) Dr. Timmer who compares this statement carefully with the rules and information given by the Hindu Scriptures comes to the conclusion that this has probably indeed been customary. [2])

To return to the natural hierarchy. In the natural hierarchy there cannot be one moral standard for all. As we saw in Chapter III the exigencies of social life are the greater the higher the Varṇa. The normal standard of one high up in the natural hierarchy will be the ideal for a person lower in the scale, and will be entirely unintelligible to a person at the bottom. It is illogical to require and expect the same conduct from these three people, to preach to them the same

---

[1]) *Arr. Ind.* 11 : 9; quoted from B. C. J. Timmer, *Megasthenes en de Indische Maatschappij*, p. 114.

[2]) *Op. cit.* pp. 118—120.

moral law and to put before them the same ideal. The Christian Church has tended to do this with the positing of 'the Christian duty'. The Church pointed to the goal but did not show the steps. In this respect it failed to show sense of reality and a sense of proportions. One standard of good and evil cannot be upheld in accordance with the natural hierarchy. What may be unintelligible and seem stupid to the man low in the hierarchy may be deemed good by the man in the middle and be just perfectly natural and evident to the man at the top. The unintelligible and seemingly stupid maxim will be of no use to the man at the bottom, whereas a simpler, less exalted rule might be appreciated and followed by him, and in the course of time lead him on, to understand and follow more exacting and nobler rules, and rise accordingly in the natural scale.

The Indian scriptures provide a profusion of instances to illustrate this in application. They will be found in many places in this book. We want to mention here only the eight different grades of marriage for the four Varṇas. [1]) They are:

1. The Brāhma rite: the gift of a daughter after decking her with costly garments and honouring her (by presenting jewels), to a man learned in the Veda and of good conduct.

2. The Daiva rite: the gift of a daughter who has been decked with ornaments to a priest who is officiating at a sacrifice.

3. The Prājāpatya rite: the gift of a daughter after the father has addressed the couple with the text: "May both of you perform together your duties" and has shown honour to the bridegroom. (Yājñavalkya calls this marriage Kāya).

4. The Ārsha rite: the gift of a daughter, after that the father received from the bridegroom for the fulfilment of the sacred law (i.e. not with the intention of selling his child) a cow or a bull or two pairs.

5. The Gāndharva rite is the voluntary union of maiden and lover which springs from desire.

6. The Rākshasa rite is the forcible abduction of a maiden against her will, after a fight with her relatives.

7. The Āsura rite: the bridegroom gives as much wealth as he can afford to the kinsmen and to the bride herself, according to his own will.

---

[1]) *Manu* III : 27—34; *Vishṇu* XXIV : 17—25; *Yājñ.* I : 58—61; *Artha-śāstra* III : 2 : 2—9.

8 The Paisācha rite is the seducing of a girl who is sleeping, intoxicated or disordered in intellect

The first four are for Brahmans, the 5th and 6th are for Kshatriyas, the 5th, 7th and 8th are for Vaisyas and Śūdras The Śāstras discourage the 7th and the 8th altogether, as immoral, and the last four for Brahmans

If we read the Gospels we cannot escape from the conclusion that Christ also distinguished grades of morality and sociality, and organs with different social functions, and had a clear sense of distinguishing between reality and the ideal Especially St Matthew and St Luke contain significant matter on this point It would lead us too far to go into this in detail, we refer to the source, giving the main points in a footnote [1])

The tendency to weave all pieces on the same loom has also appeared in criminal law Law in Western countries, under the influence of the above mentioned tendency of the Church, and perhaps psychologically strengthened by modern ideas of equality, has been generally until very recently to hold all people (exc children, idiots and the mentally weak) to be equally responsible for their actions That this is really illogical, is clear That for practical reasons however the principle of equality has been generally adhered to is quite understandable

[1]) *St Matthew* 7 1—2 (everybody decides his own standard), 7 3—5 (everybody to judge only himself) 7 16—21 (different trees, different fruits) 8 20 (different standards for different groups, the Sannyāsin) 10 38—39, 20 16 (test of Varna), 10 41 (degrees of vision and fruits) 13 10—11 (also *St Mark* 4 33—34) (degrees of realization of truth) 19 16—17 (only God is good not one moral standard) 20 26—28 (also *St Mark* 9 35, 10 42—45) (the greatest is the server the first shall be the last and has the greatest task and responsibility), 22 21 (also *St Mark* 12 17) (distinction between the spiritual and the social) 25 40 (the 'least of the brethren degrees), 25 2—33 (social and non social groups) *St Luke* 6 39 (can the blind lead the blind ?), 6 40 (everyone that is perfect shall be as the master), 6 41—42 (everybody to judge himself), 6 43—44 (different trees bear different fruits), 8 10, 10 21 (inequality in realization of truth), 3 10—14 (different rules for different groups), 10 29—36 (degrees of 'neighbour hood, degrees of soul relationship) 12 47—48 (degrees of responsibility) 12 51—53 (Christ come to bring division), 17 7—10 (servant and master) 22 26—27 (the greatest is the server) *St John* 8 1—11 (everybody to judge himself only) 12 47 (not judgment, but salvation) 14 2 (in my Father s house are many mansions), 17 16—22 (the hierarchy), See further the letters of the Apostles The spiritual hierarchy is mentioned often in the New Testament

The scale of natural hierarchy is kept in internal equilibrium by the general principle, which everybody may easily verify for himself, that on the whole the higher a person's place in the natural scale, the more severely he will judge himself and the less severely others, and that on the whole the lower a person's place, the more severely he will judge others and the less severely himself. [1]

If the class-consciousness in the modern sense tends to separate people, the sense of Varṇa, the realization of the natural hierarchy, tends to unite people into a whole.

If the population classes and the castes predominate in the social mind and do no more correspond to the Varṇas, we get what the Śāstras so often warn against, the 'mixture of Varṇas', to which we shall devote a special Chapter.

If we protract the conception of organs with special functions in the whole from any delimited group of men, be it a tribe or a state or a continent, to the world as a whole, we see that the conception of autarchy is entirely anti-social in the wider sense. No organ in a body can be self-sufficient; if it desires and tends to grow out into an independent organ, or rather body, it becomes a cancerous tumour [2]. Free-trade, not necessarily coupled with an entirely free production and competition ('Śūdras' and 'Vaiśyas') but controlled to some extent by some international body ('Kshatriyas') is thus a natural and scientific consequence of the organic and hierarchic theory. The present day super-nationalism and policy of protection is from a sociological standpoint unscientific up to the degree of stupidity. Surely not the realization that it is wrong or immoral (which so many know) but the realization that it is unscientific and stupid and that in the end it will not pay, will eventually lead to the policy of co-operation and internationalism. For after all we are living in a mental age, and the mind will bring succour where the emotions fail and where the spirit is yet relatively helpless.

Also the hierarchical graduation applies to the world at large. The constitutional hierarchy is the fundament of what is commonly called civilization, the natural is the basis of culture. Nobody will contradict that Africa falls into a lower place in the natural as well as in the constitutional hierarchy. In what organic and hierarchic

[1]) Cf. *St. Luke* 6 : 41—42; *St. Matthew* 5 : 22 and 7 : 1—5.
[2]) Cf. G. Simmel, *Soziologie*, p. 429.

relation the Great Powers stand to one another nobody will be able to decide. Continuing our line of thought we might say that the highest in the constitutional hierarchy is the nation that has the most powerful army, the most poisonous gasses at its disposal, and has the most powerful finantial position. And the highest in the natural hierarchy that nation will *prove itself* to be which most strongly manifests the spirit of internationalism, which most convincingly takes the initiative to disarmament, to the abolishment of the unnatural economic measures of protection, to a revision of the Treaty of Versailles etc. Whether the two hierarchies cover each other or not, only history can prove. As in the case of the individual man: does his class and position correspond to his Varṇa? His *conduct* indicates it.

As it is, Europe has no cause to look down upon the Indian caste system which is in spite of all its shortcomings still organic, since Europe has developed separative nation-castes which for the moment tend to grow away more and more from the organic basis.

Internationalism (which, as we shall see in Chapter VIII, yet gives full scope to the expression of nationalism) is nothing but (speaking mystically) the sense of social unity plus the urge to the expression of unity, or (speaking sociologically) the sense of sociality plus the urge towards integration.

To conclude with a few words about the religious and occult doctrines of hierarchy. They do not fall within the scope of this book, yet we may not pass on without just mentioning them. Many of the ancient religious and philosophical systems pictured the world and the cosmos on the basis of some great organic Being or Man, the Cosmic Christ of the Gnostics and the Purusha of India being the best known instances. And all the ancient (as well as many modern) theological and theosophical doctrines and mythologies have mentioned, taught or proclaimed their hierarchy of devas, angels or nature-powers. Lucifer appears under different names as a symbol of the anti-social element of power and privilege which developed the hierarchy of power from the natural hierarchy.

As a recent book on the spiritual aspect of Hierarchy expresses it: "Hierarchy is not coercion — it is the law of the world-structures. It is not a threat — but the call of the heart and a fiery admonition directing towards the General Good." [1]

[1]) *Hierarchy, 1931, (Signs of Agni Yoga)* p. 5.

C. CONCLUSIONS. We have distinguished between the natural hierarchy (which is the basis of Varṇa) and the constitutional hierarchy, and seen that the characteristics of the natural hierarchy are:

1. If the actual social hierarchy corresponds to the natural hierarchy, every individual naturally falls into his proper place. If not, he yet betrays his hierarchical degree to those persons who have the sense of Varṇa.

2. There is not one moral standard but there are grades of sociality.

3. In connection with this there are organic groups each with a specific function, differing in social usefulness (e.g. Varṇas).

4. There is a tendency towards social integration, it is the manifestation of that socializing element of human nature which is called either the consciousness of kind, fellow-feeling, or just: love.

5. The natural hierarchy is based upon individual responsibility, and thus always tending towards equilibrium.

On the other hand the characteristics of the constitutional hierarchy, is so far it does not correspond to the natural, are:

1. Every individual comes into his place by the application of some amount of power, either by himself or by his group.

2. Not his degree of sociality, but his trade or profession, his wealth or his social power count in the social estimation.

3. The groups (of every conceivable kind) may or may not be organic, may tend to be social, unsocial, or anti-social. The Indian caste system is largely organic, the groups of Western society seen as a whole are dangerously tending towards the anti-social, both if considering the nation-castes of the world, and the different population classes which more or less agree in the different countries.

4. There is a tendency towards a class-struggle, it is the manifestation of the desire for power and privilege.

5. There is a tendency of individuals to strive towards the summit, this tends to upset equilibrium. That equilibrium is yet maintained in society is due to the psychological influence of the natural hierarchy. Which force will prove the strongest in this present period?

We have seen that due to the confusion of the two hierarchies the *word* has become unpopular, and that the realization of hierarchy or sense of Varṇa has been largely lost by modern man. Insight into the nature of hierarchy has to be won again, this knowledge has to come forward again out of the social unconscious into the light of day. Only then the socializing forces of man may be liberated more profusely and the internal harmony of society improved.

Thus there are three distinct happenings; 1. the mental act of realization; 2. the awakening of the sense of social unity and sociality, followed by 3. the urge towards integration.

Hierarchy has some more implications which do not fall within the scope of this book, we may mention only that in the natural hierarchy there is a passing on of power and knowledge downwards, whereas in the constitutional hierarchy power and knowledge extend through the upward movement of the individual. [1])

[1]) The organic conception of Society was specially brought forward by: Eucken, *Geschichte und Kritik der Grundbegriffe der Gegenwart*; Van Krieken, *Die sogenannte organische Staatstheorie*; H. Spencer, *Social Organism, Essays* I; Kistiakowski, *Gesellschaft und Einzelwesen*; E. Kaufmann, *Über den Begriff des Organismus in der Staatslehre des 19. Jahrhunderts*.

Chapter VI

Equality and Inequality. The Vertical View of Society and the Horizontal View of Humanity

A. PROPOSITION. Though the theory of Varṇa implicates the social inequality of man, it does not contain any principle of a spiritual or essential inequality. In this Chapter we want to compare the social inequality and the spiritual equality of man, or the vertical and the horizontal view of society. We want to make clear that the two views, each with a different set of ideals, have to be clearly distinguished. This was not always accomplished in history. The confusion may have very unfortunate results.

As to India, we want to point to the fact that at all times in its history the principle of man's spiritual equality was recognized and applied.

In Section C we want to try to determine the relation of caste and religion. In section D we shall consider the question of equality in connection with law.

Finally we shall come to a new definition of Dharma.

B. EQUALITY AND INEQUALITY. The social theory of Varṇa implies a 'vertical' scale: the natural hierarchy. But this does not mean that men are essentially unequal. If the Indian scriptures again and again point to social inequality, they also stress the spiritual equality of men. Not the spiritual nature as manifested imperfectly in social life, but the spirituality 'an sich', as basic truth and fundamental factor of human life. The spiritual nature of man is manifested only relatively and to a different degree in different men of different Varṇas. If it manifests (let us presume) fully, in the case of those who have reached the summit, it also manifests the inner unity, and the theory and ideal of the "all men are brothers" has become a fact through them; the saint and sage know no fundamental difference between themselves and others. Men feel unequal in so far as they cannot yet manifest the spiritual forces.

The main schools of Hindu philosophy hold that Brahman is the origin of all things, of all beings, and that Brahman is the goal, the supreme realization, and that into which all will eventually dissolve. How could there be a fundamental inequality in accordance with this doctrine? Inequality arises only in creation, in time and space, bringing differentiation of form and function.

To continue this line of thought: Brahman is truth, is perfect, is eternal, is one. Thus the essential nature of all created things or beings is truth, and perfect and eternal and one. The higher the degree of realization (and true realization must naturally be followed by application) the greater the manifestation of this oneness or unity, which if applied to society is a synonym of sociality.

The essential spiritual equality of men is expressed in the philosophical works. Since this is so well known and so clear we need not quote any texts. In the Dharma-śāstras we find confused thoughts on the matter. But the Śūdra is taken as being religiously adequate. "By following his own religion even a Śūdra enjoys the celestial region." 1) The Śūdras were even free to practise religious rites (Ishṭa) but they were not allowed to recite Mantras which was the privilege of the Āryas. 2) Another Dharma-śāstra proclaims that the Śūdra may perform religious works but not Vedic rites. 3) These religious works (Pūrtta) however are stated to be means to attain spiritual emancipation, whereas religious rites (Ishṭa) are only means to attain celestial regions. 4) Yet he may attain heaven by serving Brahmans. 5) And sometimes even various religious rites are allowed to him in addition to Śrāddha. 6) Works of industrial art are especially recommended to the Śūdra out of all Varṇas, which is remarkable unless we remember the productive, physically creative Dharma of the Śūdra-varṇa. 7) One notices the variety of

1) *Atri* I : 18, *Hārita* II : 10, 14.
2) *Vyāsa* I : 6. Cf. *Manu* X : 126—128; *Gautama* X; *MBh. Śānti-parvan* 60; *Atri* I : 46.
3) *Likhita* 6.
4) *Likhita* 1.
5) *Manu* X : 122, *Gautama* X : 56.
6) *Yājñ.* I : 121, *Gautama* X : 65.
7) *Atri* I : 15, *Yājñ.* I : 120, *Manu* X : 99, *Gautama* X : 60.

views. In the following statement no difference whatever is made between the Varṇas: "Men of all Varṇas, if they fulfil their [assigned] duties, enjoy [in Heaven] the highest imperishable bliss. Afterwards, when a man who has fulfilled his duties returns to the world, he obtains by virtue of a remainder of merit birth in a distinguished family, beauty of form, beauty of complexion, strength, aptitude for learning, wisdom, wealth, and the gift of fulfilling the laws of his Varṇa or order." [1]) The effort is certain to bear its fruits. This conviction was expressed in the assurance of heavenly happiness or of a favourable next incarnation. Quite apart from its possible truth, a to the priests convenient doctrine when the rise to a higher caste in the same life had been made impossible when the castes had become hereditary and exclusive. [2]) Still it was not always supposed that the fruits of actions were to be reaped in the next world, and Manu states: "Śūdras who are desirous to gain merit, and know their duty, commit no sin, but gain praise, if they imitate the practice of virtuous men without reciting sacred texts. The more a Śūdra, keeping himself free from envy, imitates the behaviour of the virtuous, the more he gains, without being censured, exaltation in this world and the next." [3]) The conception of religious worship is expressed like this: "These (four) Varṇas worship Hari their father by means of their several duties discharged with faith for the purpose of purifying themselves, since they are born of Him, along with their powers and duties." And regarding the Śūdra: "From the feet of the glorious Lord, service was born (which is useful) for the acquisition of virtue or righteousness, and in the beginning the Śūdra was born of it (service) by means of which Hari is propitiated." [4]) "All men must serve those who belong to higher Varṇas." [5])

In the idea of service the Śūdra touches the Brahman, both serve, the former with his hands and his devotion, the latter with his superior knowledge, implying full responsibility for others as a teacher and guide. Culture is founded upon mutual service or social service or just: service. Service is the performing of one's Dharma. And "Man reaches perfection by each being intent on his

[1]) *Āp.* II : *1* · *2* : *2*—3. For the Śūdra cf. *Manu* IX : 335.
[2]) *Manu* X : 42, *Āp.* II : *5* : 11 : 10—11; *Chhāndogya-Up.* V . *10* : 7, *Yājñ.* I : 96.
[3]) *Manu* X . 127—128.
[4]) *Bhāg.-P.* III . *6* . 34, 33.
[5]) *Gautama* X : 66.

own duty." [1] We have to be careful not to confuse the vertical and the horizontal in this. By this statement and similar ones is indicated that from a spiritual standpoint the work of all four Varṇas — of whatever kind -- is leading towards perfection. It cannot mean that a man low in the scale, for instance a Śūdra by Varṇa, could reach 'perfection' by a great jump. Such would be entirely in discrepancy with the doctrine of karman. It may however mean that a man of low caste may really be an unrecognized true Brahman, and thus reach perfection. As was the case with the Brahman Ṛishi Kausika who received religious instruction from a meat-seller of Śūdra-caste and said to him: "In my opinion you are a Brahman even in this life; because a Brahman who is haughty and is devoted to degrading vices is no better than a Śūdra, and a Śūdra who restrains his passions and is ever devoted to truth and morality I look upon as a Brahman, in as much as character is the basis of Brahmanhood." [2] In a society which has moved far away from the manifestation of a natural hierarchy, there may be, by force of circumstances, little relation between the cultural development of an individual, and his occupation.

But in the "man reaches perfection by each being intent on his own duty", the stress is laid on the word *own*. By this *Varṇa* is clearly implied. We shall recur to this in the next Chapter.

In our quotations from the Dharma-śāstras the trouble is that sometimes the lower caste Śūdra is meant and sometimes the Śūdra by Varṇa. Some of the compilers thought along the horizontal line and some along the vertical. Sometimes they also thoroughly confused Varṇa and caste and for this reason the rules on the privileges and disabilities of the Varṇas deserve to be treated with the greatest suspicion. [3] The word Varṇa is sometimes used in the sense of a Caste. Yet now and then there was an effort to see more clearly and to put side by side the Varṇas and the castes, as for instance the statement that the pursuits in life of the men of mixed races or mixed castes of all races including the untouchable [except wretches and sinful outcasts (fifth class)] are those as followed by the Varṇas. [4]

[1]) *Gītā* XVIII : 45.

[2]) *MBh. Vana-parvan* 3 : 75—84; quoted by N. K. Dutt, *Origin and Growth of Caste in India*, p. 170.

[3]) See S. V. Ketkar, *History of Caste in India*, p. 124.

[4]) *Bhāg.-P.* VII : *12* : 30.

It may happen that the horizontal ideal (of man's equality) filters into the social theory and creates confusion. Movements propagating the equality of men, in so far as they were not the manifestation of a class-jealousy, economic or otherwise, but of the humanistic ideal, were the outcome of the intuitive realization of the fundamental oneness and equality of all men. It was a mystic realization (however much the upholders of equality, excepting some categories like for instance the Christian socialists, might repudiate that imputation) and a dangerous one, for it was projected on to the world of social realities. The circumstance that the realization was of mystic nature explains the fanaticism of the proclaimers of the 'égalité, liberté, fraternité'. The realization of oneness and equality was projected on to the mental picture of human society — which was a confusion of a spiritual and a social ideal — and forces were set to work towards social application. The adherents of these movements overlooked that society is by its very nature ever tending towards a hierarchical inequality and that their efforts were bound to be useless in so far they were directed against hierarchy. Their efforts were anti-hierarchical, not only directed towards the constitutional hierarchy, but also against the conception of natural hierarchy, and consequently anti-social. They endangered the internal equilibrium of society in two ways. First by forcibly upsetting the equilibrium of the constitutional hierarchy, secondly by propagating thoughts and ideals entirely opposed to the conception of the natural hierarchy, and by that postponing a natural adjustment. History since the French Revolution provides the illustrations.

Also in various periods of Indian history, as we have seen in Chapter II, the horizontal ideal was somewhat confused with the social. This always happened in periods when caste had become over-tyrannical, and it always was the manifestation of a religious movement. [1]) We tend to conclude that at all times when the social hierarchy has become tyrannical to a degree surpassing its limits, suffering stimulates the inner forces of man, and the horizontal view of the human family comes forward again to the light of recognition. Whatever form it will take depends upon the psychology and the need of the time and of the country in question. It may take many forms between a spiritual and a materialistic manifestation. In so far it is spiritual (in the widest sense, incl. religious, mystical,

[1]) Excepting modern movements of equality imported from the West.

ethical, etc.) it is conducive towards the awakening of the social conscience and by that to an improvement of the state of the depressed classes. In so far it is materialistic, it is dangerous on account of either or both of the above mentioned reasons.

It is significant that the Śūdra low castes, which one might expect to be more democratic than the higher castes, have been and are really far less so. The hierarchical sense is so strong in humanity, that, as Dr. Ketkar remarks, even the lowest feel a very great pride on even a very slight superiority over their neighbours. [1]) As has been remarked by various sociologists, like Simmel, hierarchical tyranny is generally far greater in a democratic state than in a monarchy. [2])

The sense of spiritual equality, naturally combined with applied brotherhood, is found in people on the highest rungs of the natural hierarchy. These persons may also generally be considered to be on the highest rungs of the social hierarchy in India. If the class of Sannyāsins and fakīrs contains many who are nothing more than mere beggars and parasites, it still contains some who belong to the flower of mankind. The class is respected and feared. Also in the Brahman caste there are still many true Brahmans.

As we have seen, in ancient times in India it was possible for men in the highest ranks of the natural hierarchy to become Brahman disciples. When the Brahmans had developed into a caste, closed to outsiders, the ideal and order of the Sannyāsin met a social need. Men (and women) of all castes could become Sannyāsins, and, to whatever caste they might have belonged before, from that moment they became of equal status, and holy men beyond the differences of caste. The order of Sannyāsins was, like the order of Buddhist monks, in some way a reborn Brahman Varṇa, with the difference that the true ancient Brahman was a full member of society, living with wife and children in a well regulated if simple home, and performing his religious rites, whereas the Sannyāsin and the Buddhist monk are celibate, homeless, and wandering about, in so far they are not living in monasteries. The Sannyāsin has also renounced ceremonies and rites. *If they do their job* in society they need not be considered to stand outside or above ordinary life, as has often been brought against them.

Also in their ranks distinctions and grades have arisen but again

---

[1]) S. V. Ketkar, *History of Caste in India*, p. 99.
[2]) G. Simmel, *Soziologie*, p. 105.

and again it has been expressed that they are equal. As for instance Nārada proclaims about the Bhakti-saints: "Amongst them no distinction is to be made of caste, learning, beauty, birth, wealth, occupation, etc. Because they are His." [1]) Or as for instance Bhartṛihari expresses that they know themselves to be beyond the social distinctions: "When accosted by people who loquaciously express doubt and surmise, such as "is he a Chaṇḍāla, or a twice-born, or a Śūdra, or an ascetic, or perhaps some supreme Yogi with his mind full of discrimination of Reality", the Yogis themselves go their way neither pleased nor displeased in mind." [2]) And the Gītā expresses that they regard everything with an equal eye: "Sages look equally on a Brāhmaṇa adorned with learning and humility, a cow, an elephant, and even a dog and an outcaste." [3])

C. CASTE AND RELIGION. On the relation of caste and religion we find opposed views. For instance: The problem of caste is a purely social problem and not one of religion. Most reformers made the mistake of regarding it as a religious problem. This is one view, as expressed by Swami Vivekananda. "A man from the highest caste and a man from the lowest may become a monk in India and the two become equal. In religion there is no caste: caste is simply a social institution." [4])

Yet if in true religion there is no caste, this does not imply that in caste there is no element of religion. There is a great deal of it we are afraid. We do not mean religion in the true sense, but in the form of stereotyped privileges and antiquated customs. Accordingly the opposite opinion is also found that the problem of caste is mainly religious. As an authority on caste wrote: "a man may become a Brahmo or agnostic and yet remain in caste, but if he espouse Christianity or Mahommedanism, his own parents would exclude him from their house and disallow every kind of intercourse except on the most distant terms", because he would have become impure. [5]) Yet it is not all religious, for, as the same author mentions, if a man marry a widow he loses caste, though such marriage is not in any way against Śāstric injunctions, while

[1]) *Bhakti-sūtra* 72—73.
[2]) *Vairāgya-Śatakam* 96.
[3]) *Gītā* V · 18.
[4]) *Complete Works*, Vol I, p. 20. Cf. also Vol. III, p. 132 and Vol. V, p. 19, 235.
[5]) J. N. Bhattacharya, *Hindu Castes and Sects*, p. 17.

the keeping of a Mohammedan mistress, which is a serious and almost inexpiable offence, is not visited with any kind of punishment by castemen. Sir Surendranath Banerji wrote: "you cannot think of a social question affecting the Hindu community that is not bound up with religious considerations." [1])

It is hard to take sides in this matter. The difficulty probably arises from the vagueness of the conceptions 'religious' and 'social'. Does religion mean the mystic realization, the love of God and man, the dynamic impulse of brotherhood, or the form-side of the established religions?

It will probably be correct to say that some of the evils of the caste-system in India are due to established religion, to orthodox Hinduism, and in so far as this is the case have to be remedied by living religion. In Chapter II we have shown how this was periodically attempted in Indian History. In the campaign of Mr. Gandhi and others for the rights of the Untouchables against the orthodox Brahmans we may follow it at the present time.

The attitude of world-negation and the spiritual nihilism which has often been brought up against the philosophy of several Hindu-sects as well as of forms of Buddhism by Western thinkers, may be explained partly from the suffering caused by the social and spiritual bondage of the caste system. If a better social status and a higher personal consideration by public opinion and by established religion might not be reached in ordinary social life, freedom could always be attained by retirement from ordinary conditions of life to a lonely existence of asceticism in the woods or to the wandering life of a begging monk. Religion often escapes the bondage of established forms to flourish and live an unhampered life elsewhere. The more so if there is social delimitation of personal freedom. But the natural reaction to the system and the life abandoned is one of negation. This is a weakness to be overcome. When the Hindu outsiders became a recognized organ in the social system in the order or Āśrama of Sannyāsa, the philosophy of some of their categories as well as that of Buddhism tended to become one of negation. This may have been promoted by the gradual dilution of the spiritual quality. In contradistinction to the above tendency the philosophy of most of the religious castes and sects was a positive one. [2])

---

[1]) *A Nation in making*, p. 396, quoted by O'Malley, *India's Social Heritage*, p. 169.

[2]) For instance as beautifully expressed in the text: "I do not desire

The caste spirit has infected to some extent the social system of the lower classes of Moslems, though it is utterly at variance with the precepts and traditions of Islam. [1]) Also Christianity has been influenced by caste feelings. The oldest Christian Church in South India, the Syrian Church, was treated by the Hindus as a caste of good status, equal to the Nairs. The members of this Church behaved in every way as a caste and made no efforts to make converts. [2]) The Roman Catholic Church upheld the caste-distinctions in South India. In the seventeenth century there were really two sections in the Church, there were priests for the Untouchables, dressed as Untouchables, and priests for the Brahman converts, dressed like Brahmans. The two categories held aloof from each other as if they themselves were Untouchables and Brahmans. And even now there are partition walls or railings in many Churches to separate the descendants of Untouchables from the converts of higher origin. Or there are two churches at either end of a village for members of the two communities. The Protestant missions in South India with a single exception have for the last hundred years refused to recognize caste distinctions. Yet caste prejudices are present everywhere in some degree. [3])

In conclusion a few remarks about Christianity and caste-separatism in general. On the whole the Roman Catholic Church much opposes the development and the preservation of caste feelings and generally in Roman Catholic countries not much of caste can be found. On the other hand caste feelings are promoted much more easily in Protestant countries. [4]) On both rules there is a notable exception. South India is the one exception, and the other is provided by Protestant Java, where the Eurasians are almost regarded as Europeans. This compares favourably with the status of Eurasians elsewhere.

from the Supreme Lord that highest salvation attended with the eight perfections, nor do I ask liberation or exemption from future births. I seek to live within all corporeal beings, and endure their pains, so that they may be freed from suffering." (*Bhāg.-P.* IX : *21* : 12).

[1]) L. S. S. O'Malley, ***India's Social Heritage***, p. 30.

[2]) *Ibid.* p. 32.

[3]) *Ibid.* p. 33—36.

[4]) It is probably fundamentally a question of race mentality. In that case both the different religious tendencies and the different manifestations of class or castefeelings could be explained from the different social mentalities of the different Latin and Teutonic races. But see p. 85.

D. LAW AND EQUALITY. The need of Law arises in proportion to the degree of 'mixture of Varṇas'. [1]) If in a society the social constitution were modelled faithfully upon the social composition, there would be no need of civil law. The greater the 'mixture of Varṇas' the more the protection of law is required. Law is then a makeshift, not a remedy. The remedy is the inducing and stimulating of social-psychological forces to diminish the 'mixture of Varṇas'.

Megasthenes was surprised at the honesty and truthfulness of the Hindus. [2]) In the 13th century Bedi-ez-zaman wrote: "The Indians.... are free from deceit and violence." [3]) Marco Polo was struck by the prevalence of the same virtue: "You must know that these Brahmans are the best merchants in the world and the most truthful, for they would not tell a lie for anything on earth." [4]) Also Nicolaus Damascenus wrote: "They rely more on their mutual good faith than on juridical securities." [5]) They were able to take legal proceedings as to pledge and deposit, but probably it happened only rarely. Merchants had to find their security for the observance of contracts in morals and public opinion, rather than in law. This was only possible because the standard of morality was high and commerce not yet much developed, so that trade with persons entirely unknown to the merchants hardly existed. The solid organization of the village, of the family, and of the caste-guilds, and their control over their members provided a high moral standard and a fear not to be able to live up to it. The protection of civil law was not yet needed to the extent it is now. The sense of Varṇa was still strong, and what the sense of Varṇa could not accomplish, was effected by the fear of public opinion. [6]) If this had not been the case surely also a more developed commercial law would have resulted.

The people of the India of recent times are however very much in

[1]) This Section will be more clearly understood after reading the next Chapter.

[2]) *Aelianus* V. H. IV : 1; *Strabo* XV : 1, Ch. 53. See M. Elphinstone, *History of India*, Vol. I, p. 243; B. C. J. Timmer, *Megasthenes en de Indische Maatschappij*, p. 240—1.

[3]) M. Müller, *India, what can it teach us*, p. 275.

[4]) Marco Polo, *Book concerning the kingdoms and marvels of the East. Newly transl. and ed. with notes, maps and illustr.* by H. Yule. Vol. II, p. 350.

[5]) B. C. J. Timmer, *Op. cit.* pp. 250—252.

[6]) See Chapter IX C.

need of the protection of civil law, partly on account of the shortcomings of Caste, partly on account of causes as generally found all over the civilized world. The law of 1858 (of which the law of 1850 was an anticipation) provided equality for all concerning civil rights. There are however still many inequalities left in fields where civil law is connected with religious tenets. Many Hindu thinkers may be heard to observe that if polygamy is bad, it should be bad for all and it should cease to be a privilege for the Mohammedans and for Hindu princes, and that if it should not be bad, it should cease to be penal to Christians. A Mohammedan, if he wants to make a gift of his entire estate, can do so only if he adopts Christianity. Why should one to get rid of a wife, be put to the necessity of changing his religion? A Hindu may marry a first cousin only if he adopts another religion. A Moslem may make an endowment for the maintenance of his children and descendants with an ultimate gift for charity. A Hindu cannot do so. [1])

It seems to be the best policy that in a society where there is a great 'mixture of Varṇas', there should be equality of all before the law, not as an application of the principle of equality (as considered in this Chapter), but as a safeguard against even greater 'mixture of Varṇas'. [2])

The institution of suspended sentence and probation is a sign that the recognition is steadily growing that the dissimilarity of psychology and conduct, the difference of the degree of sociality, has to be taken into account.

We have to leave this Section at these few remarks.

E. CONCLUSIONS. We have seen that, though the theory of Varṇa implicates social inequality, it does not contain any principle of a spiritual or fundamental inequality. The principle of spiritual equality (if the word 'equality' be proper) stands outside the social theory, but manifests at times in society in the form of ideals of and as an urge towards brotherhood or comradeship. This may be in the form of a religious or humanistic movement, or it may take the form of a political or economic (r)evolution. The theory and ideals of Varṇa may also come to

[1]) Instances from K. P. Jayaswal, *Adjustment of social institutions to modern conditions*, in *Prabuddha Bharata*, Vol. XXXVI, pp. 384—392.
[2]) As regards punishment cf. *Manu* VII : 24, quoted on p. 133.

the foreground again at the same time, in particular if the movement be religious.

The horizontal view of humanity and the vertical view of society were not always clearly distinguished, with unfortunate results.

We pointed to the fact that in all periods of Indian history the principle of man's spiritual equality was recognized and applied.

In so far the evils of the caste system are due to defects of the established religion they have to be remedied by living religion. In so far they are not they have to be impaired before all by an awakening of the sense of Varṇa. There are movements in India now in both directions.

Continuing the line of thought of the Conclusions of the last Chapter we have now come to the point where we may distinguish: 1. The sense of Varṇa or hierarchy. 2. The sense of unity and oneness. The former is a social sense (i.e. of creation: differentiation in time and space, in form and function), the latter is a spiritual or mystic sense, inspiring brotherhood. Together they form the sense of sociality (with the urge to integration as natural outcome) in the individual as part of and from the standpoint of the social mind plus the social unconscious (and thus in him only partly conscious), and the sense of individual place, work and worth in the individual from his own standpoint (about which more in Chapter VIII). This sense of sociality (with the urge to integration as the natural outcome) plus the sense of individual place (with the urge to work as the natural outcome) are together nothing but the sense of Dharma (with the urge to perform it as natural outcome). Dharma has thus a two-fold nature in two ways, which do not cover each other. In one way it is partly social, partly mystical. In the other way it is partly collective-psychological, partly individual.

In Section D we considered briefly the conception of equality before the law. It seems that the greater the 'mixture of Varnas' in a society the more the protection of law is required, and it seems to be the safest policy that the principle of equality before the law is upheld, not as an application of the principle of equality as considered in this chapter, but as a safeguard against an aggravation of 'mixture of Varṇas'. We cannot here go deeper into this question to which a special study ought to be devoted.

Chapter VII

The danger of „Mixture of Varṇas"

A. **PROPOSITION.** The scriptures often dwell on the danger of a confusion of the Varṇas. What did the old sages and the compilers of the Dharma-śāstras mean by this, what was their fear, what was their intention? What was implied by this danger we want to try and determine in this Chapter. It seems that we must distinguish clearly between a 'mixture of Varṇas', dangerous from the standpoint of hierarchy, and a mixture of the castes, objectionable from the standpoint of caste.

We shall also point to the fact that from the Purāṇic information about the Kali-yuga we see that a 'mixture of Varṇas' was foreseen. The ancient compilers of the Purāṇas must have noticed the tendency in its first stage and forecasted its ultimate development.

B. **MIXTURE OF VARṆAS.** In the Dharma-śāstras stress is often laid on the danger of a 'mixture of Varṇas'. Sometimes however it is clear that a danger to the caste system is meant. [1]) Two conceptions of 'mixture' are found, the one applying to caste, the other to Varṇa. In places where the first conception is represented, nothing is stated to the effect that persons of one caste might not take on the profession of another caste. Though that was always discouraged elsewhere, and allowed only in exceptional cases and in times of distress [2]), it is not in these places regarded as the cause or as a characteristic of a mixture of castes. Such mixtures are then stated to have resulted from intermarriage of the different castes corresponding to the four Varṇas, and all sorts of combinations of marriages of the four groups are mentioned to account for the existence of the so-called

[1]) See p. 67.
[2]) *Gautama* VII; *Manu* X : 81—122; *Yājñ.* III : 35—44.

'mixed castes'. [1]) All authorities on caste agree that these theories of which the Dharma-śāstras abound are highly fanciful in their details. Also adultery is stated as a cause of mixture of castes. [2]) These views are significant in some respects. It is clear that the danger of a mixture of the castes was pictured by those who were afraid of either or both of the following things: 1. That the partitions between the hereditary classes might disappear with the consequence of a social anarchy and a loss of privileges of the higher castes. 2. That society might split itself up into ever more and more castes.

Intermarriage between the different castes is sometimes forbidden [3]) and sometimes allowed [4]) and in some Śāstras compromises are found [5]). In the Mahābhārata we read: "All sorts of men are continually begetting children on all sorts of women." "Birth is difficult to be discriminated until action is shown." [6]) A great deal of caste- and race-admixture had been going on since a long time and purity of race had long been lost. Perhaps a remainder of racial feelings may have manifested as a desire of the higher castes to protect their fairer complexion. At any case the tendency to make the caste endogamous and exclusive steadily gained ground.

The fear of a confusion of the social groups was so great that we read in Baudhāyana that the mixture has to be prevented by all means even if the Brahmans and the Vaiśyas have to resort to arms, a function which is normally sinful for them. [7]) Sometimes the two conceptions of a mixture of the castes and a mixture of the Varṇas are found in a combined form. Manu states: "(The king) should carefully compel Vaiśyas and Śūdras to perform their own work; for if these two Varṇas swerved from their duties, they would throw this (whole) world into confusion." [8]) Elsewhere we find: "He who follows the duty of his *own* Varṇa, and acts thus, forsooth repairs to the celestial region." [9]) Atri mentions: "By following these Institutes (for the Varṇas) which have been described by

---

[1]) *Manu* X : 8—41; *Gautama* IV : 16—21; *Vasishṭha* XVIII; *Baudhāyana* I : *8* : 16 : 6—12, I : *9* : 17; etc.
[2]) *Manu* VIII : 353.
[3]) *Āp.* II : 13 : 4—5.
[4]) *Baudhāyana* I : *8* : 16 : 2—5; *Manu* IX : 85.
[5]) See also S. V. Ketkar, *History of Caste in India*, Vol. I, p. 146.
[6]) See the quotation on p. 114.
[7]) *Baudhāyana* II : *2* : 4 : 18.
[8]) *Manu* VIII : 418; cf. VIII : 172, and *Artha-śāstra* I : 3 : 13—14.
[9]) *Hārita* II : 10.

me, the Varṇas attain a most excellent condition and great honours in this world. The king, who punishes them who, renouncing their own Dharma, follow another's, becomes glorified in the celestial region." [1])

A moral element, indicating a sense of Varṇa, is shown by the following opinion or injunction: "Killing domestic or wild animals degrades the perpetrators to the status of a mixed caste." [2])

The danger of confusion in the pure sense of Varṇa is met only in the older works. By the later confusion of theory and ideal with the actual conditions of class the 'danger of mixture' was applied to caste, and instead of working as a warning and in favour of natural class, it contributed to the crystallization of caste.

What is a 'mixture of the Varṇas'? In the 18th Chapter of the Bhagavad-gītā, after the enumeration of the duties of the four Varṇas, we read: "Man reaches perfection by each being intent on his own duty (karman)". [3]) And: "Better is one's own Dharma though destitute of merits than the well-performed Dharma of another. He who performs the Dharma laid down by his own nature incurs not sin." [4]) Elsewhere we read: "Death in the discharge of one's own Dharma is preferable, the Dharma of another is full of danger." This is the pure Varṇa doctrine, and here we have the danger of the 'mixture of Varṇas'. The Brahman must live and behave as a Brahman and each of the Varṇas according to its own standard and function. If a man of lower Varṇa poses as one of a higher, say a Brahman, performs the social task (not even to mention the spiritual task) of a Brahman before he has attained the capacities of a Brahman, he endangers the organic health of society, he lowers the Brahman standard, he mixes the functions.

It should be observed that the expression 'mixture of Varṇas' is really not accurate, for a mixture of Varṇas is impossible on account of their very nature. It is clear that a confusion was meant of Varṇa with social class, of natural with constitutional Hierarchy. The 'mixture of Varnas' exists according to the degree of non-correspondance between the two hierarchies. This was the thought the composer of the Gītā had at the back of his mind, and this non-correspondance he expresses as sinful for each individual case.

[1]) *Atri* I : 16—18. See also p. 128.

[2]) *Vishṇu* XXXIX : 1.

[3]) *Gītā* XVIII : 45. Cf. *Artha-śāstra* I : *3* : 13—14.

[4]) *Gītā* XVIII : 47, cf. III : 35.

On all Varṇas, but especially on the Brahman, lies the responsibility. As Śrī-Kṛishṇa expresses it: "These worlds would fall into ruin, if I did not perform action; I should be the author of confusion of Varṇas, and should destroy these creatures." [1])

The second Chapter and in a way the whole of the Gītā is devoted to a sermon to Arjuna reminding him that he is a Kshatriya and that his duty is to fight for the righteous cause. "If thou wilt not carry on this righteous warfare, then casting away thine own Dharma, and thine (Kshatriya) honour, thou wilt incur sin." Etc. [2]) He would be deemed a coward. It would be a flight, and not the least a flight in the psychological sense. What would be a sin for the Brahman (presume he should do it — and if he did he would not be a true Brahman) may be the duty of a man of lower Varṇa.

The lesson of the Gītā is: do not shrink from your task before it is fulfilled. And then (and not before) you have of its own accord risen to a higher stage. This is also expressed by the sermon held by Śrī-Kṛishṇa to king Yudhishṭhira, who, after the war of Kurukshetra, wearied to death by the horrors of war and the weight of responsibility, wished to retire and become a Sannyāsin. Kṛishṇa reminded him of his Dharma to rule as a king, from which he should not shrink on account of any personal feelings of dislike. [3]) The bent of his nature was to rule, therefore he should be king.

How great a 'confusion of varṇas' has come into being in modern society! So many persons are performing 'the work of others', or are jealous of 'the work of others', and striving for it. There is also a 'mixture of Varṇas' in politics: universal suffrage is a distribution of the functions of the Kshatriya-varṇa, the ruling and regulative powers, etc., over all classes.

Light may fall on several social problems, as for instance the question of conscription, if they are considered from this line of thought. One man may feel it to be his duty to serve in the army or in the navy, whereas another might consider it immoral. They may be both right — for themselves.

On the whole Christ's words apply to modern society very well indeed: "Every kingdom divided against itself is brought to desolation; and every city or house divided against itself shall not

[1]) *Gītā* III · 24.
[2]) *Gītā* II : 33.
[3]) *Kāma-gītā.*

stand." [1]) Significant is also the favourite maxim of an imperial Inca, Tupac Inca Yupanqui: "Science was not intended for the people, but for those of generous blood. Persons of low degree are only puffed up by it, and rendered vain and arrogant. Neither should such meddle with the affairs of government, for this would bring high offices into disrepute, and cause detriment to the state." [2]) If we substitute 'character' for 'blood' we have the pure Varṇa doctrine. In ancient Peru, like to some extent in ancient India, character was determined largely by the race, because the ruling-class or caste of Incas belonged to a race with a culture far superior to that of the people. Hence the stress on race.

A 'mixture of Varṇas' in the larger sense we have in the different aspects of nationalism, or rather 'state-ism', of the present day. 'Inter-nationalism' or rather 'universalism' is then an aspect of Varṇa.

The hereditary system may also tend to cause a 'mixture of Varṇas', for the children need not belong to the Varṇa of the parents. The hereditary system is bad, i.e. socially inefficient, if there is any compulsion, direct or implied, to follow a certain profession. Family traditions, ideals and opportunities have to be passed on, not the occupation, the office or the title. The Varṇa (a title was originally largely a Varṇa-degree) has to be demonstrated and won by the children. Yet it would be wrong to abolish the family-hereditary system, at least in the West, because: 1. in modern Western society it has adapted itself already largely to changed conditions; and 2. on the whole the children of parents of a certain Varṇa will be more likely to belong to the same Varṇa than children of parents of lower Varṇas. Of course the same applies to the social classes.

The action of some of the early Russian Communists against the family-system may have been partly a reaction to the evils of the Russian hereditary family system. Later there was a gradual return to the normal family life.

C. THE KALI-YUGA. It is significant that the Purāṇas contain forecasts of the 'mixture of Varṇas'. This indicates that the process had begun, and had been noticed, that its development was foreseen, and considered to be inevitable and not to be completely remedied till the extreme had been reached

[1]) *St. Matthew* 12 : 25.
[2]) W. H. Prescott, *The Conquest of Peru*, p. 70.

at the end of the Kali-yuga, in which Age we are at present. Reading the passages applying to the Kali-yuga we often have occasion to wonder, and we get a feeling as if a visitor from some other planet were caricaturising conditions of our present time. We shall quote from two Purāṇas some lines of interest for our subject.

"The glorious Hari will appear as the punisher of Kali .... when the Pākhaṇḍas (miscreants) will form the Brahman population and Śūdras will be the kings of men." [1]) Then natural conditions will evolve again out of the old class system. "In that age of Kali people become greedy, are given to impious habits, destitute of mercy, are inimical for no cause, impure by birth, and too full of thirst for worldly things, the most important place being taken by Śūdras, fishermen and the like." [2]) "Low people conduct business transactions and merchants behave dishonestly even when there is no calamity, people will take to pursuits condemned by the righteous, thinking them to be good. Servants will abandon their penniless masters though they are good in all respects; masters will forsake the servant in difficulty though he be in the family; so also people will cease to support cows when they cease to yield milk." [3]) Śūdras will be worshipped, and the ignorant will administer justice, poverty will prevail as a result of the confusion of Varṇas. People will be generally atheistic. Etc. etc. And the Vishṇupurāṇa states that "in the Kali-Age people will not observe Varṇa, Āśrama and institutes, ... all celestials will be considered in equal light, and all orders of life will be common alike to all persons .... Every trifling property will make men proud of their wealth.... Wives will desert their husbands when they will lose their wealth, and the rich only will be considered by women as their lords. He who will distribute great wealth will be considered as master of men, and prestige will no longer be a title to supremacy. Accumulated wealth will be spent on ostentatious dwellings. The minds of men will be wholly occupied with earning money and that even will be spent on the gratification of selfish desires.... In the Kali-Age all people will consider themselves as equal with the Brāhmaṇas, and cows will be held in reverence only because they supply milk... Deprived of wealth people will be perpetually subject to famine and other afflictions; and they will never enjoy pleasure and

---

[1]) *Bhāg.-P.* II : 7 : 38.
[2]) *Bhāg.-P.* XII : 3 : 25.
[3]) *Bhāg.-P.* XII : 3 : 35—36.

happiness.... The women will have many children and little means.... Princes will plunder their subjects instead of protecting them and under the pretext of levying customs they will rob merchants of their property. In the Kali-yuga everyone possessing cars and elephants and horses will be a Rāja; everyone who is feeble will be a slave.... Respect for the teachers declines.... Principle caste will be the Śūdra...." [1]) "Wealth will be the test of pedigree and culture, passion will be the only tie of marriage...., earth will be respected for its mineral treasures.... external marks will constitute the only distinction of orders.... gifts only will constitute virtue." [2])

D. CONCLUSIONS. We have distinguished between the 'mixture of castes' and 'the mixture of Varṇas'. If the first applies to India, the latter conception is seen to be significant for the state of modern social conditions in India as well as elsewhere.

By 'mixture of Varṇas' is meant the non-correspondence of Varṇa with class or caste, which may develop to different degrees. It entails many social problems.

This 'mixture of Varṇas' was noticed and its development foreseen in the Purāṇas. The process of confusion must have begun in an early age.

[1]) *Vishṇu-P.* VI : *1.*
[2]) *Vishṇu-P.* IV : *24.*

Chapter VIII

Varṇa and the Individual

A. PROPOSITION. The line of thought taken in this Chapter follows from the conclusions arrived at in the former Chapters. We want to point out that the theory of Varṇa stresses the import of the individual, yet is not an individualistic theory in the ordinary sense; and that it brings forward the social benefit, yet does not consider the group or the state to be of more weight than the individual. Thus it reconciles and balances somewhat opposed conceptions.

The conception 'Varna' we shall furthermore analyse in connection with the natural hierarchy.

B. VARṆA AND THE INDIVIDUAL. Dharma can be realized only by the individual for himself. The true Brahman, who is supposed (in former lives) to have passed through the lower stages, is able to approximately recognize (not realize) the Dharma of others. The same applies to the ruling and regulating Varṇa as regards the lower Varṇas.

Dharma is entirely individual as regards action, karman. A group consists of individuals; it is really not the group that acts, but the individual members. Of a finished product one may say that it was produced by a group of workers, but it is more correct to say that A. produced one special part, B. some other, C. the third, and so on. Every worker, like every worker in the social machinery, performs his own individual little task.

Dharma is also individual as regards the work which ought to be done. In accordance with the organic aspect of society no two persons can have the same or an equal function. The functions may be complementary and so appear to be common. Since no two persons are alike, how can they be expected to have equal social duties. If a person is taken to substitute another in a particular bit of work, or appointed to fill a particular office until then held by somebody else, there are sure to appear great changes in the quality of the work to which the person in question contributes his little bit. If perhaps the difference in material output be negligable in the case of a working man, whose task is simply to turn a handle, he will yet bring a mental influence to bear upon his fellows different from that of his predecessor. It may be beneficial to the spirit of co-operation, etc., and consequently to the work, or it may be an influence for the worse.

A community, a state, or a society are built up only by the efforts of their individual members. But for them they are helpless abstractions.

So far the theory of Varṇa is individualistic. But it is more than that. For man may be in his form life a separate individual, yet his mind is united to the mind of humanity. He may from this standpoint be symbolized as the centre of a number of concentric circles, the smallest being his family, the largest humanity, all possible kinds of human communities and societies intervening. There is a constant mental interplay going on between himself and the members of the different groups, and the individual is more than only himself, in him work the social mind (and the collective unconscious). In his achievements there are elements betraying his period, his belief or his creed.

The theory of Varṇa recognizes the intrinsic worth and the place of every individual, moreover linking him up with all others in the vertical scale of a hierarchy. And, as we have seen before, furthermore the individual members of society are united in the horizontal circles of the life of the heart.

Perhaps we may say that the Varṇa theory is individualistic and liberal in manifestation, i.e. social action, but communistic in essence.

The communistic *life* gives full scope to the expression of individuality in the *way and form* of fulfilment of the organic function. Applying this to the individual states in the world at large, internationalism or rather 'universalism' gives full scope to the expression of nationalism. The one cannot exist without the other, they are two sides of one coin.

Instead of the 'égalité' the other French maxim "Chacun son

goût, et Dieu pour tous", is to be upheld, since it is more scientific, if taken in a somewhat more exalted sense than popularly understood.

The individual — to truly deserve that name — must influence the groups in which he works to a larger extent than they do him. This is possible only to the individuals high in the natural hierarchy, hence they are 'born' to be leaders. Persons high up in the social hierarchy may be influenced more by the people than they are able to influence the mass, they are the typical popular heroes and figureheads of certain movements, who on the whole rise and fall quickly, and are forgotten soon after.

As we saw in Chapter III C the higher an individual's place in the natural hierarchy the more freedom he enjoys, the more scope there is for the expression of individuality, or, as it is then called, personality.

People of the lower Varṇas are obsessed and swayed by the group mind, by mass-psychology; the Dharma of the men of the highest Varṇa is to lead and support the social mind.

The (true) Brahmans must be the upholders of Varṇa, as the Śāstras always proclaim. It is their calling to help others to gain insight into their task and place in the organic and hierarchic whole. Every individual must bring forth his Dharma from his subconscious life and thus consciously realize it. Of old it was the task of the priest to aid him in this process of birth, now, in so far as the father and the priest are not competent, it is the task of the teacher, the psychologist, the sociologist.

If the Brahman helps the people to gain insight into their special Dharma, it is the duty and the function of the ruling Varṇa to lend them a helping hand in making it possible for them to discharge it. The Śāstras stress the import of the king and exalt him even at times to the expense of (caste) Brahmans. [1])

To understand why in India Sva-dharma [2]) became to be considered as subsidiary to caste-dharma, it is necessary to critically analyse the conception of Varṇa.

The theory of Varṇa is a convenient variety of the theory of the natural hierarchy, and for that reason we use it so often in this book. Apart from the division of society into *four* Varṇas, the reason

---

1) E.g. *Atri* I : 27—29.

2) Sometimes Sva-dharma is taken in the sense of hereditary duty. We take it here in the sense of individual Dharma, one's proper Dharma.

for which we have gone into in Chapter I B, we have to remember that the conception of a hierarchy without marked steps is impractical for the holding up of ideals. For this reason the theory presents four systematized general standards of morality (which in reality do not exist) and four systematized groups of ideals. Regarded in this light Varṇa is a kind of working hypothesis for educational application, a useful invention, based upon the theory of the natural hierarchy. The Dharma of a Varṇa is equally a useful invention, based upon and presenting the (theoretical) average of the individual Dharmas of the members, which are again divided hierarchically and organically within the bounds of the Varṇa in question. If this is kept in view, there is no danger that the Varṇa-dharma (and if there is 'mixture of Varṇas': the caste-dharma) will be held to be superior to the Sva-dharma, the Dharma of the individual.

This was lost sight of in India, Varṇa was generally taken in a far too dogmatic sense, the individual Dharma became largely subsidiary, 'mixture of Varṇas' was promoted, and caste-dharma overruled Sva-dharma.

The social use of the conception of Varṇa is its educative importance. It is of use to the members of society to determine their own place and work and to get inspired by a set of ideals akin to their own nature.

If in India the caste-dharma was generally considered to be of more weight than the Sva-dharma [1]), in the West a similar confusion of conceptions arose in the theories which laid undue emphasis upon what we might call the state-dharma, to the detriment of the freedom of the individual to determine and perform his own Dharma. Needless to say that these theories have been put into practice in several states.

C. CONCLUSIONS. We have seen that the theory of Varṇa stresses the intrinsic worth of the individual yet is not an individualistic theory in the ordinary sense (also because it does not concern itself with the mutual rights of individual and state); it brings forward the social benefit, the common good, yet is not a theory of caste- or state-supremacy. It is perhaps

[1]) In spite of sayings like the following, as found also in the Dharma-śāstras: "It is not our Āśrama in itself that produces Dharma, Dharma must be practised. Therefore let no one do unto others what he would not have done to himself." (*Yājñ.* III : 65).

not incorrect to say that the Varṇa-theory is individualistic and liberal in manifestation, i.e. social action, and communistic in essence.

Apart from the reasonable division of society into *four* Varṇas, which however can never be carried through in too strict a sense, since there will always be individuals that are in a transitional stage between two Varṇas and perform several kinds of social functions [1]) — if we critically consider the conception of Varṇa we come to the conclusion that in a way Varṇa is a kind of working hypothesis for practical purposes, based upon the theory of the natural hierarchy, and invented for its great educational value. [2]) For this reason we prefer on the whole the use of the conception of Varṇa to that of the natural hierarchy. This may safely be done as long as 'Varṇa' is not taken in too dogmatic a sense.

[1]) In a way all people, if only to a very slight extent, have the opportunity to perform the functions of the other Varṇas. For instance the father must be somewhat of a Brahman in the education of his children.

[2]) Cf. p. 76 regarding the Āśrama system.

Chapter IX

Varṇa and the Social Mind

A. PROPOSITION. In this Chapter we propose to consider and determine the importance of different social-psychological factors like personal example, public opinion, class honour, in relation to the conception and the sense of Varṇa. We shall also try to determine the connection or correlation between Varṇa and the population classes, after defining the conceptions of the social composition and the social constitution.

On account of the fragmentary nature and the general character of this Chapter there will be no summary of conclusions at the end.

B. EXAMPLE. Personal example is an important, perhaps the greatest educational factor, which leads people step by step from the lower grades of the natural hierarchy to the higher. As the Bhagavad-gītā says: "Whatever a superior person does, that is followed by others. What he demonstrates by action, that people follow." [1] So, from the pinnacle of the hierarchy, people are drawn up step by step, each being the example of the man next below and forming the ideal of a group further below.

C. PUBLIC OPINION. Public opinion contains a mass of conceptions of value, with resulting judgments, which happen to be the fashion in a particular society at a particular time. It consists of elements which result from the sense of Varṇa plus elements which are the reflection of the moral standard of groups or classes of the constitutional hierarchy. Hence public opinion may contain immoral elements if considered from the higher

[1]) *Gītā* III : 21.

grades of the natural hierarchy. It is hard to circumscribe public opinion, for there exists no public opinion including all members of a society, and all social groups have their own particular public opinion. Some always stand outside or above. For public opinion mainly represents the social views and the standard of honourable conduct of a particular social group, or of a particular individual in a group. This social group or this individual may be one high in the scale, but is more often one 'low' in the natural hierarchy, and in that case many will 'stand above it'.

Public opinion may evoke fear which the sense of Varṇa can never do. Public opinion may form an important sanction of rules of public convention. Varṇa can never have anything to do with a heteronomous sanction. May not criminal law be largely legalized public opinion? It betrayed the influence of the 'low' social groups all through history and contains only in recent times elements of the conceptions and moral standards of higher groups.

To the extent public opinion contains elements of Varṇa it is a great socializing factor. It exerts also a great casteforming influence. The Brahma-Varṇa and to a minor extent the ruling Varṇa are the leaders of public opinion. If there is 'mixture of Varnas', Brahmans and nobles who really belong to a lower Varṇa will bring into public opinion elements of lower conceptions and lower standards.

An important element of public opinion is the sanction it carries. From fear of being excommunicated people (in castes as well as in other social groups) are often forced to conform to certain conventions. Otherwise they expose themselves to being regarded as in some way inferior, impure, immoral or ridiculous.

Persons high in the constitutional hierarchy not being high in the natural hierarchy tend to take the sanction of public opinion far more seriously than the threat of punishment by civil or criminal law. We believe this was taken into account in cases as mentioned in the following quotations. Another motive may have been the shielding of the Brahman caste as a whole against physical violence. The following was enjoined as punishment for different crimes: "Tonsure (of the head) is ordained for a Brāhmaṇa instead of capital punishment, but men of other castes shall suffer capital punishment [1]). Great emphasis was laid on the prohibition to kill a Brāhmaṇa,

[1]) *Manu* VIII : 379.

the Vishṇu code advises to banish the Brahman culprit and enjoins that "a headless figure be painted on his forehead in the case of Brahmanicide; for drinking spirituous liquor, the emblem of wine; for theft, a dog; for violating a preceptor's bed, the female organ." [1]) And there were injunctions for Kshatriyas and for women, meant to make them ridiculous or socially impossible as punishment for certain misdeeds, by shaving their heads, by shaving them with the urine of an ass, by making them ride through the village on a donkey, etc. [2]) And even now in some cases the breaker of certain caste laws may be subjected to a humiliating punishment such as being paraded through the village seated backwards on a donkey, with his face covered with lime and with half his head shaved. [3]) In mediaeval Europe there were customs of a similar character. Only then they were generally followed by punishments of penal law.

From the standpoint of Varṇa we may say that a person who acts in a socializing way from fear of public opinion, does so only in appearance and will betray his lower Varṇa to the disappointment of his fellows when on a certain day for some reason he will not be afraid. It is equally possible that some day a man 'disappoints' his fellows by demonstrating to stand above public opinion because he really belongs to or has risen to a higher Varṇa. To make this clear let us give an example. In the beginning of the war of 1914 public opinion in the countries at war held that young men had to join the army. If some did not, it may have been due to indolence or cowardice, and public opinion may then *perhaps* have succeeded in awakening the manhood of the laggards. But some of those who remained may have been 'Brahmans' with a Dharma different from that of a soldier. They stayed, and rightly so. If only the 'Brahmans' who were less sure of themselves had also stayed, instead of being swept off their feet by mass-psychology, by 'participation mystique', by fear of public opinion!

To return to our subject. Typical phenomena of public opinion are the judgments pronounced and the valuations expressed. They may sometimes be useful in opening the eyes of people as to their own follies or their personal unimportance. But on the whole the

[1]) *Vishṇu* V : 2—7.
[2]) *Manu* VIII : 370, 375, 384.
[3]) L. S. S. O'Malley, *India's Social Heritage*, p. 26.

element of fear which public opinion inspires will work towards a 'mixture of Varṇas', as we saw above.

Public opinion is formed by a concord of expressions of value about others. In a society where the organic and hierarchic composition of society is not commonly realized, there is a general tendency of people to judge others according to their own standard. We cannot stress enough that it is highly illogical and unscientific thus to set all clocks by Greenwich time, which is being done at the present time far more than one might think. Judging people according to one's own standard tends to evoke in them an inferiority complex, which may easily be followed by jealousy. In how many cases a happy and harmonious family life has not been made impossible by a disdainful or slighting attitude or even subconscious feeling of one member towards another or the others. The inferiority complex remains long after its causes have been removed. An interesting sociological problem is that of the prestige of labour. In mediaeval society the social consideration of labour was great, the guilds were internally hierarchically composed and mutually organically interrelated, and the sense of Varṇa was strong. But in the centuries to follow the social consideration of labour sank with great strides. In our century Labour has been exalted so highly and at the same time the desire of members of the labour classes to climb higher in the hierarchy of power has been demonstrated so convincingly that we hardly need to draw the attention to the inferiority complex (and the perhaps subconscious jealousy) of the labour classes.

But if the sense of Varṇa is strong, it will be generally recognized that *all* work is socially useful, from an economic standpoint even relatively equally important. The sweeper's work is as necessary as that of the doctor, the merchant or the research student, and there is not the slightest reason why the one should look down upon the other. If one does, he betrays his lower Varṇa. The function of the highest Varṇa is not to sit upon a throne of self-righteousness, but to serve the other Varṇas with its greater insight into phenomena, and with its deeper realization of the nature and the oneness of humanity.

The judging of people lower in the social scale applies to the constitutional hierarchy. The 'lower' may be purely imaginary from the standpoint of Varṇa.

In the natural hierarchy someone will not seriously try to judge or to express his opinion about somebody higher in the scale, for the simple reason that his experience and knowledge are not sufficient. Therefore we find among the caste regulations prohibitions of criticism of people of higher rank. Contemptuous expressions like "he is a bad Brāhmaṇa" were punishable by a fine. And if any one of a lower caste spoke ill of the habits of one of a higher caste, the fines imposed were to increase from 3 paṇas upwards commencing from the lowest caste. [1]) And "one who indulges in talks affecting the interests of royalty, one who vilifies the king.... should have their tongues cut off, and be banished." [2]) The tendency of recent forms of government to prohibit free criticism of its decrees and policy may be understood in this light. It is indeed illogical that people should criticise things they know nothing of. But if the classes corresponding to the lower Varṇas are not competent to criticize, the 'Brahmans' indeed are quite competent, even much more so than the rulers, and their advice and criticism have to be taken into account.

The question of judging others could not have been expressed more clearly than in the text: "Judge not, that ye be not judged. For with what judgment ye judge, ye shall be judged: and with what measure ye mete, it shall be measured to you again." [3]) If one man judges another, he betrays his own standard, his Varṇa, his place in the natural hierarchy, and according to that standard he will be judged himself. A special form of this 'judging', and on account of its self-righteous nature a particularly obnoxious one is gossip. The perpetrators of this social crime often betray their own subconscious and suppressed desires, for self-righteousness is always a delusion as regards one's own character and possibilities.

In conclusion we want to remark that the influence of public opinion on caste is considerable. The author of a recent book goes as far as to say that the relative position of the different castes depends not on any authoritative order of precedence but on public opinion as to whether they are high or low. It is based partly on traditional beliefs as to origin in one or other of the Varṇas, but more largely on ideas as to the relative purity in a ceremonial, and not in a physical sense. [4]) This shows that caste has possibilities, and may once more be influenced by the ideal of Varṇa. This writer

[1]) *Artha-śāstra* III : *18*.
[2]) *Yājñ*. II : 305.
[3]) *St. Matthew* 7 · 1—2.
[4]) L. S. S. O'Malley, *India's Social Heritage*, p. 16.

points to the fact that the ultimate sanction of caste rules is excommunication, which cuts off a man and very often his family from all communion with his fellow caste men. This course is often temporarily followed by his fellow caste men in self-defence, until the charge against him has been decided by a caste tribunal, for if they remain in communion with him and he is eventually outcasted, they are liable to be excommunicated themselves. The high castes have rarely any organization for dealing with social offences. The community merely passes a tacit verdict and by common consent ceases to have anything to do with a man believed to be guilty of a breach of caste rules. The low castes on the other hand have a systematic organization to uphold the social code. The judicial body, or the caste headman, are however largely the instruments of public opinion within the caste concerning caste peculiarities. [1])

Public opinion upholds the caste system and there cannot be said to be anything like a revolt against the supremacy of the Brahmans, though in some parts of the country their right to lay down the law in religious and social matters is disputed. The lower and untouchable castes, in spite of desiring a leveling of castes, or an abolishment of the system, are only striving for a higher position in the hierarchy for which they invoke the aid and the recognition of the Brahmans.

If public opinion exerts such a caste-forming influence, it seems to be the main factor to reform caste. Those who are competent to lead public opinion must realize their calling and carefully set to work in so far they are not already doing their little bit. As we wrote in the conclusions of Chapter VI, this work will have to consist partly in the exerting of a religious or humanistic influence, and partly in the awakening of the sense of Varṇa.

D. CLASS HONOUR AND GROUP HONOUR. In class honour and group honour the element of Varṇa is very strong. It may go together with a selfrighteous attitude towards other classes and groups, higher or lower, with racial valuations and with valuations of conventions of the constitutional hierarchy.

Sometimes a different moral standard is upheld for mutual contact between members of the class or group and for contact

---

[1]) *Op. cit.* p. 22—25.

with outsiders. (E.g. in some gangs of thieves it is considered most dishonourable if one member steals from another. Something similar is often told of gypsies.)

Typical shades of group honour are presented by the standards of the different trades and professions — old-fashioned merchants' honour, bankers' honour, doctors' honour, etc. and by family honour. Caste-honour is only a special form of class-honour.

E. THE SOCIAL COMPOSITION AND THE SOCIAL CONSTITUTION.

It is important to notice that we use the conceptions social composition and social constitution in a sense somewhat different from that used for instance by Giddings. This scholar compares the social composition to that of living cells into a larger organism, and the social constitution to the differentiation of an organism into specialized tissues and organs. [1]) We cannot accept the theory that either biological or sociological cells (individuals) could combine into an organism without an implied and immediately manifested differentiation of function or 'organization' (organ-formation). In primitive forms of life cells have not integrated into one body by chance, it happened for profit, for mutual benefit. We cannot accept a basic distinction, or a stage of transition between integration and 'organization', though the one or the other may specially come to the foreground.

In primitive society of the ancient past every family or tribe or nation (internally hierarchically and organically composed) may have been self-sufficient, but as soon as it contacted other families or tribes or nations, it at once by association assumed an organic relation towards them. This relation was partly intellectual, consisting of an inspiration by special ideas and ideals; and partly economic, consisting of an interchange of raw materials or useful articles. In early ages intercourse was far more extensive than was formerly imagined, as is now generally recognized. Religious conceptions travelled over the earth and adapted themselves to the psychology of the different ethnical groups. It has been proved that even in very early ages there was an extensive 'international' trade in raw materials. [2])

[1]) F. H. Giddings, *The Principles of Sociology*, p. 73.

[2]) To give a single example from the early stone age: rough stones only found in Pressigny in France, and meant to be manufactured into

So we mean by the *social composition* the natural organic and hierarchic relation between different individuals and groups as a result of contact by association. Regarding the original prehistoric society we may perhaps only speak of the social composition of the family or of the tribe. In the course of time the circle widened, and now we may also speak of the social composition of human society of the world. In the social composition the social-psychological predisposition of persons is denoted.

By the *social constitution* we mean the actual cast of (a) society. There always is some 'mixture of Varṇas', to however slight a degree. Therefore in the social constitution the work and hierarchic place of persons in society do not correspond to their organic predisposition, to their Dharma, and to their place in the natural hierarchy. If there were no 'mixture of Varṇas' the social constitution would correspond to the social composition. This must have been the case in the earliest stage of man's history. [1])

Because there is 'mixture of Varṇas' the social constitution comes foremost in the social mind, and the social composition is perceived only by those who have the sense of Varṇa. In animal societies there is only question of the social composition of the herd, of the hive, and so on. In such societies there can be no "mixture of Varṇas'.

Thus the social composition is primary, the social constitution secondary.

The social composition develops according to the socializing instincts and intuitions of humanity. The social constitution develops largely by means of mental activity through the selfish unsocial desires.

We cannot accept a basic distinction between an organism and an organization. The distinction is only one of consciousness. An organism is the outcome of subconscious or unconscious activity, an organization besides also partly the result of conscious planning. But what do we really know as yet about the consciousness of an organism?

Organization — in the popular sense of the word — not to cause an aggravation of 'mixture of Varṇas', must be accomplished as much as possible according to the 'organ-realization' in the social

axes, knives and arrow-heads have been found in several localities in Belgium, and even as far removed from the place of origin as Budel in the Netherlands.

[1]) See pp. 43 and 126.

composition. [1]) This is very important, and has to be generally realized to a far greater extent than is the case at present.

F. THE DIFFERENT ORDERS OF POPULATION CLASSES. Professor Giddings distinguishes three fundamental or *primary* orders of population classes, viz. *social classes, vitality classes* and *personality classes*. In Chapter V B we compared the Varṇas with the social classes and we need not recur to it. It would provide an interesting field of study to discover the correlation, if there is any, between Varṇas and the vitality classes. Rest the personality classes. They are: 1. *The geniuses and talented*; 2. *The normally endowed*; 3. *The defective*. It is hard to make out the connection of these classes with Varṇas, since the conceptions 'genius' and 'the normal' and 'the defective' are so hard to define. If — and this applies to any category of classes — if a definition stresses the degree and kind of mental development, the connection with Varṇa is little; if it implies the degree of efficiency of the physical instrument, the connection is even less; if it mentions the degree of sociality of the personality, or of personal responsibility in connection with knowledge, the relation to Varṇa is more evident. To me the genius and the defective do not seem to form the terminations of one catena.

As *secondary* population classes Giddings mentions *political, industrial, economic classes*, etc. It is clear that there is connection with the organic aspect of the Varṇa system. These classes are considered by Giddings to be secondary because they are created only through the evolution of a social constitution. [2]) We do not consider them secondary in the light of the basic organic and hierarchic composition of society. Secondary they can be only in so far they represent — as classes of the social constitution — a later stage in the evolution of human society.

[1]) Cf. Giddings' conclusion, quoted on p. XIV.
[2]) F. H. Giddings, *The Principles of Sociology*, p. 125.

Chapter X

Conclusions

A. MAIN CONCLUSIONS. If we try to summarize our main conclusions we come to the following concretion. The 'first aspect of Dharma' (which we considered in Chapter II) partly applies to the composition of society as a hierarchic and organic whole (systematized in 'Varṇas') and partly to the horizontal composition of humanity. The 'second aspect of Dharma' applies to social organization.

The system of four Varṇas is a kind of working hypothesis for practical purposes, based upon the theory of the natural hierarchy. This must always be remembered when the conception of Varṇa is brought forward. Another — not yet mentioned — imperfection of Varṇa has to be realized, viz. that no fixed standards of 'the four' Varṇas can be accepted for all times. In different periods of history in various cultures the Varṇas correspond to different degrees in the natural hierarchy. We may probably not judge one period by the standards of another. Does even time hold a hierarchic element? [1])

Having determined the limitations of Varṇa, we can safely use the conception. For practical purposes we prefer it to the conception of the natural hierarchy.

The *theory of Varṇa* relates to the natural hierarchy that *is*. Only those who have the 'sense of Varṇa' will recognize grades of Varṇa as hidden by the cloak of the social constitution owing to 'mixture of Varṇas'.

The *ideal of Varṇa* relates to the natural hierarchy that *ought*

[1]) In the Śāstras we find that the duties of man vary in the different Yugas. *Manu* I : 85; *Parāśara* I : 21; etc.

and is *desired* by those that have the sense of Varṇa, to be manifested as completely as possible in the social constitution.

The sense of Varṇa and the realization of Varṇa are the only primary factors equal to the task of remedying the social tendency of 'mixture of Varṇas'. Hence the function of the social mind is all-important. The function of the two highest Varṇas is to call forth from the social unconscious the insight into the organic and hierarchic composition of society. Their task is to lead public opinion. Their task is — this stands partly outside the theory of Varṇa — to awaken the heart of humanity. Their task is further to form the 'second aspect of Dharma' as much as possible according to the 'first aspect'. Regarding law this means the laying down and the application of legal rules as much as humanly possible according to justice and equity.

The *sense of Varṇa* (which is the *sense of hierarchy*) is the intuitive sense of the organic and hierarchic composition of society and more in particular the sense of the organic relation of one's own Varṇa with the Varṇa below and with the Varṇa next above. Sense of the function of a Varṇa much higher in the scale cannot be expected, and the functions or even the existence of the highest rungs of the natural hierarchy cannot be commonly sensed. The *realization of Varṇa* is the conscious recognition, intuitive and mental, of the principle of Varṇa in general, or in particular of Varṇas up to a certain degree. 'Esoteric' knowledge includes some aspects of the knowledge of higher Varṇas. There can be drawn no hard and fast line between the esoteric and the exoteric, all depends upon the degree reached by the individual person in the natural hierarchy. Because knowledge is inextricably connected with conduct and thus with social responsibility, the higher degrees guard their knowledge with care, as a provision against 'mixture of Varṇas'. For that reason the Brahmans (as many other priesthoods) originally jealously guarded the Vedas. When they developed into a caste, their precaution became however unfounded and unscientific, i.e. against the theory of Varṇa.

The teachings of some great Teachers have been applied to all types and classes of men, and it has often been overlooked that they gave teachings for their disciples side by side with teachings meant for other people.

I wrote that the realization of Varṇa is in a more particular sense insight into the organic relation of one's own Varṇa with the

Varṇas below and with the Varṇa next above. In relation to this it is also the sense of one's own particular place, of one's Dharma. This will be demonstrated by action and conduct, for nobody will proclaim "I belong to the Brahman Varṇa" or "I am a noble", if he truly belongs to those categories. For the same reason that no true gentleman will announce himself to be a gentleman. His peers, that is to say those that are nearest to him in degree, will tacitly recognize him as such.

The knowledge of the organic and hierarchic composition of society is stored in the social unconscious, and man must again consciously realize it, and propagate it as an ideal and as a path with steps leading to a goal, visioned dimly in far-off heights. There will be always higher rungs to be reached by him in the natural hierarchy. Dharma always holds out further prospects in the distance. The stage reached is not of importance, but the movement onwards is. As Cervantes expressed it: "The road is always better than the inn."

Of course Varṇas are not classes which could be 'instituted'. They can but be realized in the social composition, endeavours may be made to make them part and parcel of the conscious store of conceptions and values of the people, and there can be individual efforts of application in the social constitution.

B. AFTERTHOUGHTS. Fascism and National-Socialism may perhaps be understood to be in essence movements and endeavours of the ruling and regulating Varṇa and of persons supreme in that Varṇa, to make an end of 'mixture of Varṇas' as regards matters of government. It is against the theory of Varṇa that classes corresponding to lower Varṇas should have legislative powers or should criticize the government policy. The legislative powers belong to the ruling and regulating Varṇa, and it is the function of the highest Varṇa to criticize and lead. Philosophy and religion must be above the state, and there must be no 'mixture of Varṇa' between them. Neither must the Church aim for temporal power nor the state for spiritual power. In India there was generally a healthy organic and hierarchic co-operation of the two. If 'religion' and 'philosophy' have to stand above the State this does not imply that any organization — Church or Sect — may dictate the State, for if there is 'mixture of Varṇas', Church and religion, Sect and philosophy, need not cover one another.

The freedom of the individual may — according to the theory of Varṇa — never be menaced or violated. [1]) The new world must come of itself by the way of the social mind, and all efforts to bring it by force are unnatural (i.e. against the theory of Varṇa) and bound to bring much social suffering and to entail much waste of energy.

Modern man as a politician is something of a democrat in his heart, grateful to the past achievements of Liberalism and Socialism, he will have to become something more, of which many aspects of Fascism, National-Socialism and Sovjetism are the first visible, as yet sometimes perhaps pre-natal, signs. The latest economical theories propagating an internationally regulated and rationalized production combined with the application of free trade are much in accord with the theory of the organic and hierarchic composition of society.

The intellect may no longer be man's master and its own end. It has to become the obedient instrument of man. The same applies to the products of the intellect: machinery. The rational with all its technical creations is not to be thrown overboard as is propagated by so many of the younger idealists, it is only to be used in the right way, in subordination to sociality and humanity, to culture and happiness.

Eucken's and Nietzsche's ideas on culture may be seen in a new light in relation to the theory of Varṇa. This applies also to the thoughts of many writers, both of to-day and of the past. At the present hour there are far too many unconnected social theories and ideals. There are hundreds of loose ideals of different types. This is a promising sign of life. But some theory is wanted to connect them all into one body, some set of conceptions is required to interrelate them as parts of one system. The theory of the vertical composition of society together with the theory of the horizontal composition of humanity provides the links and an all-embracing doctrine. Care has to be taken that it is not systematized and dogmatized too much, for the different ideas and ideals form part of the life of man and not of any circumscribed dogmatic theory.

As an instance of how the theory of Varṇa may offer a solution to a social question that provides a field for the most vehement dissention between different persuasions and views of life, we may mention the question of birth control. Sexual self-control and

---

[1]) It may be limited, if necessary, by the *proper* men of the ruling Varṇa.

abstinence may be seen to be the rule for the 'Brahman', and the use of contraceptives may be regarded as helpful to people of the lowest Varṇa. Both courses are socially useful — if followed by the right persons. It is a question which everybody must decide for himself.

The inner division of modern man has to be remedied. When that will be on the way of accomplishment, the outer division of society will be remedied of its own accord. Forms must not be changed before the indwelling life has altered. The social mind is all-important. The social leaders must work on and by the social mind. Regarding certain aspects of this the 57th sign of the I-Ging, the ancient Chinese *Book of Transition*, gives: "Penetration generates gradual and subtle effects. It should not be brought about by violence, but by uninterrupted influencing. These effects attract less general attention than those won by infraction, but they are more persevering and deeper. In order to be able thus to work, it is essential to clearly realize one's end, for something will be attained only if the penetrative influencing is continually going on in the same direction. .... The penetrative quality of the wind is due to its incessancy. That makes it so powerful. It uses time as means to the effect. Similarly the thought of the ruler has to penetrate into the social mind. To that effect a continuous influencing through elucidation and commandment is required. Only when the commandment has entered the social mind, a corresponding course of action is possible. Unprepared action scares people and works alienating." [1])

That the new world must come — so to speak — of itself by the way of the social mind, and cannot be created by force, was sensed for instance by the emperor Aśoka when he had engraved the following words: ".... in order that our sons and grandsons may not think .... that conquest by the sword deserves the name of conquest; that they may see in it nothing but destruction and violence; that they may consider nothing as true conquest save the conquest of Dhamma!" [2]) Hundreds of years before his time the same thought was expressed in the Mahābhārata: "The victory that is achieved without war is much superior to the victory that is achieved through war." [3])

[1]) R. Wilhelm, *I-Ging, Das Buch der Wandlungen*, Vol. I, p. 166.
[2]) *Piyadasi's Rock Edict* XIII.
[3]) *MBh. Śānti-parvan* 94 : 1.

In the theory of Varṇa specialization and integration are held in equilibrium. Neither of these two social tendencies may come forward to the cost of the other.

Ideals have to be handled and applied carefully. No ideal may be considered as final and become its own end. The intrinsic worth of an ideal lies in its relation to other ideals and in the fact that it is a step leading to a higher ideal. It is wise not to put one's immediate ideal too high, otherwise there is danger of becoming an impractical dreamer or a dangerous fanatic owing to mental confusion.

Every ideal must form the step and the means to an end, to a higher ideal, and justify that higher ideal. And not the reverse. The same applies to theories.

In modern society respect for high offices has been lost to a large extent. This is due only to 'mixture of Varṇas'. For the right men are not always in the right place. People must learn to respect the office apart from the person that holds it, and yet respect the person for what he is worth.

It must also not be forgotten that if there is a great 'mixture of Varṇas', there may be many 'Brahmans' among the working-people. This is a reason the more for respecting labour.

Regarding the world at large it is to be hoped and to be expected that a renewed general insight into the composition of human society in different national and regional organs with special Dharma, coupled with insight into the horizontal nature of humanity as a brotherhood, will lead to a manifestation of internationalism (or rather 'universalism'), in healthy balance with nationalism. Not an anti-organic, anti-social policy of 'splendid isolation', but co-operation will eventually be the watchword of public opinion. That is to say, if the cultural leaders prove equal to their task.

C. INDIA. In Chapter VI we concluded that in so far the evils of the caste system in India are due to the shortcomings of the established religion they have to be remedied by inspired religion, and that in so far they are not they have to be impaired by a renewed social sense of Varṇa. This applies to the problems of social intercourse, in particular those of untouchability and food, further of permission to enter temples considered as specially holy, of marriage, of widowhood, etc. The lessons derived from history will have to be realized, fresh Dharma will have to come forth from the soul of the people, to be strengthened if possible by the authority of ancient texts.

No serious student of caste will propagate the abolishment of the caste system. A social system which has a history of thousands of years cannot be expected to change its whole nature in the course of one or two decades. Neither will it be possible to 'reinstate' the four original classes. Mr. Gandhi is the greatest exponent of this point of view. [1]) He has not given a complete programme by which he would reinstate 'the four classes.' He stresses birth and heredity. As we have seen, though birth and heredity are extremely important, to lay undue emphasis upon them in the form of rules is against the theory of Varṇa. There would also be much difference of opinion about the question into which one of the three lower Varṇas a caste ought to be included. The complications would be endless. Only the Brahman castes may correspond to some extent to the ancient Brahman class.

To propose to abolish caste by slow consolidation of the smaller groups into larger ones is also to miss the real problem, as Dr. Ghurye writes in the Conclusions of his book *Caste and Race in India*, to which we refer. He mentions that this method has been tried in the Bombay Presidency for the last twenty years and more with disastrous results. [2]) Ghurye's opinion is that the problems of caste arise mainly out of pride of caste (he calls it 'caste-patriotism' [3])), and that it is this feeling that must be killed. He thinks that the State, the Census and every educated and progressive Hindu ought to ignore caste altogether and to denounce all expressions of this 'caste patriotism'. He also believes in the enthusiasm of youth and in the efficacy of inter-caste marriages. These and his other thoughts and suggestions are quite in keeping with our conclusions that the theory and ideal of Chāturvarṇya have to come forward again in the consciousness of the people, not as the model on which to remould the caste system by legislation, but as the fundamental theory of the composition of society. Public opinion will do the rest — and the problems of caste will solve themselves, and the new classes will emerge from the crumbling remains of the old

[1]) M. K. Gandhi, *Young India*, pp. 479—83.

[2]) See G. S. Ghurye, *Caste and Race in India*, pp. 182—188.

[3]) It is a pity to use a word — like 'patriotism' — which has a favourable meaning, in an unfavourable sense.

castes. The ideal of Chāturvarṇya will serve as a beacon during this process which may be a long one.

Of course Mahatma Gandhi's principles of harmlessness and non-violence, of spiritual striving and organic growth, are entirely in accord with the theory of Varṇa.

Much depends upon the *true* Brahmans, in all the racial and cultural groups. This applies also to the Hindu-Mohammedan problem, to the psychological basis of which a recent excellent book is pointing. [1])

Among the Brahmans by caste are still many true Brahmans. This holds a promise. Let us say with Vivekananda: "Anyone who claims to be a Brahman should prove his pretentions, first by manifesting that spirituality and next by raising others to the same status ....Arise (Brahmans!) and show your manhood, your Brahmanhood, by raising the non-Brahmans around you — not in the spirit of a master — not with the rotten canker of egotism crawling with superstitions and the charlatanry of East and West — but in the spirit of a servant. For verily he who knows to serve knows how to rule." [2]) The Swami holds out as the hierarchical ideal, and as the ultimate end of social life, the "raising of all humanity slowly and gently towards the realisation of that great ideal of the spiritual man, who is non-resisting, calm, steady, worshipful, pure and meditative. In that ideal there is God." [3]) Mr. Gandhi formulates his own ideal as follows: "My consolation and my happiness are to be found in service of all that lives because the Divine essence is the sum total of all life." Both leaders carried on the flaming torch of an ancient ideal. The Bhāgavata-purāṇa puts the ultimate end and highest ideal beautifully into the mouth of Śrī-Kṛishṇa: "This is the utmost limit of usefulness of their fellows, namely, that everyone should sacrifice his own life, wealth, thought and word, and do always what is beneficial to others." [4])

In conclusion a political remark. It is to be hoped that the ultimate form of the Indian Government will be one in accordance with the ancient Hindu tradition of the 'divine king', may the true Kshatriya be called upon to rule again under the spiritual guidance of the true

[1]) Atulananda Chakrabarti, *Cultural Fellowship in India.*
[2]) *Complete Works*, Vol. IV, p. 246.
[3]) *Op. cit.* Vol. III, p. 197.
[4]) *Bhāg.-P.* X : *22* : 35.

Brahman. This is also in accordance with the traditions of Islām. May not some one of the unscientific and surely temporary democratic forms of government of the West be imitated, and may democracy, socialism, communism, bc rccognized for what they surely *fundamentally* are: aspects of the underlying doctrine of the heart, of the horizontal view of humanity.

BIBLIOGRAPHY

Some works and articles dealing of the social theory and the social constitution of India

Alberuni's India, Account of the religion, philosophy, literature, astronomy, chronology, customs, laws and astrology of India about A.D. 1030. (Ed. E. Sachan). 1887.

ABUL FAZL 'ALLAMI, *Ain-i-Akbari*, transl. by H. Blochmann and H. S. Jarrett. 1873—'94.

A. BARTH, *Religions of India*. 6th ed. 1932.

A. BARTH, *A view of the Hindu Law* (in: *Revue Critique I, 1878*) *A prospectus of the Hindu Law* (in: *Revue Critique II, 1882*).

B. H. BADEN-POWELL, *The Indian Village community*. 1896.

A. BAINES, *Ethnography* (*Castes and Tribes*). (Encycl. of Indo-Aryan Research; 1912.

K. M. BANERJEA, *Essay on Caste*.

SURENDRANATH BANERJEA, *A Nation in making*. 1935.

L. D. BARNETT, *Antiquities of India. An account of the history and culture of ancient Hindustan*. 1913.

J. N. BHATTACHARYA, *Hindu Castes and Sects*. 1896.

K. K. BHATTACHARYA, *Tagore Law Lectures*.

E. A. H. BLUNT, *The Caste System of Northern India*. 1932.

M. C. BOUGLÉ, *Essais sur le Régime des Castes*. 1908.

M. C. BOUGLÉ, *Remarques générales sur le Régime des Castes* (*l'Année sociologique IV, 1899—1900*).

S. C. BOSE, *The Hindus as they are, a description of the manners, customs, and inner life of Hindu Society in Bengal*. 1881.

E. BURNOUF, *Essai sur le Véda ou Etude sur les religions, la littérature et la constitution sociale de l'Inde*. 1863.

Cambridge History of India. Vol. I. 1922.

Caste, in: *Encyclopaedia of the Social Sciences*. 1930—.

Caste (*Papers on India Reform*). Compiled from Muir, Max Müller, Sherring, Wilson, etc. etc. 1896.

Caste, in the Vth Supplement of the *Encyclopaedia Brittannica*.

Caste, by E. Gait in the *Encyclopaedia of Religion and Ethics*. 1908—26.

K. CHATTOPADHYAY, *The Origin of Caste* (in: *Vishwa-Bharati Quarterly, II 1924—25, pp. 347—58*).

R. Chanda, *The Indo-Aryan Races.* 1916.
H. Cowell, *A short treatise on Hindu Law.*
Atulananda Chakrabarti, *Cultural Fellowship in India.* 1934.
Mc. Crindle, *Ancient India as described by Megasthenes and Arrian, and ancient India as described in Classical Literature containing extracts from the writings of Strabo, Diodorus Siculus, etc.* 1877.
W. Crooke, *The Tribes and Castes of the North-Western Provinces and Oudh.* 1896.
J. Dahlmann, *Das altindische Volkstum und seine Bedeutung für die Gesellschaftskunde. 1899.*
J. Dahlmann, *Das Mahābhārata als Epos und Rechtsbuch.* 1895.
A. C. Das, *Rigvedic Culture.* 1925.
Bhagavan Das, *The Science of Social Organization. 1932.*
B. Datta, *Das Indische Kastensystem* (in: *Anthropos. XXII, 1927, pp. 142—159*).
M. Desai, *Gandhiji in Indian villages.*
H. H. Dodwell, ed., *The Cambridge Shorter History of India.* 1934.
J. A. Dubois, *A description of the character, manners and customs of the people of India.* Transl. G.U. Pope, 1862.
N. K. Dutt, *Origin and Growth of Caste in India.* 1931.
N. K. Dutt, *The Aryanization of India.* 1925.
R. C. Dutt, *History of Civilization in Ancient India.* 1893.
R. Fick, *The Social Organization in North-East India in Buddha's Time.* Engl. transl. by Maitra, 1920. (German edition 1897).
M. K. Gandhi, *The story of my experiments with Truth.* 1930.
G. S. Ghurye, *The ethnic theory of Caste* (in: *Man in India IV, 1924, pp. 209—71*).
G. S. Ghurye, *Caste and Race in India.* 1932.
Hand-book of Castes and Tribes employed on Tea estates in N.E. India. 1924.
E. B. Havell, *The History of Aryan Rule in India.* 1918.
A. Hillebrandt, *Altindien und die Kultur des Ostens.* 1901.
E. W. Hopkins, *The social and military position of the ruling caste in ancient India as represented by the Sanskrit Epic* (*Journal of the American Oriental Soc. XIII, 1889*).
E. W. Hopkins, *The mutual relations of the Four Castes according to the Mānava-dharma-çāstram.* 1881.
E. W. Hopkins, *The Great Epic of India.* 1901.
E. W. Hopkins, *India old and new.*
D. Ibbetson, *Panjab Castes.* 1916.
B. A. Irving, *The Theory and Practice of Caste.* 1853.
S. Iyengar, *Life in Ancient India in the Age of the Mantras.*
L. K. Anantha Krishna Iyer, *The Cochin Tribes and Castes.* 1909.
C. S. Ranga Iyer, *Father India.* 1927.
C. S. Ranga Iyer, *India in the Crucible.* 1928.
J. Jolly, *Recht und Sitte.* (Encycl. of Indo-aryan Research). 1896.
H. Kern, *Indische Theorieën over de Standenverdeeling* (*Verspreide*

Geschriften XIII). Versl. & Meded. Kon. Ac. v. Wet., afd. Lett. reeks 2, dl. II 1872.
F. E. KLAY, *Ancient Indian Education*. 1918.
S. V. KETKAR, *The History of Caste in India*. 1909.
S. V. KETKAR, *An Essay on Hinduism*. 1911.
E. J. KITTS, *A compendium of the Castes and Tribes found in India*. 1885.
C. LASSEN, *Indische Altertumskunde*. 1847—61.
N. N. LAW, *Studies in Ancient Hindu Polity*. 1914.
N. N. LAW, *History of education in ancient India*. 1917.
A. C. LYALL, *Asiatic studies, religious and social*. 1844, 1899, 1906—7.
G. MACMUNN, *Moeurs et coutumes des basses classes de l'Inde*. 1934.
R. MAJUMDAR, *Corporate Life in Ancient India*. 2nd ed. 1922.
J. MATHAI, *Village communities in British India*.
D. K. MAVALANKAR, *Castes in India*. 1930.
J. D. MAYNE, *A Treatise on Hindu Law and Usage*. 1914.
H. S. MAINE, *Dissertations on early Law and Custom*. 1883.
H. S. MAINE, *Ancient Law*. Notes by Sir F. Pollock. 1906.
A. R. DE LA MAZELIERE, *Essai sur l'évolution de la civilisation indienne*. 1903.
R. MICHELS, *Probleme der Sozialphilosophie*. 1914.
R. L. MITRA, *Indo Aryans*. 1881.
A. MORAHT, *Die lutherische Mission und die Kaste in Ostindien*.
J. MUIR, *Original Sanskrit Texts on the Origin and the History of the people of India, their religion and institutions*. 1868—73.
J. MUIR, *On the relations of the priests to the other classes of Indian society in the Vedic Age* (*Journal of the Royal Asiatic Soc. 1866 pp. 272 sqq.*).
MAX MÜLLER, *Caste* (In: *Essais de mythologie comparée, 1873, pp. 370—73*).
MAX MÜLLER, *Chips from a German workshop*. 2nd ed. 1868—75.
MAX MÜLLER, *India, what can it teach us?* 1883.
P. L. NARASU, *A Study of Caste*. 1922.
LALA BAIJ NATH, *Hinduism, ancient and modern*. 1899.
J. H. NELSON, *A view of the Hindu Law as administered by the High Court of Madras*.
J. H. NELSON, *The scientific study of the Hindu Law*.
J. C. NESFIELD, *Brief view of the caste system of the North-Western provinces and Oudh*. 1885.
C. OCHS, *Die Kaste in Ost-Indien und die Geschichte derselben in der alten lutherischen Mission*. 1860.
H. OLDENBERG, *Aus dem alten Indien*. 1910.
H. OLDENBERG, *Buddha*. 1890.
H. OLDENBERG, *Zur Geschichte des Indischen Kastenwesens* (in: (*Z.D. M.G.*) *51, 1897, pp. 267—290*).
L. S. S. O'MALLEY, *India's social heritage*. 1934.
L. S. S. O'MALLEY, *Indian Caste customs*.
J. C. OMAN, *Cults, Customs, and Superstitions of India*. 1908.

J. C. OMAN, *Indian life, religious and social.* 1889.
F. E. PARGITER, *Ancient Indian Historical Tradition,* 1922.
L. LAJPAT RAI, *Arya Samaj.* 1915.
S. RADHAKRISHNAN, *The Hindu Dharma.*
S. RADHAKRISHNAN, *The Hindu View of Life.* 1927.
S. RADHAKRISHNAN, *The Heart of Hindusthan.* 1932.
RÉMON, *La contrainte sociale et caste* (in: *Revue Int. de Sociologie 35*).
HAYAVADANA RAO, *Indian Caste System, a study.* 1934.
H. H. RISLEY, *The people of India.* 1915.
H. H. RISLEY, *The Tribes and Castes of Bengal.* 1891.
T. W. RHYS DAVIDS, *Buddhist India.* 1903.
R. V. RUSSELL, *The Tribes and Castes of the Central Provinces of India.* 1916.
J. SAMUELSON, *India, past and present, historical, social and political.* 1890.
Santana Dharma, ed. by the Bharata Dharma Mandali. 1924.
H. B. SARDA, *Hindu Superiority.*
BENOY KUMAR SARKAR, *The positive Background of Hindu Sociology.* 1914.
J. SARKAR, *India through the Ages, a survey of the growth of Indian Life and Thought.* 1928.
R. SCHMIDT, *Das alte und moderne Indien.* 1919.
L. v. SCHRÖDER, *Indiens Literatur und Cultur in historischer Entwicklung.* 1887.
E. SENART, *Les castes dans l'Inde.* 1927. Engl. transl.: *Caste in India.* 1930.
MAHENDRANATH SIRCAR, *Comparative studies in Vedantism.* 1928.
M. A. SHERRING, *Natural History of Caste.*
M. A. SHERRING, *Hindu Tribes and Castes.* 1879—81.
J. S. SIROMANI, *Commentary on Hindu Law.*
G. SLATER, *The Dravidian element in Indian Culture.* 1914.
V. A. SMITH, *Oxford History of India,* 1919, 1928.
A. STEELE, *The Law and Custom of Hindu castes within the Dekhan provinces.* 1868.
O. STEIN, *Megasthenes und Kautilya.* 1921.
SHAMA SHASTRI, *The evolution of Caste.*
E. THOMPSON, *The reconstruction of India,* 1930.
E. THURSTON, *Tribes and Castes of Madras.* 1909.
E. THURSTON, and RANGACHARI, *The Castes and Tribes of Southern India.* 1909.
B. C. J. TIMMER, *Megasthenes en de Indische Maatschappij.* 1930.
C. V. VAIDYA, *Epic India.*
C. V. VAIDYA, *The Riddle of the Ramayana.*
C. V. VAIDYA, *Mahabharata criticism.*
C. V. VAIDYA, *History of Mediaeval Hindu India, 600—1200 A.D.* 1921—26.
S. V. VENKATESWARA, *Indian Culture through the Ages.* 1928—1932.
S. V. VISHWANATHA, *Racial Synthesis in Hindu Culture.* 1928.

S. V. VISHWANATHA, *International Law in Ancient India*. 1925.
VIVEKANANDA, *Complete Works*. 1922—26.
M. WEBER, *Indische Studien*. 1850—98.
M. WEBER, *Gesammelte Aufsätze zur Religionssoziologie*, II, *Hinduismus und Buddhismus*. 1921.
J. T. WHEELER, *The history of India from the earliest ages*. 1867.
W. J. WILKINS, *Modern Hinduism, Religion and Life of Hindus in North India*. 1887.
J. WILSON, *Indian Caste*. 1877.
MONIER WILLIAMS, *Religious Thought and Life in India*. 2nd ed. 1885.
H. ZIMMER, *Altindisches Leben*. 1879.

Texts used

The Sacred Books of the East, transl. by various scholars and ed. by F. Max Müller. 1879—. (The Sacred Laws of the Āryas, the Vedas, the Upanishads, the Bhagavad Gītā, Buddhist Texts, etc.).
The Sacred Books of the Buddhists, transl. by various scholars and ed. by F. Max Müller. 1899—.
Original Sanskrit Texts on the Origin and the History of the people of India, their religion and institutions, ed. by J. Muir. 1873—90.
The Dharma Śāstra, (Yajñavalkya, Hārita, Uśanas, Aṅgiras, Yama, Atri, Samvarta, Kātyāyana, Vṛihaspati, Dakshi, Śātātapa, Likhita, Vyāsa, Parāśara, Śaṅkha, Gautama, Āpastamba, Vasishṭha, Vishṇu), ed. and publ. by M. N. Dutt. 1908.
Kauṭilya's Arthaśāstra, transl. by R. Shamasastry. 3rd ed. 1929.
The Rāmāyan of Vālmīki, transl. by R. T. H. Griffith. 1870—74.
The Mahābhārata, transl. by P. C. Roy. New ed. 1925—30.
Śrīmad Bhāgavata Purāṇa, transl. by S. Subba Rau. 1928.
The Vishṇu Purāṇam, transl. by H. H. Wilson. 1864—77.
Vishṇupurāṇam, ed. and publ. by M. N. Dutt. 1896.
Etc. etc.

INDEX

LIST OF NAMES

LIST OF SUBJECTS